Lague • Frank Lalli • Dave Laventhol • Dave Lawrence Jr. • Grace Lichtenstein • A. J. Liebling • John Lindsay • Walter Lippmann • Sterling Lord • Eulia Love • Clare Boothe Luce • Marshall Lumsden • Joan Luther • Mary Lou Luther • Stan Mack • Norman Mailer • Leonard Maltin • Carson McCullers • Wanda McDaniel • Ralph McGill • Mary McGrory • Diana McLellan • Willie Morris • Mary Murphy • Al Neuharth • Bob Novak • Pat Oliphant • Bill Paley • Gene Patterson • Mary Pitzer • Tom Plate • Edwin Pope • Burt Prelutsky • Richard Reeves • Mary Reinholz • Rip Rense • James Reston • Tim Robinson • Lynn Rosellini • Harry Rosenfeld • Richard Rovere • Mike Royko • Rollene Saal • William Safire • J. D. Salinger • Pierre Salinger • Mike Salisbury • Maggie Savoy • Dick Schaap • Jean Seberg • Diane K. Shah • William Shawn • Gail Sheehy • Bobby Shriver • Art Siedenbaum • Jeff Silverman • Gene Siskel • Red Smith • Michael Sragow • Ben Stein • William Styron • Arthur Sulzberger Jr. • Walter Thayer • Bruce Thurlby • Grant Tinker • Reva Tooley • Garry Trudeau • Priscilla Tucker • Joe Urschel • Abigail Van Buren • Richard Wald • E. B. White • John Hay Whitney • George Will • Nick Williams • David Wise • Jules Witcover • Tom Wolfe • Stanley Woodward • Ed Yoder • Paul Ziffren • Steve Zousmer

THE LAST EDITOR

THE
LAST
EDITOR

How I Saved
the *New York Times*,
the *Washington Post*, and
the *Los Angeles Times*
from Dullness and
Complacency

JIM BELLOWS

**Andrews McMeel
Publishing**
Kansas City

02 03 04 05 06 QUF 10 9 8 7 6 5 4 3 2 1

Library of Congress Cataloging-in-Publication Data

Bellows, James G.
   The last editor : how I helped save the New York Times, the Washington
Post, and the Los Angeles Times from dullness and complacency / Jim Bellows.
     p. cm.
   ISBN 0-7407-1901-7
   1. Bellows, James G. 2. Newspaper editors—United States—Biography.
I. Title.

PN4874.B3699 A3 2002
070.4'1'092—dc21
[B]

2002018351

BOOK DESIGN AND COMPOSITION BY KELLY & COMPANY

For the girls:

Keven, Amelia, Priscilla,
Felicia, and Justine

CONTENTS

◆

FOREWORD

◆

by Jimmy Breslin

The first time I saw him he was standing in the conference room of the newspaper and he had a piece of paper tacked to the wall. It was the dummy for the first page of the second section of the newspaper, the split page.

He said this was the space for the column he wanted me to write. Now he told me what it was he wanted in it.

He writhed. He mumbled. He didn't finish a sentence. I didn't know what he was saying, but I knew exactly what he meant. He talked with hands and excited eyes.

Nor did I have any unique method of translating his shoulder shrugs and mumbles. Everybody on the newspaper—and I've seen him on two, this one, the old *New York Herald Tribune* and then the *Washington Star*—knew what he meant. The list of those who went to the top, whatever that is, because of him is astonishing.

Then on this day he said, "Great," and he left with a laugh.

This was the start of a livelihood for me, and just another small challenge for Jim Bellows.

He likes nothing more than a fresh challenge. I think this one worked for him.

Since then, he has found challenges everywhere. He switches jobs, he switches industries, he even switches technologies.

He does this with ease because he is a kid at heart and kids can change on a dime. He is a smart, tireless, eager, good kid—even in his seventies.

I met him in newspapers. His great respect for good writing and his good ideas left us all whirling through days of excitement. I know of no newspapers that have come close to it. He would praise and then fight for anything he liked. If the idea wasn't his, he fought even more furiously.

Not surprisingly, he inspires loyalty, without demanding it, and he, in turn, is incredibly loyal, the textbook example of the friend for life.

I cannot recall a single solitary time when I didn't know exactly where he was and what he would do with any question.

I cannot recall a week in which I have not spoken to him. And each time I see somebody from the days with Bellows, any days, anywhere, the question is always the same: "Spoken to him? Seen him?"

Always in this climate there was a crackle, a joyous eruption upon reading or hearing something he loved, crystals of excitement snapping and filling the air and the story getting better on the machine at your hands. Going to work each day, the sky was brilliant, the breeze pleasant. On the worst days, the cold February rain mixed with sleet was refreshing. Because right upstairs in that old city room was air with the fragrance in it of the love of life. Often I feel this way when I go to work and don't realize that it is different, and then suddenly something will happen—a horn, a growl, a cough—and that is enough to jar me, to make me realize it is not the same. Bellows is in my life forever but he just isn't in this particular room right now.

■ Jimmy Breslin's column on sports began in the *New York Herald Tribune* in 1962, shortly after publication of his book *Can't Anybody Here Play This Game?* His column, which broadened its coverage to the entire city, ran until the very end of the *Herald Tribune*'s life.

RÉSUMÉ

"The longest résumé in the history of journalism."
—*Washington Journalism Review*, June 1992

1947–50   *Columbus (Georgia) Ledger:* reporter

1950–57   *Atlanta Journal:* copy editor, news editor

1957–59   *Detroit Free Press:* assistant city editor

1959–61   *Miami News:* managing editor

1961–67   *New York Herald Tribune:* editor

1967–74   *Los Angeles Times:* associate editor

1975–78   *Washington Star:* editor

1978–81   *Los Angeles Herald-Examiner:* editor

1981–83   *Entertainment Tonight:* managing editor

1983–86   ABC News: executive editor, *World News Tonight*

1986–88   Prodigy: editorial director

1988–89   *USA Today on TV:* executive producer

1989–90   MediaNews Group: vice president of editorial

1991   TV show: *Crusaders,* consultant

1992–94   *TV Guide:* West Coast bureau chief

1994–97   Excite: executive editor

1998   *Los Angeles Daily News:* consultant

1999   Eguard.com, Gator.com: consultant

2000–01   *The Last Editor*

INTRODUCTION

◆

Let me give you my Top 10 list of reasons why I wrote this book:

10 ➤ To answer my daughter Justine's letter urging me to write it. She was born when I turned 50 and kept running into people who asked her about my career. She didn't know what to tell them. So she wanted more information on the old man, and she was insistent. "Do a book, Dad—please!"

9 ➤ To give the reader a cross-country trip through the U.S. media, from newsrooms to television to magazines to the Internet.

8 ➤ To entice young people to sign on to the adventure of a career in covering the news, especially kids who are shy and insecure, as I was for most of my life.

7 ➤ To talk about work in general, and why it shouldn't be something ancillary to your life, but something that nourishes your soul and is a lot of fun.

6 ➤ To share the newsroom story about how Tom Wolfe took on *The New Yorker* magazine and landed us in a fight with America's literary establishment.

5 ➤ To tell how Jimmy Breslin and his column gave the *New York Times* a good run for its money on local news, and how our "City in Crisis" series gave New York a new mayor.

4 ➤ To describe the remarkable group of American women journalists whose careers I promoted, and the marvelous work they did in my newsrooms.

3 ➤ To recapture the day when a bull invaded the newsroom of the *Miami News* and soiled a few rugs.

2 ➤ To recount my adventures with the Ku Klux Klan on Stone Mountain and tell you where J. Edgar Hoover stood. Aside.

1 ➤ To look back on the first eighty years and take stock.

It has been suggested to me that one way to tell a life story is in strict chronological order. No fanfare, no big stories up-front. But I have been hopelessly corrupted by my newspaper years. In my newsroom, the big story goes on page one. And in my memoir, the big stories get the spotlight—at least at the beginning, before I settle into the coherence of chronology.

If I had wanted smoothness and security, I would have traveled a different road. The "second paper" in town has usually been my home. Second papers have more excitement than number one. Easy Street is not a good address for innovation. That's why I have always been more comfortable working for the struggling underdog. Even on the Internet, Excite ate the dust of Yahoo!, and AOL ultimately eclipsed Prodigy.

The underdog position may be the reason why I have had some influence on the papers that have crushed and survived me. The *New York Herald Tribune* made the *New York Times* a livelier paper than it was before. ("Who says a good newspaper has to be dull?" we needled, and the good gray giant heeded our slogan.) The *Washington Star* made the *Washington Post* a less institutional paper, a result to which Ben Bradlee and Kay Graham also contributed, not to mention Richard Nixon. And the *Los Angeles Times* was put on its mettle by the *Los Angeles Herald-Examiner,* the hoary old Hearst warhorse that I resurrected.

The subtitle of this work proclaims that I saved America's three most powerful newspapers from dullness and complacency. What unspeakable bravado! But as you read, you will see how I managed that feat, and its impact on modern journalism.

There was just one little problem in writing this book. I am not a writer.

I have few complaints about my life, but if there were one thing I could change, I would want to be a writer. Not just a writer, but a superlative writer. That's why I have such an affinity for good writers and such a keen appreciation of their skill, why I have taken such pride in motivating them and showcasing their work, why my newsrooms became literary Camelots.

Though I spent my first few years in newspapers as a reporter, I was tapped early on to be an editor. I'm not sure whether that was because I was a lousy writer or a good editor. So here I was in my late seventies, owing my youngest daughter a book, with time on my hands and not enough talent to write the damn thing. But no one knows more good writers than I do, so I set about finding one to work with me. There were a lot of false starts, but Gerry Gardner and I began to work together about two years ago.

It has been challenging and difficult for me, the daily deadline kid, to hang in for the long haul required to turn out a book, though it's been great fun to sort through boxes in the garage, take down the files from the shelves, revisit good times, reacquaint myself with great friends, and feel renewed gratitude for all my good fortune.

But best of all is the truly stunning amount of help I've gotten from former colleagues all over the country. You can see the galaxy of their famous names on the endpapers. I've been amazed to read what so many people have contributed to this book. It made me realize that this renowned "mumbler" hit on a surefire management technique to get people to dig deep and give their best to meet any challenge—you just ask for help. People appreciate being needed. It unleashes their best.

My early life taught me that lesson. Because I was quite small for my age until I reached 17, I was always the underdog. I needed help, and I asked for it. And even when I got bigger, and had even acquired some impressive titles, I always identified with the have nots. It was never me versus them.

It was always us.

I was raised with all the old-fashioned values, thank God. I believe each one of us has a responsibility to make a difference in the world, and journalism has allowed me to fulfill that responsibility. Journalism is not just a profession, it's a calling. Members of the Fourth Estate perform a public service, I believe, and can have a great time doing it. I did.

Sure, I've had my share of failures, both professional and personal. I once said in an interview with the *Boston Globe* that I was abrasive, which was good, because life is a series of scrapes. At least mine has been, but I've never met a challenge I didn't like. A lot of the newspapers I poured my heart into are gone. But success to me is getting things done and doing them well. I feel pretty good about how I've spent my life.

I once saw a newspaper story about a judge who asked a man why he stole 100 television sets. The fellow frowned and said to the judge, "This is not a simple life, your honor, and there are no easy answers." Amen.

But I do know that the joys of life are not in the destination but in the unsought surprises along the way. I've set down some of them on these pages.

So onward and upward with the press. Your timing is exemplary. You are reading this book while there are still newspapers around to read and remember with love.

THE LAST EDITOR

CHAPTER 1

◆

Tom Wolfe and *The New Yorker*

"Jim Bellows loved a brawl. I think if a month went by without a brawl, he thought it was a pretty dull month."

Tom Wolfe was recalling my relish at the literary controversy he landed us in with his articles on *The New Yorker* magazine.

It was 1965, the year that Norman Mailer marched on Washington, France left NATO, and the first U.S. combat troops landed in Vietnam, so it was not exactly an uneventful time. But the Tom Wolfe–*New Yorker* flap was still memorable. It was unsettling, potentially damaging, and the most fun I'd had in years.

I had set out to redesign the Sunday edition of the *New York Herald Tribune* for its publisher, John Hay "Jock" Whitney. Jock had made me editor of the paper and I was trying to create a lively alternative to the *New York Times,* New York's venerable newspaper of record.

"Who says a good newspaper has to be dull?" we used to ask in our ads.

The centerpiece of our new Sunday edition was a new supplement called *New York.* It turned out to be so successful that it outlived the newspaper as the independent *New York* magazine. It contrasted nicely with the Sunday *Times Magazine,* which in those days was a little dull. *Times* readers were accustomed to spending their weekends with articles like "Brazil: Colossus of the South." Their covers featured pictures of an ox with a Cambodian native behind it pushing a plow.

The literary stars on our new magazine were a couple of extraordinary young men whom I had managed to bring aboard the paper. One of them

William Shawn's Hand-Delivered Letter to Jock Whitney

To be technical for a moment, I think that Tom Wolfe's article on The New Yorker *is false and libelous. But I'd rather not be technical. . . . I cannot believe that, as a man of known integrity and responsibility, you will allow it to reach your readers. . . . The question is whether you will stop the distribution of that issue of* New York. *I urge you to do so, for the sake of* The New Yorker *and for the sake of the* Herald Tribune. *In fact, I am convinced that the publication of that article will hurt you more than it will hurt me. . . . As the editor of a publication that tries always to be truthful, accurate, fair, and decent, I know exactly what Wolfe's article is—a vicious, murderous attack on me and on the magazine I work for. It is a ruthless and reckless article; it is pure sensation-mongering. It is wholly without precedent in respectable American journalism. . . . If you do not [cancel the article] I can only conclude—since I know that you are a decent man—that you do not understand Wolfe's words. For your sake, and for mine, and, in the long run, even for the sake of Tom Wolfe and his editor, Clay Felker (God help me for caring about them), I urge you to stop the distribution of that article.*

Letter sent the Thursday before publication, April 11, 1965

was a sportswriter named Jimmy Breslin, whose book about the New York Mets' abysmal season, called *Can't Anybody Here Play This Game?*, had been published in 1963. I put Jimmy to work writing a sports column, but I sensed that he was wasted there—Jimmy Breslin had enormous potential. So I asked him to write about the city. And the rest, as they say, is history. Then he started to write for *New York* magazine as well.

The other star of the *Trib*'s new Sunday supplement was a young fellow named Tom Wolfe.

Tom had been working as a reporter on the paper, covering hard news for the main sections. I wanted articles that were readable *stories,* not just news reports. Not every reporter is able to write that way—but God knows, Tom Wolfe could do it. He could take the everyday fact and make you see it anew. He had met all the tests of a daily journalist regarding clarity and speech, but he had gone far beyond that.

Tom was a remarkable communicator of energy and grace. His prose rollicked along with unexpected words embedded in pages that were covered with a confetti of punctuation marks. If his prose was eye-catching, so was he—his trademark was a gleaming white suit.

It didn't take editorial brilliance to put Tom Wolfe to work writing features for *New York.*

■ **A Letter from J. D. Salinger to Jock Whitney**

With the printing of the inaccurate and sub-collegiate and gleeful and unrelievedly poisonous article on William Shawn, the name of the Herald Tribune, *and certainly your own will very likely never again stand for anything either respectworthy or honorable.*   ■

And since a magazine is only as good as its ideas, I brought aboard a young fellow named Clay Felker to edit *New York.* Felker was a font of them. He came over from *Esquire,* where he and Harold Hayes had battled for the top spot and Clay had lost. One of the reasons he lost may have been that he was lobbying his boss to do an article satirizing *The New Yorker.*

"When you can edit as good a magazine as *The New Yorker,* we'll talk about it," was the reply.

Great minds think alike. Tom Wolfe had the idea of doing a profile on William Shawn, the editor of *The New Yorker.* When Clay Felker suggested a sendup of the legendary magazine, Tom leaped at the idea.

E. B. White's Letter to Jock Whitney

Tom Wolfe's piece on William Shawn violated every rule of conduct I know anything about. It is sly, cruel, and to a large extent undocumented, and it has, I think, shocked everyone who knows what sort of person Shawn really is. I can't imagine why you published it. The virtuosity of the writer makes it all the more contemptible, and to me, as I read it, the spectacle was of a man being dragged for no apparent reason at the end of a rope by a rider on horseback.

April 1965

Richard Rovere's Letter to Jock Whitney

Physically and atmospherically The New Yorker *office Tom Wolfe describes is a place I have never visited. The editor of the magazine described by him is a man I have never known. Unless I have lost all judgment and power of observation, the piece you published is as irresponsible as anything I have ever come upon outside the gutter press.*

April 1965

They agreed that *The New Yorker*—that great ornament of contemporary writing—had in fact become somewhat tedious.

The New Yorker had had its fun with *New York* magazine. Lillian Ross had written a piece for the Talk of the Town in a parody of Tom's coruscating style. It was about a playground in Central Park and the main character was a young mother called Pam Muffin. Clay Felker was engaged at the time to the actress Pamela Tiffin. Well, they had had their fun. Now we would have ours.

Tom called up William Shawn and when he finally got him on the phone, told him he wanted to do a piece on *The New Yorker* for *New York* magazine, and he wanted to interview him.

"We have a policy at *The New Yorker*," said Shawn coolly. "That is, if someone doesn't want to be profiled, we drop it. I would like you to show me the same courtesy."

Tom explained that it was, after all, *The New Yorker*'s fortieth anniversary, and Shawn was, after all, a famous figure in publishing. So Tom was going to do the piece.

As he set out to write the article, the first thing Tom realized was that you cannot write a parody of a dull magazine. Not for more than half a page.

"Once you get the joke, it gets duller than dull. It's the Law of Parody."

So Tom decided to change the tone completely. He set out to write it in the style of sensational tabloid journalism. Something on the order of the old *Police Gazette*.

"I thought, the wilder and crazier the hyperbole, the better," said Tom. "I wanted to paint a room full of very proper people who had gone to sleep standing up."

Tom was working in the satiric tradition established by *The New Yorker* itself. Back in the 1930s *The New Yorker* had done a savage sendup of *Time* magazine and its famous editor, Henry Luce.

Luce went through the roof. *The New Yorker*'s founding editor, Harold Ross, had sent a copy of the article to Luce ahead of time, and Luce went berserk. He confronted Ross in Ross's apartment and threatened to throw him out of the window. Tom never dreamed that Shawn's reaction would make Luce's seem mild.

Tom's piece turned out to be very long, so we broke it into two parts. The first part was almost exclusively about William Shawn—his life, his mannerisms, and the atmosphere he had created at *The New Yorker*. It kidded the magazine's offices, its customs, and its editorial procedures. Tom pictured the hallways filled with aged messengers bearing a blizzard of multicolored memos: "They have *boys* over there on the

Tom Wolfe Replies and Pays Tribute

A lot of people are going to read the letters and wires by Richard Rovere, J. D. Salinger, Muriel Spark, E. B. White and Ved Mehta, five New Yorker *writers, and compare their concepts and specific wording and say something about— you know?—funny coincidence or something like that. But that is unfair. These messages actually add up to a real* tribute *to one of* The New Yorker's *great accomplishments: an atmosphere of Total Orgthink for many writers of disparate backgrounds and temperaments. First again . . . they are evidence, I think, of another important achievement of* The New Yorker. *Namely, this wealthy, powerful magazine has become a Culture-totem for bourgeois culturati everywhere. Its followers—marvelous!—react just like those of any other totem group when somebody suggests that their holy buffalo knuckle may not be holy after all. They scream like weenies over a wood fire.*

April 25, 1965, in *New York*

19th and 20th floors, the editorial offices, practically caroming off each other—bonk old bison heads!—at the blind turns in the hallways because of the fantastic traffic in memos. They just *call* them boys. Boy, will you take this, please. . . . Actually, a lot of them are old men with starched collars with the points curling up a little, 'big bunch' ties, button-up sweaters and black basket-weave sack coats, and they are all over the place transporting these thousands of messages with their kindly elder bison shuffles shoop-shooping along."

He called Shawn "The Colorfully Shy Man" and portrayed him as diffident, excessively polite, and soft-spoken. He pictured Shawn draped in layers of sweaters as he went pat-pat-patting through the corridors.

The first section was headlined: "TINY MUMMIES! The True Story of the Ruler of 43rd Street's Land of the Walking Dead!"

New York was printed on Wednesday for the *Trib*'s Sunday edition. On Thursday, I sent a copy over to William Shawn at *The New Yorker*. Like Tom, I was innocent enough to think that the old spirit of *The New Yorker* still flourished. After all, who had engaged in satire more than the good old *New Yorker*? They had always gloried in puncturing pretension with a satirical needle. I suppose it makes a difference who is feeling the prick of the syringe.

■ Clay Felker Recalls Tom Wolfe's Firepower

It was a real explosion. Wolfe did this incredible piece of reporting, and it wasn't that many years before that he had done his doctoral thesis at Yale in American Studies. You know, you don't get many pieces written with that kind of intellectual firepower.

And it was really a blow to The New Yorker, *and the incredible thing was it was the making of* New York *magazine. Up until that point, we were not selling that much advertising. I think we were averaging 15 pages a week, and then we went double and it never went away, because it put us on the map nationally.*

From interview with Digby Diehl, March 1, 1997 ■

William Shawn went berserk.

Within hours a hand-delivered letter arrived on Jock Whitney's desk.

"This is beyond libelous," said Shawn. "This is murderous."

Now, Jock Whitney had been America's ambassador to the Court of St. James's. So part of him was a very dignified gentleman. And part of him was a newspaper publisher.

"With one stroke," wrote Shawn, "this article will take the entire reputation of the *New York Herald Tribune* and thrust it down into the gutter, along with . . ."

I don't remember the exact citations. Mussolini? Or the man who kidnapped the Lindbergh baby?

A Letter from
William Styron

I was quite amused to read in Newsweek *that William Shawn feels that Tom Wolfe's brilliant study of himself and* The New Yorker *"puts the* Herald Tribune *right down in the gutter. . . ." I have become fairly resilient over the years in regard to criticism, but since the only real whiff of the gutter was in a review of one of my books in the pages of* The New Yorker, *I found Shawn's cry of Foul woefully lacking in pathos.*

When Jimmy Breslin learned that Shawn was desperately trying to keep the *Tribune* from publishing Tom's series, he called Shawn on the telephone and said he had a method by which this could be accomplished if Shawn would meet him at Toots Shor's bar. He never dreamed that Shawn would show up. Jimmy was at the bar talking with friends when he noticed a little man crawling up behind him. Jimmy took him over in the corner and said:

"I can stop the publication. It's very simple—we just blow up the building!"

Shawn left in a hurry.

But the letter to Whitney was just the beginning.

Letters rained in from America's shocked cultural establishment. Not one of the letters came to me (the editor), Tom Wolfe (the writer), or Clay Felker (*New York*'s editor); they were all directed to Jock Whitney, the publisher. So I suspect the outpouring was orchestrated. Jock Whitney was a leader in the cultural community—these were his friends.

Maureen Dowd's Review of Tom Wolfe's <u>Hooking Up</u>

Even after the cascade of bitter and nostalgic books written about [The New Yorker] *by Shawn protégés, Wolfe's send-up is still a scaldingly funny, perceptive portrait of the weirdo Whisper Zone, horsehair-stuffing days of Shawn. Fury over the piece . . . reached from Walter Lippmann to President Johnson's aide Richard Goodwin to J. D. Salinger. . . . But Wolfe weathered it because he was lucky enough to work for an editor whom I was once lucky enough to work for at the* Washington Star—*James Bellows, a newspaperman with verve and bravery in equal measure, who always backed up his reporters and who loved nothing better than to do a joyous rain dance in a hail of criticism.*

New York Times, November 5, 2000

J. D. Salinger, John Updike, E. B. White, Muriel Spark, Hannah Arendt, Richard Rovere . . . Virtually all of them had ties to *The New Yorker* of one kind or another. They either worked there or had contracts as contributors.

Perhaps they were troubled to see Tom describe *The New Yorker* as "the most successful suburban women's magazine in the country." Or "a national shopping news."

But why had Shawn become so unhinged? His frenzy seemed inexplicable. I reread the article. Yes, it made fun of his whispers, his reclusiveness, his sweaters. But still . . .

Tom's best guess was that Shawn was enraged because he feared the piece would expose his affair with the *New Yorker* writer Lillian Ross. True, the article had mentioned their contacts, but only in a professional context—the fact that she could always get through to him on the phone immediately; the fact that they would often go off to lunch at some remote pastrami joint. In 1998 Lillian Ross wrote a memoir called *Here But Not Here* about her long affair with Shawn. So that may have been what set him off.

But whatever the reason for Shawn's meltdown, it was a strategic blunder. When Jock Whitney received Shawn's letter, he came into my office and showed it to me.

"Jim, what do we do about this?" said Whitney.

"Here's what we do," I said and called to my secretary.

"Jane, get me the press section of *Time* magazine, and then get me the press section of *Newsweek.*"

Tom Wolfe on William Shawn, "The Ruler of 43rd Street's Land of the Walking Dead"

Stories about Shawn help explain why he is so . . . retiring. *Why he won't allow interviews, why he won't let his picture be taken, why it* pains *him to ride elevators, go through tunnels, get cooped up—why he* remains anonymous, *as they say, and slips* The New Yorker *out each week from behind a barricade of . . . pure* fin de siecle *back-parlor horsehair stuffing.*

The Shawn legends! The one of how he tries to time it in the morning so he can go straight up to his office on the 19th floor, by himself on the elevator and carries a hatchet in his attaché case so he can chop his way out if it gets stuck between floors . . .

He always seems to have on about 20 layers of clothes, about three button-up sweaters, four vests, a couple of shirts, two ties, it looks that way, a dark shapeless suit over the whole ensemble, and white cotton socks. Here he is in the hall, and he lowers his head and puts out his hand.

"Hello Mister—" he begins nodding, "—Taylor—how—are—you," with his head down nodding down, down, down, down, "—it's—nice—" his head is down and he rolls his eyes up and looks out from under his own forehead "—to—see—you—" and then edges back with his hand out, his head nodding, eyes rolled up, back foot edging back, back, back, back "—very— good—to—see—you—"

April 11, 1965, in *New York*

I sent over Shawn's letter. I let them know that *The New Yorker's* lawyers were seeking an order of prior restraint to keep us from publishing Tom's article. If that wasn't a story, I didn't know what was.

The first part of Tom's article ran on Sunday, April 11, 1965; on Monday morning, *Time* and *Newsweek* arrived at several million homes. The press sections of both were all about *The New Yorker* and their reaction to Tom's story. You can't buy that kind of publicity.

My view has always been that we had every right to dismember *The New Yorker*, and to do it with irreverence and gusto. Tom's pieces were funny as hell, but they were not mean or malicious. William Shawn was a public figure. Every highly visible editor of every newspaper and magazine in America is a reasonable target for satire. That's true of Henry Luce, Ben Bradlee, William Shawn, and me.

> ## Breslin to Whitney When Our Circulation Began to Rise
>
> *When I started here, I thought I was just going to be writing for 300,000 people or so every day. And I approached my job with that attitude. But now I awake each day to find myself in an immense publication. The responsibility for going directly to over one million people each day is becoming awesome. It is clear to me that I need something to calm my nerves. . . . I need a raise.*
>
> Letter in 1965

The New Yorker has always been skillful at dishing it out; they should have been able to take it. And Tom's lampoon captured the essential truth of the magazine.

During the following week I noticed that Tom Wolfe and Clay Felker were not their usual exuberant selves. They knew that Jock Whitney had received letters from notables in the literary community, as well as the journalistic and political worlds.

Walter Lippmann had said, "Tom Wolfe is an incompetent ass."

E. B. White had said, "The piece is sly, cruel and undocumented."

Richard Rovere had said, "It is as irresponsible as anything outside the gutter press."

Lyndon Johnson's aide Dick Goodwin had said, "Here at the White House . . ."

J. D. Salinger emerged from his own reclusiveness in the wilds of New England to write Whitney: ". . . the name of the *Herald Tribune* and certainly your own will very likely never again stand for anything honorable."

Tom's first reaction was that it had all been a prank.

"I know what this is," he said. "This is some kind of *superprank*. I pranked them, and now they are outpranking me."

He vacillated between this hopeful view and a more apprehensive one: "I thought the sky was going to fall down. Because you think if people this famous—Lippmann and Alsop and Salinger—think you've done something dreadful, you must be in serious trouble. I thought, can I survive this?"

None of the complainers tried to dispute or debate Tom's argument—that *The New Yorker* had grown prosaic and overrated. Most of the letters were a shrill cry for "dignity."

Nowhere was this more the case than in a piece by the *New Yorker* writer Dwight Macdonald in *The New York Review of Books*. It was a strange argument. Macdonald basically agreed with Tom's assessment of *The New Yorker*, then framed the case in his own terms: This was all

---

■ Wire to Me from Art Buchwald When Breslin Was
  Planning D.C. Trip to Cover LBJ's Inaugural Ball

UNDERSTAND BRESLIN COMING DOWN FOR INAUGURATION. I FEEL THE TRIBUNE WOULD BE MAKING A MISTAKE IN SENDING HIM HERE AT THE HEIGHT OF THE SOCIAL SEASON. BRESLIN'S MANNERS AND CLOTHES JUST WOULDN'T FIT IN.

WITH THE TYPE OF PEOPLE EXPECTED NEXT WEEK, THE GREAT SOCIETY IS NOT EQUIPPED TO TAKE CARE OF PEOPLE LIKE BRESLIN.

BUCHWALD   ■

Breslin's Reply to Buchwald—Sent over My Name

TO ART BUCHWALD: HUMORIST
WASHINGTON BUREAU

THANKS FOR OFFERING US SUCH PROFOUND EDITORIAL ADVICE. AM CONFERRING WITH BRESLIN, AND WE HOPE SHORTLY TO COME UP WITH A COMPROMISE. MEANWHILE, MR. BRESLIN HAS SENT MARVIN THE TORCH AND BAD EDDY TO WASHINGTON TO PERSUADE YOU THAT THE GREAT SOCIETY INCLUDES JIMMY BRESLIN TOO

BELLOWS

P.S. JIMMY WANTS TO KNOW WHAT ROUTE YOUR CHILDREN TAKE WHEN THEY GO TO SCHOOL—AND WHAT TIME?

■ Art Buchwald was the *Trib*'s most successful expatriate talent. After 14 years of writing a satiric column for the Paris edition, Art and his cigar moved to Washington, where his column dealt with social and political issues and was nationally syndicated.

about the New Journalism that Wolfe and his buddies had launched at the *Trib*. It was about the *form* in which Tom was writing, which was an affront to traditional journalism. The *Herald Tribune* was in a dilemma, said Macdonald—"caught between deficits and respectability."

The New York Review of Books called the *Trib*'s writing "bastard journalism." We were "exploiting the factual authority of journalism and the atmospheric license of fiction." Tom came to the defense of our New Journalism in an article in *New York*. He pointed out that traditional journalism was often "lazy, slipshod, superficial, and incomplete."

But this New Journalism, complained Macdonald, isn't *accurate*. Here's how Tom answered *that*:

> I am the first to agree that the New Journalism should be as accurate as traditional journalism. . . . I contend that it has already proved itself *more* accurate than traditional

journalism—more painstaking, more patient, and more ambitious in its reporting, far more complete in the picture it gives; in fact, that it offers the reader more of the truth than he is likely to get in any other way.

And so Armageddon approached. And America's literary giants piled on Tom Wolfe. And he feared he would be crushed.

Johnny Carson once said that three days after death, hair and fingernails continue to grow but phone calls taper off. Well finally the phone calls tapered off.

The dust began to settle. And a strange thing happened.

Tom started getting invitations to parties from people he didn't even know.

He was suddenly the hottest thing in town. And by sheer coincidence (some thought it was a plan!), two months later Tom's first book appeared. It was called *The Kandy-Kolored Tangerine-Flake Streamline Baby* and it became an overnight best-seller.

Newsweek on the Tom Wolfe–New Yorker Flap

"Libelous . . . murderous . . . ruthless . . . reckless . . ."

These strong, sometimes intemperate words came from New Yorker *editor William Shawn, a journalist with a legendary reputation for his judicious use of the language. . . . So disturbed was Shawn that before writing the letter, he tried unsuccessfully to reach Whitney and made his plea at least four times by phone to* Trib *editor James Bellows. But his cry went unheeded. . . . Beneath his byline, the 34-year-old Tom Wolfe, the* Trib's *hottest writer, explained it all in some 4,600 words—not counting exclamation points, ellipses, and "zonks." E. B. White, Robert Benchley, James Thurber, Dorothy Parker—writers who made* The New Yorker's *reputation—were all "tiny giants"! And because Shawn is bent on perpetuating their style, he has made the magazine's West 43rd Street offices a mausoleum of reverence and turned his present staff into "tiny mummies"! . . .*

Newsweek, April 1965

The New Yorker made a tactical error in going through the roof about Tom Wolfe's piece. Thanks to the boost given by their rage, within eighteen months *New York* magazine became the hottest magazine in America.

And Tom Wolfe was suddenly famous. All thanks to the bonfire of vanities on West 43rd Street.

"It taught me a lesson," reflected Tom Wolfe. "You can be denounced from the heavens, and it only makes people interested."

A Note from Tom Wolfe to Jim Bellows
After the Death of the Trib

I went down to the building of the alleged World-Journal-Tribune *yesterday and watched the Hoboken ferry come in about 92 times, and it really hit me what the end of the* Herald Tribune *means. I began to reflect a little, and one of the things that kept occurring to me was what a critical part you played in my good fortune.*

One of the things I remember was the day I went over to Jersey and did a story, and after it was in, you came over and told me I had done a great job. And that really gave me a lift. You created an atmosphere at the Trib *in which people had the freedom to swing from their heels and try to find the top of their form, because you gave the whole thing a sense of adventure.*

I think the last four years of the Herald Tribune *will go down in the books as the last great experiment, the last great hour of American newspapers.*

CHAPTER 2

◆

Ben Bradlee and The Ear

In January 1975, I was off on another suicide mission, this time to try to save the venerable *Washington Star*. The *Star* had been the pre-eminent newspaper in the capital during the years of World War II. It had an illustrious history and a great lineup of writers. But newsprint was scarce during the war, and the *Star* had used most of its space for advertising; the *Washington Post* used theirs for the news. Also, the *Star* was the victim of nepotism: The three families that owned the paper used it as an in-house welfare system. And nepotism led to stagnation. Besides, when TV arrived, afternoon papers had the life expectancy of fruit flies because people got their news at nightfall from television.

Another thing that damaged the *Star* was the increased prestige the *Washington Post* gained from two youngsters named Woodward and Bernstein who happened to unseat a president.

Still, I couldn't dream that the city of Washington didn't have enough people who read without moving their lips to support two newspapers.

So the year after Nixon left town on a rail, I arrived. A Texas multi-millionaire named Joe Allbritton, who had made fortunes in funeral homes and banking businesses, had bought the paper and hired me to become its editor. He knew of the changes I had wrought at the *New York Herald Tribune* in its glorious final days and thought I could bring similar incandescence to the *Star*, perhaps with a better outcome.

Joe found me at the *Los Angeles Times*, which I affectionately called the "velvet coffin" because of the generosity it showed its editorial staff.

I was the associate editor in charge of "soft news," and one of the popular features I had introduced was a gossip column by Joyce Haber.

"Are you going to start a gossip column in Washington, Jim?" I was asked at a farewell party.

"Oh, I don't think so. Gossip is trivial. Washington is a serious place."

That's how I saw it, in my naïveté. Washington was sober, solemn. Look at all that white marble, the Library of Congress, the Capitol dome. Boy, did I have the wrong number.

On my first trip to the capital, I attended a couple of dinner parties and observed, to my astonishment, that Washington *ran* on gossip. Everyone loved to talk about everyone else. Who was doing what to whom? A famous Washington hostess summed it up when she said, "If you don't have anything nice to say about someone, come sit by me."

Gossip made the Washington world go round.

So I decided that maybe a gossip column wasn't such a bad idea. I discussed it with the other *Star* editors, especially the talented head of our soft news section, Mary Anne Dolan. She suggested a perky Brit named Diana McLellan who could write with wit and flair.

I called Diana McLellan to my office.

"Diana," I said, "we are going to start a gossip column and you're going to write it."

She was aghast.

"Mr. Bellows, gossip isn't very nice. It's tacky and tawdry. There would be a public outcry. People would cancel their subscriptions. It would inflict pain. There's nothing you can say that would make me write a gossip column."

"We begin next Monday," I said.

"I'll get on the phone," said Diana.

Women's Wear Daily had a well-read column called The Eye. We called our column The Ear.

I knew it would take two people to do the job. The column would run without a byline, seven days of the week. I thought it would be controversial and people would want to see it daily. Two writers would assure that we'd never miss a day; not illness, vacation, rain, nor sleet would halt the column. So Louise Lague, a tall talented reporter, joined up the next day as Diana's partner.

The Ear was the wickedest thing to hit the capital since the Nixon administration. It was audacious. It was insolent. It was fun. And it quickly became "must" reading throughout Washington.

Did Ethel Kennedy buoyantly drive her convertible up the curb at Roger Mudd? . . . Did a southern congressman get pinched for propositioning a lady cop? . . . Did a prominent senatorial widow get arrested for shoplifting in Georgetown? . . . The Ear learned of these succulent happenings. Reporters in the *Star* newsroom, scrambling to save the paper, fed these items to Diana and Louise. Congressional staffers were good sources. Also, disgruntled bureaucrats. Also, certain politicians with a sense of humor, if that isn't an oxymoron. Also, hairdressers and florists. Gossipers all.

Diana McLellan profiled in the <u>Philadelphia Inquirer</u>

The Gossips

She is seated at a corner table with a good view, but alas, nothing worth reporting happens.

"I can tell what sort of gossip day it is going to be by the weather. I think it's something to do with the air pressure. If it's one of those rainy days when you can barely drag yourself out of bed, you know there will be no gossip today . . ."

Are you snobbish? "The thing I dislike in people is a lack of self-knowledge. People who can't stand back from themselves and see why they're doing things. I'm snobbish about people who are narrow-minded . . ."

Do people woo you? "I don't set myself up as a wooable. I don't go courting. If you're going to write a slightly outsiders column, you can't go on the toady circuit."

by Carol Horner, 1978

> ■ Ear-Say
>
> *Since its first appearance ten months ago in the Washington* Star, The Ear, *the brassy daily oracle, has become the most talked-about gossip column in a town that takes chitchat to heart. The Ear draws more phone calls and mail than any feature in the paper. "You're a dirty fun of a snitch," wrote one fan. A local socialite is planning an "Ear Ball" honoring Washingtonians mentioned in the column. The* Star *mails a gold-colored ear-shaped pin to all whose names have appeared.*
>
> *"New York's Great White Way is not so bright and glittering anymore," says the managing editor of the Fort Lauderdale* News. *"The center of gossip today is Washington."*
>
> *Time* magazine, May 10, 1976 ■

Sometimes the column would bother its subjects. When The Ear printed something that annoyed Washington's mayor, Marion Barry, he had all the cars towed from outside the paper's offices.

But there was a measurable statute of limitations of people's irritation with The Ear:

> Busy people forgave you faster than idle ones.
>
> Southern congressmen forgave you before northern ones.
>
> Writers and editors forgave you when they could pay you back.
>
> Cabinet members forgave you sooner than senators.
>
> Academics *never* forgave you.
>
> And Kennedys got even.

The success of The Ear was a testament to the fact that Washington was at heart a small, provincial, southern town. It might have been the Capital of the Free World, but it loved its gossip. John F. Kennedy once said, "Washington is a combination of northern charm and southern efficiency." It was also a combination of dish and dirt.

I urged Diana and Louise to include coverage of the media, and it was fun to treat reporters as though they were movie stars. They loved it. I trace a lot of today's media self-importance to the unaccustomed attention we gave them. Robert Redford played a Washington journalist. Now there are a dozen Washington journalists playing Robert Redford.

We started to send out little gold ear-shaped lapel pins to the people who were mentioned in the column. Some were enraged at having been kidded in the column, but the sheer cheek of the thing soon got to them. Eventually most of the honorees cheerfully wore their ears. At first, people assumed the lapel pins meant the wearer was deaf, and they would raise their voices. That's all we needed in Washington—more raised voices.

For a few years we held an annual Ear Ball, to which we invited everyone who had ever been mentioned in the column. This generated some wildly variegated crowds. G. Gordon Liddy showed up, fresh out

---

Louise Lague Recalls My Arrival at the <u>Star</u>

For people who hasten to report what is fresh and new, journalists are astoundingly cynical about change. So we approached Jim Bellows' appearance at the Washington Star *with great caution. He was an outsider, not rising from within, always a source of suspicion. But he had the right stuff. . . . Bellows reinforced a spirit of serious play at the* Star. *From him I learned for the first time that an afternoon newspaper was not a must-have item by definition, but rather a product that had to be magnetic and engaging and sell itself day after day. Bellows taught us how to* sell *news, and that there was no shame in doing so.*

We were used to feeling redundant but dutiful at our second-string afternoon paper. Every day from our ugly gray building in the wrong part of town, we humbly followed a stunning feature act—the Washington Post—*powerful enough to unseat a President, and so glamorous that Robert Redford and Dustin Hoffman were making a movie about it, for godsake.*

Bellows, however, would tolerate no feelings of inferiority. He planned to turn the Star *from an also-ran into something fantastic that readers couldn't wait to bite into. He was ready to spread the gospel.*

Letter, March 2001

of prison; members of the party leadership; White House speechwriters; hairdressers, interior decorators, and local socialites . . .

The success of The Ear was a testament to more than Washington's provincialism. It was also a testament to Diana McLellan's wit and vivacity. Diana was the daughter of an RAF brigadier general who eventually became defense attaché for the British embassy in Washington. She grew up all around the world, including Wales, Rhodesia, and London. "You become more aware of what makes things work when you have to confront things new all the time" (not unlike constantly changing newspapers). As a teenager she was an art student. "I wasn't going to be a writer at all. I was precocious and snobbish," she said.

Louise Lague was Rhode Island–born, left-handed, five-eight, green-eyed, and of French-Canadian descent. Only 26 when The Ear was

My "Ear" Columnists Wish Me a Happy Birthday

Through toil and stress, and thick and thin
You're there, Chief, with your glasses in
Your mouth; your cards upon the table.
Even at your great age, chief, you're able
To soothe the savage beasts—like Ben—
And wield, toujours, a winner's pen.
Bust not a gut, nor hit the floor
At hitting two score, ten and four!
Despite your Earaches, trauma, tension,
It ain't time for that old age pension.
Age will not wither, custom stale,
Jim (Abdul!) Bellows, sexy male.
Kind Muses! Hover round his head,
And keep that inspiration spread;
His rising Star prod from behind
And jam with juice his fruitful mind.
Peace, perqs and puissance push his way,
On this, his glorious Natal day.

Louise Lague and Diana McLellan, November 12, 1976

launched, she was a bright and funny writer but wary of hurting people's feelings. Her motto: No scolding, no finger-pointing, but lots of verve, italics, and exclaiming. It was always: "How *heartwarming* to see Senator So-and-So taking his secretary to lunch at the Jockey Club! *That* is appreciation, darlings!"

So before there was *Thelma and Louise* there was Diana and Louise, who came close to the edge, but never drove off. Diana and Louise rarely went to parties, as most gossip columnists do, relying instead on personal contacts and the stream of phone tips that flooded in. In fact, at first few people knew who actually wrote the column. The big weapon in their closet was the message machine. In those days, before everybody had one, theirs was a treat to listen to. I remember them setting it up before they'd go out to lunch, and when they came back, there'd be a stream of whispered murmurs on the machine.

"Through some outrageous fortune," recalls Louise, "we could pretty much tell what was true and what wasn't." (I wish I had known that when I was carefully vetting the column each day.) "The day we were asked to judge a dog show, I knew this thing was *big.*"

In a short time, Diana and Louise's identity became the worst-kept secret in Washington, right up there with the guest list for the Lincoln Bedroom.

And with their help, gossip stepped out of the closet and became almost respectable. Diana's explanation for the popularity of chatter: "It's because we don't have *opinions* to gossip about anymore."

The biggest celebrities in Washington were Ben Bradlee and his lovely roommate, Sally Quinn. The movie blockbuster *All the President's Men* was lighting up Washington's screens at this time. Ben Bradlee, the charismatic editor of the *Washington Post,* was a combination of all that is admirable in journalism and pop culture. He and Sally Quinn were the beautiful people of the Potomac. So we started making them regulars in The Ear. We called them "The Fun Couple."

It was nothing personal.

All right, perhaps I was a little annoyed at how the *Washington Post* always referred to the *Star* as "the financially troubled *Washington Star.*"

For a while I thought that was our name: *The Financially Troubled Washington Star*.

And you must understand something else.

After Watergate, Ben Bradlee was a huge, heroic, larger-than-life figure. Jason Robards had just won an Academy Award playing Ben on the screen. Robards/Bradlee was a noble, witty, astute editor in power stripes. (My contract for this book requires that if movie rights are sold, I must be played by my fellow Kenyon College graduate, Paul Newman.)

Ben Bradlee could be forgiven for being a little puffed up by the attention. So when The Ear targeted his Achilles' heel it must have

---

Letter to Me from Ben Bradlee

The Washington Post
1150 15th Street, N.W.
Washington, DC 20071

Dear Jim:

You apparently don't think it's terrible to write what you do write about the Post.

But to us, your references to the Post, *to Mrs. Graham, and to others, including me and Quinn, are without exception sneering, impugning, belittling and ridiculing. And when it is known that you are personally involved in their editing, it is only natural that I feel you are something of an authority on what is shoddy and disgraceful in journalism.*

The question is really what do you want to do about it? If you want to do nothing, that's fine with us.

If you want to talk about it, let's talk.

Sincerely,

Ben

April 4, 1977

■ D.C. Shootout: Bradlee vs. Bellows in Big Macho Duel

No wonder the Washington Post's *Ben Bradlee and the* Washington Star's *Jim Bellows don't like each other. They're just alike. They both started out as Navy men in World War II and ended up editing rival Washington papers. They even look alike and have the same deep voice. They're the same person. Bradlee and Bellows's alliterative feud borders on self-loathing.*

Washington's B-B war is just that. It is carried on with an air-rifle intensity, but the frequent hits smart. Which is all as it should be. In the old Front Page *days, Chicago was the home of organized crime and press wars. But Richard Nixon brought organized crime to Washington and with it came in-town media competition. The Bradley-Bellows fight fits the town perfectly. Who would want Washington's two leading editors to get along?*

Aaron Latham in *More* magazine, September 1976 ■

---

been particularly annoying. But after all, he was cavorting about with a much younger woman in his own newsroom. Did he expect that to go unnoticed?

On top of that, much of the news about Bradlee and Quinn was coming to us from his own newsroom. Ben threatened to fire anyone caught leaking information to The Ear, but still it came.

Some of the leaks may have been inspired by jealousy. Sally Quinn was not uniformly adored in the *Post* newsroom. Some of her fellow journalists grumbled that the stories she brought in would not have been assigned to her if not for her relationship with the editor.

Most people gave Ben a wide berth. And here, The Ear had the temerity to make fun of His Eminence. The Ear would do to Ben Bradlee what Nixon and Colson never managed to do—needle and embarrass him. But, of course, I had an advantage over Nixon: He only had the FBI, the CIA, and the IRS; I had Diana and Louise.

Ben was the perfect target for us, and I took delight in tweaking him. Not because I didn't like him—I admire Ben enormously—but because it worked wonders for the *Star*. When you are the second paper in a market, you have to position yourself against the first paper—you have to be sassy and irreverent, and you have to get people talking.

Katharine Graham on Changes at the <u>Star</u>

Important changes were taking place at the Star. . . . *Joe Allbritton had worked hard to turn around his staid and failing newspaper. When he first came to town, he had put in as editor Jim Bellows, a great talent who didn't try to compete with us where we were strong but went under, around, and beside us. The paper became livelier, more interesting, and scrappier. Jim started a gossip column called "The Ear," which specialized in tweaking the* Post, *which the* Star *referred to as the "O.P."—or the Other Paper. The most intimate details of the lives of many of us at the* Post *became grist for the mill of "The Ear." In particular it was savage about Ben Bradlee and Sally Quinn, referring to them as "The Fun Couple" and reporting on their every activity, no doubt with some help from reliable sources in our own city room. We all came in for attention, some of it accurate, some of it half accurate, some of it entirely fictitious.*

As I said to Joe Allbritton when I moved to Washington:

"We can't be a pale copy of the *Post*. That's not how it's done."

"How's it done?"

"We've got to get them to jump into our pond. We've got to make waves. We've got to liven things up."

The Ear, featuring Ben and Sally, was one of the ways of getting the *Post* into our pond—of livening things up.

We could see them wincing . . .

In 1975 the *Star* had run a series of articles on gays in pro football. The pieces were shepherded by the sports editor, Dave Burgin, who had worked earlier at the *Trib* and went on to become the editor of the *Orlando Sentinel,* the *Oakland Tribune,* and the *San Francisco Examiner,* among other papers.

Spurred by our gay pigskin series, the Chicago columnist Mike Royko had written a great column on the phenomenon. He observed that the macho guys who watch football on TV were now finding it disturbing when their favorite quarterback patted the tight end on the rear.

I wanted to run the Royko column in the *Star*, since it had grown out of our stories. But Royko's column was syndicated exclusively to the *Post* in Washington. So I called my pal Ben.

"Ben," I said, "I'm sure you don't intend to run the Royko column in the *Post*. You won't want to promote our series."

"So?"

"So I'd like to buy the column for the *Star*."

"I'll call you back."

When Bradlee called back he sounded a little aggressive.

"Okay, you can run the Royko column, but you'll have to say: `With the permission of the *Washington Post*.'"

"Fair enough, Ben. I'll just—"

"That's not all," said Bradlee.

"What else, Ben?"

"For *one month* you don't run my name or Sally's in that damn column of yours!"

I agreed.

"Oh, Ben—"

"Yeah?"

"Maybe you'd better send me a letter confirming the deal."

When I received the letter, I posted it on the bulletin board. The newsroom erupted in laughter and it was a big score for our side.

Ben Bradlee had been brought in to do for the *Post* what I was later brought in to do for the *Star*—brighten it up. Ben's career was a little like mine, only with security. Back in the Eisenhower years (if you will cast your mind back), the *Star* was being knocked off its upholstered throne by the *Washington Post*. Eugene Meyer, the *Post*'s owner, turned over a growing daily to his son-in-law Phil Graham, who was without newspaper experience. Graham had married Katharine Meyer, the only one of Meyer's kids who was attracted to journalism. In 1959 Phil Graham bought *Newsweek* magazine. When he died in 1963, Kay Graham assumed the leadership of the *Post*. She took *Newsweek*'s

Washington bureau chief, Ben Bradlee, to lunch at the F Street Club and asked him what he wanted to do with the rest of his life. His answer has become the stuff of legend: "I'd rather be managing editor of the *Post* than anything in the world. I'd give my left one for the job." History does not record whether Ben was ever asked to make this ultimate gift of loyalty. (There is a possible answer to this intriguing question in a recent e-mail from the *Star* associate editor Ed Yoder: "Re the story about Ben's left one, at Bradlee's retirement party at the *Post,* Kay told the famous story and then quipped, 'I accepted his offer.'")

The *Post* was prospering at that point, but it had grown dull and flabby, a typical concomitant of financial success, I have observed.

Ben was installed at the *Post* as deputy managing editor in 1964 with the understanding that he would get the top job when Al Friendly retired. But Friendly was in no hurry to go. It might have been a long wait had not Walter Lippmann and Friendly lunched one day. Over the appetizer, the columnist said: "Al, you shouldn't be an administrator all your life. You ought to start writing again." Friendly was persuaded to step down. And just 90 days after joining the *Post,* Ben Bradlee became its managing editor. Yes, Virginia, there *is* a Walter Lippmann.

Now we come to the question of accuracy and The Ear.

I must admit that The Ear wasn't always accurate.

Once The Ear ran a rumor that President Carter had bugged the house where the Reagans were staying as they waited to assume the presidency. That wasn't correct.

Then there was the item about the former secretary of state Dean Acheson having been spied at a Georgetown dinner party. Only it turned out that at the time of that particular party, Mr. Acheson was regrettably deceased. Diana made it all right with a correction: "Mr. Acheson is a teensy bit dead," she apologized.

"Oh, the shame of the first few public screw-ups," recalls Diana. "Louise and I each blamed the other in private, but if you personally wrote it, you had to set it straight. If our victim was inappropriately indignant, we added enough details to our correction so that he wished to God he'd kept his mouth shut."

Whenever The Ear made a mistake, Diana McLellan would write a correction—what she called "a grovel." She wrote with such wit that her corrections were as entertaining as her mistakes. And more lethal.

Ben Bradlee blistered us for our mistakes.

"Their record for accuracy is the worst I've ever seen!" he exploded. "They never call to check out what they print about me. They're unbelievable!"

Art Buchwald had worked for me on the *Trib,* and he was an old friend of Ben's. The ideal mediator. He arranged a lunch for the two of us at a hotel far from the center of town. You couldn't have the editors of Washington's two big dailies be seen eating together.

I explained to Ben that The Ear was just a device to get the *Post* into our pond. Ben was still fuming because The Ear had reported that his sons had had a run-in with the law—something about overparking. I

Jeremy Campbell Reports from
Washington in the <u>London Evening Standard</u>

James Bellows is perhaps the trendiest editor in America. . . . Now he is editor of the Washington Star, *a paper scorned by sophisticates in the smart houses of Georgetown and pushed to the edge of collapse by the only other newspaper in the capital, the rich, liberal and increasingly powerful* Washington Post. *The* Star *had to reach for its readers in the suburbs, on housing estates, and in shopping malls, where life, to the chic hostesses of political Washington, seems a drab panorama of car pools, school board meetings, and dinner theatre performances of* Hello, Dolly!

Bellows is an extraordinary figure to be in command of this staid newspaper which for a century was managed by three aristocratic families. He is tall, dark and Gothic, like a character in a Bronte novel. He speaks in a rapid, interior mumble, so that practiced members of his staff sometimes follow his train of thoughts by watching the movements of his hands . . .

1977

acknowledged our mistake and apologized. I agreed the kids were off limits.

And that was about it for our landmark lunch. Two checks.

Then there was the time The Ear accused the *Washington Post* of killing a column that accused a U.S. senator of repeatedly seducing a blonde constituent. Why did the *Post* spike the column? Perhaps because during the 1976 pressmen's strike, when the *Post* presses were damaged, the good senator had let the *Post* print their paper on the presses of his suburban daily. And so the *Post* was returning the favor. Said The Ear:

> *Take care of your chums and your chums will take care of you . . .*
> You must have heard by now that a Virginia constituent has accused Sen. Harry Byrd, her very own senator, of seducing her thrice while she begged him for help in finding her deserting husband. It's all in a Jack Anderson column this week, and it ran in over 900 newspapers, but *not* the *Post,* darlings. The Knowledgeables are saying that's because the senator's own sweet little rag printed the *Post* when they were having their Troubles. Ear is astonished.

My phone rang as soon as our first edition hit the streets.

"That's a cheap shot!" barked Bradlee.

"Wait, I'll look at it," I said.

"I just wanted to tell you that personally," said Ben and hung up.

I looked at the column and it seemed a little strong. I killed the last two sentences, which ascribed an ignoble motive to the *Post.* Then I called Bradlee back. But he wouldn't take my call. I got his secretary.

"I'd like to speak to Mr. Bradlee."

"He's all tied up, Mr. Bellows."

"Tell him I think perhaps Ear should run a correction."

"He's all tied up, Mr. Bellows."

"Explain to Ben that a correction would repeat in *all* editions a charge that has only appeared in *one* edition."

"He's all tied up, Mr. Bellows."

"So ask him if he wants to drop the whole matter or have it corrected."

"He's all tied up, Mr. Bellows."

"Tell him I apologize and we've knocked out the bottom line."

"I'll tell him, Mr. Bellows."

"Have him call and tell me what he wants me to do."

Ben never called back.

When the *Star* died, Ben Bradlee hired Diana McLellan to write a gossip column for the *Washington Post*.

"What the hell," Ben told a reporter who questioned his adopting a feature that had given him so much pain. "We can't afford not to take somebody's good idea."

But I ask myself: Would Jason Robards have done that?

Diana insists to this day that she and Louise were amazingly ill-equipped for the gossip game. Of course, it wasn't easy. The *Star* was on a starvation diet and I expected them to churn out seven Ears a week, plus, later, our soap-opera-in-print, "Federal Triangle." "We were stretched till we squeaked," recalls Diana. The giddy glee that seemed to hang over the column sprang, I suspect, from their deadline desperation, along with the comforting fact that we didn't use bylines.

"Looking at those hit-and-run columns today," reflects Diana, "I'm surprised we didn't have more corpses turning up at parties."

The Ear would struggle on for a total of ten years, in three Washington papers. Eventually, I'm told, it got all the trimmings—syndication, a private office, fancy lunches, even an assistant to check things out. But it was never as much fun as when Diana, Louise, and I started it on a wing and a rumor.

It didn't take Diana long to figure out the basics: "Take it easy on the little guys; the biggies can, and will, take care of themselves. And always leave a sprinkling of spice out of a particularly juicy item. It might come in handy later, to season a grovel."

Another good idea that Ben and the *Post* inherited from the *Star* was one of the funniest, most talented political cartoonists in the country,

Pat Oliphant. I had brought Pat—and his irreverence and talent—to the *Star* from the *Denver Post*. I put his cartoons on page one of the early edition, where it became a daily feature that caught people's eyes at the newsstand.

When I invited him to join the *Star*, Pat had two demands. One was that he be given a room with a door. Two was that the room have a source of running water. The door was to keep out journalists who like to hide out in a cartoonist's space. The running water was for cleaning pens and brushes. Simple enough requests.

"And a window," said Pat. "I need a window."

I showed him a room adjoining my own office. The furniture was what he called "Mafia modern," but the place did have a window. One of the panes had a bullet hole. The room had not one, but two doors. One opened to the hall, the other into my office.

"What about the running water?" asked Oliphant.

"Well, you can come through that door and walk through here and get water from there." There was a lot of arm waving as I indicated his own distant private bathroom on the far side of my office.

"Any time of the day, right?" said Pat.

"Any time of the day," I said.

And so it was that, many times when I was deep in low-voiced conference, trying to bring fresh talent to the *Star*, Oliphant would come barreling through on a mission to wash a brush, usually to the alarm of the new prospect.

"I felt that such people had a right to be made aware from the outset just what sort of Lewis Carroll scenario they were getting into," said the cartoonist.

In the bathroom, Pat tried to make as much noise as possible, running the taps loud and long with the door open and flushing the toilet for good measure. I never gave him the satisfaction of looking ruffled.

I have always been impressed by the continuing Washington soap opera, the great romances that have unfolded along the Potomac: Jack and Jackie, Bill and Monica, Ben and Sally, Haldeman and Ehrlichman.

So the idea occurred to me: Why not a daily soap opera in print? Why not a fictional satire of the Washington scene?

I told Mary Anne Dolan the idea—we named it "Federal Triangle"—and she invited selected members of the staff to join us in the great adventure:

Diana McLellan, The Ear

Louise Lague, The Ear

David Richards, theater critic

Michael Satchell, national reporter and muckraker

Gloria Berger, metro reporter

John McKelway, author of a Thurberesque *Star* column

Richard Slusser, chief obituary writer

Oliphant Reflects on My Mumbling and Arm Waving

Many people claimed they had trouble understanding anything Bellows said. The mumbling and arm waving and never finishing a sentence, that is all true. But that same strange mixture of inarticulation was in some mysterious way the source of inspiration to many people. There is something about Bellows which makes you want to do something for him that he will enjoy or appreciate. It is quite an artifice, for when he really wants you to hear something he is capable of speaking quite clearly. Not that you would understand what he is saying at those times, any more than when he is mumbling. In those days, as now, he was much given to the cryptic and the off-beat. He collected sayings, punchlines, couplets and ambiguities, and came forth with them at unexpected moments. . . . He once handed me a business-size card on which he had printed, "Begin at once and do the best you can." And, in the two or three seconds I pondered this and turned to ask him what it meant, he had disappeared. He is the complete enigma.

Letter, 2001

The "soap opera seven" would meet daily at a roundtable and work out the characters and events of our political story. The writers would alternate writing the daily pieces. Each staffer became a specialist in the behavior of one of the principals.

Here's a touch of it to give you the flavor: Baby Jill Sloane, fresh out of West Virginia, gets her first job at the Chicken and Egg Division of the Department of Agriculture. She is rooming with ex-hippie Melissa Priest and male nurse Howard Stubbs. Enter Congressman Snip Swinnerton, his wife, Cynthia. . . . Not quite Allen Drury. It all takes place in Federal Triangle, the name of an actual bus stop in Washington.

The daily headlines for the feature were like catnip for D.C. readers: "How Quick, Strong and Gentle He Was." "Cold Feet, Hot Passion and Iced Cliquot." "After the Moon Glow, a Bit of Ennui."

■ **Maureen Dowd on Working as a Reporter at the <u>Washington Star</u>**

A few simple tips about how to become a rich and famous reporter. My rule number one is grovel. I got hired for my first newspaper job in a bar, which probably explains a lot. I realized immediately I was not ideally suited to my new profession. I hated asking questions. I hated calling strangers, I couldn't write. I thought being a good writer meant I had to use the words "splendiferous" and "eschewed" a lot. . . . So what I mean by groveling is, don't ever let your ego get in the way of getting the story. If someone doesn't return your call the first couple of times try a dozen more times. Go to their house. Bob Woodward still does that when he's reporting. He just shows up at people's houses at night and that's pretty scary. If someone insults you or yells at you or treats you badly, don't slam down the phone or storm out. Keep taking notes. One of the great things about being a reporter is that you always get *the last word.*

Dowd speaking at a *Star* reunion, spring 1993 ■

To my astonishment, E. P. Dutton asked to publish a book of the soap opera, and in 1977 *Federal Triangle* appeared in bookstores everywhere. It was edited by Mary Anne Dolan. I particularly appreciated the dedication:

TO JIM BELLOWS. BLAME HIM.

What Next for Ben Bradlee?

Years from now, newspaper historians will refer to the mid-1970s era as Washington journalism's Gilded Age of Bradlee and Bellows. But now that Jim Bellows has left the Potomac swamps for the lotus land of Southern California, speculation flourishes at the Washington Post *over whether Ben Bradlee will follow suit and soon vacate his editor's chair.*

Not long ago, the Post *barely acknowledged the competitive existence of the* Star. *Now, Bradlee is accused of copying successful features of the afternoon paper, such as Ear, the popular gossip column. Bradlee is aware that the* Star's *reclamation and its reborn vitality made it obligatory for the* Post *to come up with a second act following its dazzling Watergate coverage.*

Washington Journalism Review, 1979

CHAPTER 3

◆

The Klan, Mr. Hoover, and Me

Wow!
A big story!
In the news business for about a year and this!
A tip just for me—better keep it quiet.
The biggest Ku Klux Klan meeting in 20 years!
Tonight at the top of Pine Mountain . . .

Those were the thoughts that chased one another around my head. I was a green reporter on a newspaper in a Georgia town, the *Columbus Ledger*. It was my first newspaper job. I had been hired in 1947. I had spent my time covering Rotary meetings, Kiwanis luncheons, and auto accidents. An intelligence officer from Fort Benning, the army base across the river, had his office in town, and that office was on my beat. One day he gave me the tip. What every young reporter looks for, dreams of. Especially a troublemaker like me!

I rounded up a couple of other young staffers—Carl Johnson, another cub reporter, and Joe Talbot, a staff photographer. Of course I probably should have told the city editor, or the managing editor, or *somebody* in authority where we were going. But the army officer had urged secrecy. This was my story and I wanted to cover it.

That evening found the passionate cub reporter in a car parked down the street from the old wooden church where the Klansmen were to assemble. Carl, Joe, and I watched the Klansmen arrive in twos and threes and huddle outside the church. "Parson Jack" Johnson was the Baptist minister who welcomed his brood. When the crowd had reached a critical mass, the Klansmen boarded three hulking buses that waited in the shadows and the buses lumbered off down the street. Parson Jack was leading his flock to the mountain.

We followed at a discreet distance. It was a 30-mile drive to the top of Pine Mountain. When the buses reached the crest and disgorged their passengers, we remained out of sight. We found a ditch that was deep enough, and banked high enough, to let us stand almost erect without being seen a short distance away. I estimated there were about a hundred men in white robes and hoods. They were taking some unrobed men into a tarpaper shack. It must have been an initiation, for when they came out, they all wore white. Then the Klansmen gathered around a huge cross and someone threw a match. The cross roared into flame.

"This place looks like hell," whispered Carl Johnson.

"That's exactly what it looks like," I said.

The wind was whipping the orange flames at the sky.

Standing before the hooded men was the Grand Dragon himself in his emerald robes. He was an Atlanta doctor named Samuel Green who was striving to revive the Klan across the South.

We were about two hundred feet from the flaming cross. I signaled Joe Talbot to take some pictures. He risked his head above the ditch and snapped off a couple of shots. One of the Klansmen spotted him and gave the alarm. They surrounded us, grabbed us, smashed Joe's camera, and stomped on the film. We were suddenly at the center of a threatening, shouting mob.

They handed us a bottle of whiskey.

"Drink!" they yelled.

When we refused they forced a pint or so down our throats. Then they dragged us into the shack. They jabbed a hypodermic needle into Carl's arm and Joe's leg. I had passed out. Carl and Joe clung to consciousness.

The Klansmen carried us to our car. Carl and I were placed in the backseat. Someone took my pants down and put me next to Carl in a position indicating we were engaged in sodomy. Another Klansman snapped some photos.

There was someone in the crowd who had plans for those photos. He was Fred W. New, editor and publisher of a racist rag called the *Georgia Journal*. The former editor was Parson Jack Johnson, who had shepherded the group to the mountain.

Two Klansmen then drove us to a deserted road on the outskirts of the town of Manchester. They wiped the steering wheel clean of fingerprints and fled the scene. Minutes later Manchester police found us. For them to arrive so quickly, they must have been called by one of the cross burners. Or more likely, some of the cross burners just got back into their daytime uniforms.

We were driven into town, booked for drunkenness, and thrown into a cell.

My FBI file, which covers these events, runs to 77 pages. Thanks to the Freedom of Information Act, which Congress finally passed in 1966, I was able to lay my hands on it. The file contains a series of

---

J. Edgar Hoover Reports My Case to the Attorney General

According to information furnished [name deleted], the two unrobed Klansmen gave each of the victims a pint of liquor and informed them they would either have to drink it or it would be thrown in their faces. The victims drank the liquor, as well as some vodka; however, only one of the victims, James G. Bellows, "passed out." It was reported that the other two victims were given some injections.

[Name deleted] further informed [name deleted] that Carlton Johnson was in the back seat of the automobile and that the Klan members partially undressed him and placed victim Bellows in a position that would indicate that an act of sodomy was taking place. According to the victims, a photograph was taken of Johnson and Bellows in this position . . .

Memo from James Bellows's FBI file, dated March 22, 1948

■ <u>Time</u> Magazine Reports on "Nightmare on Pine Mountain"

The Ledger's photographer, Joe Talbot, 36, stepped forward, started shooting flashbulbs.

He did not get many shots. The Klansmen grabbed him, began smashing his equipment. They also grabbed Talbot's colleagues, Reporters James Bellows, 25, and Carlton Johnson, 22, both, like Talbot, Navy veterans. What happened after that the newsmen described in print next day. The Klansmen handed them each a bottle of whiskey and ordered them to drink. When they refused, the Klansmen shouted that they would pour the liquor down them. They drank—a pint each within 30 minutes.

Talbot recalled later: "Bellows just kinda folded up on the ground. . . . They just threw him down beside the fire."

Time, National Affairs section, March 22, 1948 ■

memos from FBI Director J. Edgar Hoover to Attorney General Tom Clark, as well as reports to Hoover from the head of his Atlanta bureau. According to the file, some Klansmen didn't want us to see a cell. They had homicidal plans for us. Reported Hoover: "A threat had been made by an unknown [Klansman] that, after the men became intoxicated, they would be taken out in the automobile and [we would] wreck same." They didn't wreck same. They were content to manhandle same, get same drunk, and have same arrested.

At 1:24 A.M. the Manchester police called our city editor, Joe Hall.

"We have three of your boys in our jail," they announced.

Of course, he had no idea what we were up to.

Joe Hall drove to Manchester and tried to get us released. He was told there would be no disposition of the case till morning. Finally, at 7 A.M. they released us, on payment of a fine of $8.30 each.

Next day, Fred W. New phoned Carl Johnson at the paper. It sounded like he had photos of Carl and me in a compromising position.

NEW: Yes, oh, Carlton, I want to see you privately . . . just you and me. Got some information for you . . .

JOHNSON: What kind of information?

NEW: Just want to show you some photographs.

Reported J. Edgar Hoover: "The *Ledger* recorded the phone conversation . . . the morning after the incident, wherein New stated to Johnson 'I have some etchings I think you should see before you print any story.'"

Hoover was able to contain his rage at this report of brutality and blackmail, this assault on freedom of the press. A very even-handed man, Mr. Hoover. "The property on which the Klan meeting was held," he pointed out, "is owned by the Ku Klux Klan, and the newspapermen had not been invited."

The *Ledger* headlined the event. It was mortified at this assault on its reporters. Fury swept the journalistic community.

A GRIEVOUS CRIME AGAINST GEORGIA

SUIT AGAINST KLAN DRAGON LOOMS

KKK ASSAULT PROBE SLATED BY GOVERNOR

Staffer's Own Version of Mistreatment by Klansmen,
by Jim Bellows

More than 100 men milled on the Muscogee courthouse lawn Friday night, ready to attend Ku Klux Klan initiation rites in a tiny Pine Mountain Valley community house. The group left here at 7 P.M. in three chartered Howard buses, followed by a caravan of cars carrying officials of the robed order including the Grand Dragon himself. . . . A Ledger *reporter, photographer, and I trailed the procession and watched it travel the hour-long route to the schoolhouse some two miles outside Shiloh, Ga. . . . The uninitiated Klansmen were gathered round a bonfire outside the rectangular schoolhouse, waiting for the pledge-taking. Some talked about the March wind whipping through the mountain top. Others spoke of a coming war. And some simply wanted to know when they would be called to "take the obligation." . . . One tall, shabbily dressed youth paid his fee to a man who stepped outside of the dimly lit building. Then the first of the robed men told those gathered around the fire to line up . . .*

Columbus (Georgia) Ledger, *March 14, 1948*

Time and *Newsweek* both gave the story a big play. "Nightmare on Pine Mountain," headlined *Time*. The *Atlanta Constitution* editorialized, "The outrage was an unspeakable brutality, so diabolical in its scheme that it could have been conceived only by a sadistic pervert and executed by beasts in human form."

A *Ledger* editorial vowed: "We shall leave absolutely no stone unturned to assure that justice is done." The *Ledger*'s attorney, Bentley Chappell, would be handling our case.

The wire services took note. Reporters from the Associated Press and the International News Service cornered Grand Dragon Samuel Green. He admitted he was at the meeting but said if there were reporters there, it was news to him. He dismissed our story as a "cock and bull story cooked up to satisfy [their] editor."

I had spotted our paper's very own assistant circulation manager, Hollis Cooper, at the cross burning. The *Ledger* editor announced that Cooper had been confronted with our statements and had resigned.

New Disputes <u>Ledger</u> Men, Charges Plot

Fred New, publisher of the Georgia Tribune, *charged Monday night that the story of the Ku Klux Klan's manhandling of three* Ledger *staffers was "a cloak-and-dagger, ultra Dick Tracy story . . . cooked up by three men who had fluffed an assignment." . . . Mr. New asserted in a speech broadcast on Radio station WDAK that the* Ledger-Enquirer *management had seen in the staffers' story "an opportunity to crush a rival newspaper which is about to enter the daily field."*

Mr. New also stated . . . that "a diligent inquiry in the vicinity of the alleged incident" would reveal that the three men had gone "to a nearby night club" after leaving the Klan meeting, drank more, and "were ejected for ungentlemanly behavior." . . . He said he had not seen liquor forced on anyone. "Mr. New described the offer of liquor . . . as having been "forced on them the way a fish is forced on a hungry cat."

Atlanta Constitution, March 1948

An Editorial in the <u>Columbus Ledger</u>:
"We Accept the Klan's Challenge"

They say that history sometimes repeats its pattern. If that is true with respect to these newspapers and the Ku Klux Klan—so be it.

In the early Twenties, the Ku Klux Klan in Georgia in and around Columbus became so arrogant in its outrages that the Columbus Ledger *. . . launched a crusade which helped smash that organization of night riders and terrorists.*

On Friday night the Klan challenged again . . .

We accept the challenge.

We have apprised the Attorney General of the United States of the facts. We have apprised the governor of Georgia of the facts. We have apprised the Federal Bureau of Investigation of the facts. We have apprised the State and local law officers of the facts. We have hidden nothing and shall hide nothing.

We shall leave absolutely no stone unturned to see that justice is done, and we don't care how long it takes.

March 1948

The uproar was coming at a bad time for the state of Georgia. Southern leaders were in Washington in 1947 fighting off civil rights legislation designed to protect the rights of southern blacks. Said the *Atlanta Constitution*, without irony: "What chance do the Governors of Southern states have to convince the people of the United States that human rights are safe in Georgia?"

I was still nursing bruises on my skull, cheek, and chin. Joe and Carl had punctures on their arms and legs from the Klan's syringes. The Columbus city physician tested us to see whether dope had actually been injected in our veins as we claimed. He found it had. Reported Mr. Hoover, whose powers of deduction were impressive: "The injuries of victim Bellows appeared to have been received as a result of falling on his face." (Not the last time *that* happened.)

A hearing on our case was coming up in court. We didn't know a thing about it. We had gone back to our reporting jobs. Then suddenly one morning I read on the Associated Press ticker that our hearing was scheduled for that very day! Not only that, I read that our bonds were to be forfeited. We were to enter a plea of guilty! And we hadn't been told a thing about it. This by the newspaper that had vowed to leave no stone unturned till justice was done. There were unturned stones everywhere I looked.

I was furious. I spoke to Joe and Carl.

"We need a meeting," I said.

J. Edgar described our meeting with management to his ostensible boss, Attorney General Tom Clark: "At 2:30 that afternoon the paper held a meeting with A. H. Chapman (president of the paper), Bryan Collier (editor), Joe Hall (city editor), Maynard Ashworth (publisher), and Bentley Chappell (lawyer). Also victims Bellows, Johnson and Talbot. . . . The victims asked what was happening. Attorney Chappell said that there was no purpose in going through with the hearing, that it would not help the case, and that he saw no chance of the victims 'getting off.'" The *Ledger* president patiently explained that he had not contacted us about any of this "because he didn't know that they [we] wanted to know what was happening." Oh?

Lawyer Chappell told us that he couldn't go to the hearing that afternoon. When I protested, he said he would contact another lawyer, W. S. "Jack" Allen. He phoned Allen and let me talk to him.

Hoover reported: "Allen said that he could not go to the hearing in Manchester. He added that there was no purpose in going as he had talked to the Manchester police who were friends, and from their stories he could see that the victims would be convicted." Allen was not going to turn any stones either.

I made another heated request that Allen attend the hearing. He refused. He also refused to ask for a postponement. I hung up the phone. It was now 4 P.M. and the hearing was scheduled for 5. I phoned the judge of the Manchester police court.

■ Governor Orders State Probe of Klan Case Here

Green Cries "Politics" and Calls Story a Hoax

Gov. M. E. Thompson ordered the Chief of the Georgia Bureau of Investigation Monday to investigate personally the manhandling of three Ledger *staffers at a Ku Klux Klan meeting . . .*

Meanwhile, Grand Dragon Dr. Samuel Green of the Ku Klux Klan charged Monday that the Ledger *was using the statement by its three newsmen as a political move to tie in with the Governor's election.*

Replying to charges of the three men that they were forced to drink excessive amounts of liquor, given hypodermic injections, and left on the side of the highway, the KKK leader said he felt they became drunk, were arrested, and concocted the story as an excuse.

Columbus Ledger, *March 1948* ■

"Your Honor, my name is Jim Bellows. My case is before you today. I'm calling to request a postponement of the hearing for just a few minutes, until the other defendants and I can drive to Manchester."

"Those bonds were forfeited this morning," said the judge curtly.

I told my editor what the judge had told me and walked out of the room.

A few days later, Mr. Hoover sent another memo to the attorney general: "These individuals forfeited bonds of $8.30 each and failed to appear in court. The attorney representing these individuals telephonically advised I. H. Davis, City Recorder, Manchester, Georgia, that the collateral bond made by Bellows, Talbot and Johnson would be forfeited."

Case closed.

Not quite. Defense came from an unexpected quarter. Fred New, who had first tried to suppress the story, was now trying to keep it alive.

He wrote to the U.S. attorney general: "The management of the *Ledger* and their counsel have denied the right of trial and the right of counsel to three employees in the Manchester case. Demand immediate investigation and prosecution. *White men have civil rights too."*

A farce, a goddam farce. My paper had hung me out to dry, and a Klansman editor was defending my rights!

The Justice Department must have smelled a rat. They ordered Mr. Hoover to "interview the said victims and to inquire of them what their motives were in forfeiting their bonds. . . . Wish to be advised whether this action on their parts was attributable to outside pressure brought upon them." See why they call it the Justice Department? They were actually looking for justice.

Hoover's man in Atlanta questioned us and reported in: "Victims interviewed regarding their motives in forfeiting bonds. . . . All concurred in saying that they intended to appear at hearing but bonds were forfeited prior to time of hearing . . ."

Seven weeks after our visit to Pine Mountain, J. Edgar Hoover sent a final message to the attorney general: "The Atlanta office of this Bureau has determined from the Georgia Bureau of Investigation that their investigation has been completed and no evidence was produced that would either *prove, or disprove* [emphasis added by angry editor] the allegations of the three victims that they were manhandled at a meeting of the Ku Klux Klan."

I was mad. I went looking for another job and found it on the *Augusta Chronicle.* I called the *Ledger* and told them I was quitting, because I had just received a job offer. But, of course, that wasn't the real reason I was leaving.

Columbia Encyclopedia Entry on Samuel Green, Atlanta Obstetrician and Grand Dragon of the Ku Klux Klan

After World War II, Dr. Samuel Green of Georgia led a concerted attempt to revive the Klan, but it failed dismally as the organization splintered, and as state after state specifically barred the order. . . . With the death of its strongest post-war leader, obstetrician Samuel Green (1890–1949) of Atlanta, Klan unity broke down into numerous independent competing units.

And two days later that job offer was withdrawn.

The Augusta paper called. "Uh, sorry, but that position has been filled." I knew what had happened. The *Ledger* publisher had wanted to avoid the embarrassment of a reporter leaving because the paper had not stood by him. So he had probably called the Augusta publisher and said: "Don't hire him. He'll come back here. Where else can he go?" And return I did.

Why did the paper renege on their vow to defend us? Well, the *Ledger/Enquirer* was part of the local southern business establishment and the southern aristocracy, and I suspect they didn't think it was too smart an idea to rock the boat.

But we had performed a public service in alerting a lot of liberal Georgians—yes, there were a lot of them—to an evil in their own backyard.

My conviction remains on the books to this day. Though I lived in the state of Georgia for nearly nine more years, it never surfaced to haunt me.

In 1950, two years after my Klan fracas, the editor who helped me escape the *Ledger* was the man who had first welcomed me there with some doubt. In 1949 Jim Fain had moved on to the *Atlanta Journal,* where he became the news editor. He brought me aboard there before himself moving on to become editor of the Dayton *Daily News* and then the Austin *Statesman.*

Jim was one of three men from those early days who really helped me get my footing. The second was Joe Hall, who replaced Fain as the *Ledger*'s city editor and gave me plenty of chance to spread my wings (and even paid my bail). And the third was a courageous, talented copy desk editor named Bruce Wilder.

Bruce taught me a lot about newspapering and even more about how to overcome challenges with style and grace. I was immediately drawn to him, I guess, because my early years had presented me with my own set of obstacles, albeit less severe than Bruce's muscular dystrophy.

CHAPTER 4

◆

The Maggot Also Rises

They called me Maggot. It's right there in the 1940 yearbook.

It was at a prep school in western Connecticut called South Kent. The thing I remember most vividly is that as a senior I had only reached the height of five feet. It was embarrassing. Humiliating!

Is it any wonder I grew up feeling like an underdog?

Is it any wonder that in the years to come I would be the editor of so many "second" newspapers?

The *Washington Star vs.* the *Washington Post.* The *Los Angeles Herald-Examiner vs.* the *Los Angeles Times.* The *New York Herald Tribune vs.* the *New York Times . . .*

I grew up short and shy. And I stayed that way for a long, long time. It was true even before prep school. I remember when I was a teenager at Shaker Heights Junior High in Ohio. I was the smallest guy in the class.

In the eighth grade, during the football season, I was in my customary position on the bench, when the center was injured. The coach snapped:

"Bellows—get in there at center. You can do that, can't you?"

I detected a note of doubt.

"Sure!" I said.

And there I was, centering the ball. Suddenly everybody was running right over me.

The Milwaukee Editor Talks About His Uncle

There are only two drawbacks to being Jim Bellows's newspapering nephew. One, you can never be Jim Bellows. And, two, though we've talked about newspapers all my life—because what else is there?—he would never talk about how he got to be the legendary Jim Bellows who wasn't just my uncle.

Jim has always been too busy with the future to talk about the past. His trademark conversation stimulator is "What do you want to do with the rest of your life?" Whether you are 8 or 80, you get the same question.

Or how about a little philosophy: "Begin at once and do the best you can." It sounds so simple—you can't change the past—so why waste your time worrying about it?

That's the Jim Bellows I have always known—he's moving forward, a new idea, a new adventure.

Great philosophy for him, but this frustrated the hell out of me. Only a newspaperman understands that to a kid reporter, your heroes are not athletes or movie and TV stars. Your heroes are the guys who write, who laugh through deadlines, who could have written or starred in The Front Page *. . .*

My problem with Jim began not long after I learned to read. I couldn't have been more than eight years old before I was demanding my parents get a second subscription to the morning newspaper. I didn't like my dad taking the paper to read on the train to work . . .

I soon learned my uncle was a famous editor in far off places like Miami, New York, and Los Angeles. But it wasn't Uncle Jim who gave me the closest glimpse of his world. His late wife, Maggie, a reporter for the Los Angeles Times, *was in Chicago to cover the 1968 Democratic convention. She let me, a high school student, tag along with her for a day while she interviewed famous politicians and celebrities. I was impressed with only one person—a reporter, Jimmy Breslin. The police riots didn't come until later in the week. I missed being there when Maggie was tear-gassed. Jim's dad—my grandfather—said, "The reporters probably deserved it." I wanted to be one of those deserving reporters.*

I have now spent more than 30 years in journalism. When I'd see Uncle Jim, I craved one of those late-night sessions about newspaper life the rest of us won't ever get to live. Okay, so tell me about Breslin, I'd say. No? How about Tom Wolfe? . . . I finally tried another tactic. I suggested a book. He would mumble something about how he didn't have time, or, who cared about the past?

Three years ago he got a letter from his 25-year-old daughter, Justine. She wanted him to write a book telling the same stories I wanted to hear. At last there was hope. Saying no to Justine is not something Jim is very good at.

From one editor to another: Thanks, Jim.

Letter from Marty Kaiser, editor of the *Milwaukee Journal Sentinel*

The coach had me out of the game in a flash.

"Bellows—you're a coward!" he shouted.

I have never forgotten that moment.

Next day, the coach came by and apologized:

"I didn't realize how much smaller you were than the other boys."

Growing up smaller than the other boys defined me. I was lucky that whatever gene pool I swam out of let me use my size positively, rather than let it limit my horizons. Anything that makes a kid "different" can go either way. My size set me apart.

In my newspapering career, people would ask me: How do you get all this high-powered talent? How do you get them all singing on the same page? How does such a self-effacing guy do it? But that's the very thing that did it. I don't attract people to me because I am articulate, or tall, or handsome, or funny. I'm none of those things.

A small shy guy can't bowl other people over with the force of his personality. He has to find another way. I never had a sense of entitlement, I was just grateful to be included—so I guess I developed a collegial style, even when I later became the boss. I also usually had a pretty clear idea of where I was going, and a determination to get there—the "vision thing," as George Bush the Elder used to say. So maybe I substituted vision for power, and it worked out pretty well. For the five-foot-tall Maggot, it wasn't the best way, it was the *only* way.

I became this person not despite my size, but because of it. I played the cards I was dealt to advantage. This was how I got on the teams at school. I was a very small guy, and I made myself useful in that dimension. I wasn't threatening in any way. And I always asked for help. Hell, I *had* to ask for help.

And it has always stayed in my mind, that feeling of being the upstart, the underdog. I like it—the challenge, the long odds.

From a very young age I had to figure out how to make my life work. First came physical safety. If you don't have brute strength, you'd better have smarts. I remember one day in the schoolyard. I was in the fourth grade. I wasn't following orders fast enough and the school bully started chasing me. He was about to catch me, when I stopped short and crouched. He went flying over me and landed hard. He was pretty banged up. That won me new respect in the schoolyard. It also taught me the importance of *timing* and *risk*. In this case, the timing consisted of stopping and crouching at just the right moment; the risk was the chance of getting kicked in the head by flying feet. That was the beginning of the lesson that timing is crucial in life—in getting hired, in getting fired, in knowing when to leave and when to stay, in love and in work.

How to Live Another Year, by Ben Stein

About five years ago, on my birthday, I had lunch with veteran print and television editor Jim Bellows. "I'm 41," I said. "I've been a lawyer and an economist and a screenwriter, and now I wonder what my next goal should be."

Bellows, a laconic sort of guy, replied, "To live to be 42."

I didn't leave the restaurant that day with Jim's words ringing in my ears. I had worlds of money, power and prestige to conquer. Reaching my next birthday seemed trivial by comparison. But, a few years later, Jim's message lit up in neon. I had stopped by my house to look in on my son Tommy, who'd just turned two. I was rushing home from a business dinner and on my way to a business after-dinner drink, with an acute stress pain in my abdomen.

He was in his crib. I perfunctorily said, "Good night," all the while thinking about my next sale. I heard the voice of a little angel say, "Good night, Daddy." It was the first time I had heard him say that.

It came to me, more or less like lightning, that if I kept on living the way I was, I would be unlikely to hear his sweet voice for many more years. I instantly knew Jim was right. I had to learn how to live another year without letting my work kill me. It's not easy. Success in any endeavor usually means that obligations and duties pile up. Your ability leads others to give you additional responsibility. Your vanity and greed lead you to accept it. This means stress, conflict, sleepless nights—all of which endanger your primary goal of surviving . . .

Now, when I'm tempted to work on a Saturday rather than take my son to watch the whales off Zuma Beach, I go for son and whales instead. It's the kind of decision I can live with.

Reader's Digest, November 1991. Reprinted with permission.

■ South Kent School, 1940
  Yearbook Prize Day for Graduating Class

Prizes Awarded

The Head Master's Cup . . . Addison R. Taylor
Best All-Around Athlete . . . Robert S. Curtis
Allen Murrell Hockey Trophy . . . Howard R. Gleason
Gordon McCoun Baseball Trophy . . . C. Edwin Williams
Best All-Around Junior Athlete . . . James G. Bellows   ■

I was thirteen when I entered South Kent School in Connecticut. I had applied with my cousins to go to Kent—a big, older school—but I didn't pass the math test, so *they* went to Kent and *I* went to South Kent. Always the road less traveled.

South Kent proved a good lesson in forced growth. The school was all about self-help and equality. Boys who could afford it paid more. Boys who couldn't paid less or nothing. But there was no way to tell. We all did everything but cook the food and do the laundry. We cleaned the bathrooms, picked the apples, dug the potatoes, raked the lawns. If it snowed, we got out the shovels and cleaned off Hatch Pond, where we skated, and the road around the school. There was only one maintenance man, and he took care of the furnace.

Everyone had to participate in athletics. Whether you were a water boy or a quarterback, you participated. There were three teams in each sport: a varsity, a junior varsity, and what they called a "kids" team, composed of the smaller, lighter students. Guess which one I was on. But every team competed ferociously against other schools throughout New England.

We were not cradled through those years, and it was a wonderful place to build character. It was tough going but it was good for the soul. Every day also was chapel day at the school for everyone. But don't think there wasn't any leisure. Every Saturday night we were each given a quarter and could walk a mile down the hill to the only store in town, a shop at the train station that sold candy, among other things.

Kenyon College Awards an Honorary Degree,
Doctor of Humane Letters, to James Gilbert Bellows

We did a little research recently into your undergraduate years here at Kenyon, looking for something that might illuminate your remarkable ascendancy, in less than two decades, from reporter for the Ledger *in Columbus, Georgia, to editor of the* New York Herald Tribune. *I suppose we wanted really to find evidence that would allow us to take some of the credit for your success while seeming to give it all to you . . .*

We know, of course, of your admiration for Philip Blair Rice. As a newspaperman, you have shown the tenacity and vision that were his as a scholar. He was truly an exemplar for you, and it was at his urging that you became a journalist. So, at least through him, perhaps we may truly claim that something of what you have become you owe to your Kenyon experience.

May 30, 1965

Only one quarter, once a week. That's all the money anyone was allowed to have at school.

I think my lack of respect for amassing capital began there. That failing has remained constant my whole life—even though I've lived a pretty good one. But as exasperating to parents and wives as my indifference to security has been, it's also allowed me to leave "sure things" behind and go for the challenge.

South Kent was started on a shoestring back in the early twenties by Sam Bartlett and Richard Cuyler. Bartlett had been an All-America football player at Lafayette. We called him "the old man." He was one of those crusty New Englanders who looked as though he just walked out of the sea. I've tried to emulate Sam Bartlett in a lot of things—his independence, and the value he placed on fairness, enterprise, and accepting accountability.

When I graduated from South Kent, it was the only time in the school's twenty-year history that a *senior* won the trophy for Best All-Around *Junior* Athlete. Besides playing on peewee football and hockey teams, I had been the coxswain of the crew, the one place where there was a very special leadership role for a little guy.

Entering Kenyon, a liberal arts college in Ohio with 300 boys, I remained the runt of the litter.

Though I would finally outgrow my bantam size (I added seven inches to my five-foot frame in my freshman year at college), I never outgrew my identity.

I always understood how to deal with the establishment bullies of the journalistic world. Of course, sometimes I worked for the big guys in town. And I always noticed how eager they were to drive the smaller paper out of business, if they could. And usually they did. It always saddened me to see an underdog paper go under, and whenever I ran the second paper, I fought like hell to keep it alive—and could usually enlist the staff in my crusade.

During the years of growing up, I was shy and insecure. It was a long time before I became more confident of my own talents. It was a long process of growth, and so was my growth in the world of journalism. Because I started with no experience. I gained that experience by working like crazy for as many hours a day as it took. And I think that's another factor of my style that has helped me in my career. I learned the value of hard work from Sam Bartlett.

The "li'l ole country boy," as I wryly referred to myself, just worked his tail off and did the best he could. I adopted this appellation when I reached New York and found myself surrounded by all those glib, big-city types.

Of course, I was hardly a "country boy"—born in Detroit, raised in an upper-middle-class family in Shaker Heights, Ohio, prep school in Connecticut, and college in Ohio. But I never identified with those golden boys and girls. Though I guess I could have become more like the privileged kids I grew up with—and my parents would have been thrilled—that role never appealed to me. I seemed destined to remain an outsider.

I was the unsure, reticent naïf, the quiet, observant, diffident country mouse—and I *mumbled*! It was always easy to underestimate me, which was a great advantage. I didn't make a lot of noise. I wasn't always wrestling with my ego.

So I set out to slay the dragon, my weapon a hesitant drawl. Has it worked all that well? Well, of course every paper I've tried to save has gone down the tubes. And yes, the dragons I tried to slay all continue to breathe fire. But they were glorious contests. I've enjoyed the loyalty of wonderful reporters. I've given a start to many great writers. Together we created lively, interesting papers that gave readers their money's worth—and I've had an exciting life. I've made wonderful friends in a fascinating profession. So I didn't beat the Yankees. I got to play in the World Series. Three of them, in fact. So, yes, I'd say it's worked pretty well for me.

In the interest of full disclosure, I should say there was another formative ingredient in my youth. Yes, being undersize at eighteen had a major effect. But my character—my scrappiness—may go back to something besides height.

As a little boy, I learned that I would have to be the captain of my own destiny. My mother found herself in a difficult situation. My father's parents were wealthy but had lost most of their money in the stock market crash of 1929. So they moved in with my parents and tended to treat Mom like one of the servants they had lost.

My dad was a regional traveling salesman, so he wasn't around to lend a hand with me and my sister, or to protect Mom from his autocratic parents. She had very little time to be a doting mother. I figured out early how to do my own thing, and I have never stopped doing it. Life offered me two options: sink or swim. Swimming was more invigorating.

Also invigorating were the dinner-table disputes between me and Dad when I was a teenager. My father was way over to the right, one of Colonel McCormick's fans during the *Chicago Tribune*'s right-wing days. Sometimes he would imply that I was a Communist. My father and I had heated arguments, which my mother tried to settle as gracefully as possible, before I was ordered from the table.

My father was tall, handsome, articulate, outgoing, a real ladies' man, a salesman, a good cook—the opposite of me. I defined myself in opposition to him. I never exploded at those dinner-table arguments. I have always been wary of high-pitched, intense, emotional expression. I don't get that from my dad. He was a guy who could come to a boil. And when you're a kid, that can be scary. There was a disparity in our size: Dad was a giant, I was a pixie. Also in our psychology: he was of the get-it-out school; I was of the keep-it-in school. The buttoned-up little guy. It came from growing up with a huge man across the dinner table. Very early on I said to myself: "I'm not going to be like you. I'm not going to do it that way."

The United States entered the Second World War at the start of my second year at Kenyon College. I had not yet received a draft notice when I enlisted in the Naval Air Corps in 1942, having desperately stuffed my face with bananas for weeks to get my weight up. I needed to get to 130 pounds and the bananas did the trick. My height by then had increased to well over five feet. I was springing up like a weed. So the Naval Air Corps condescended to accept me.

When I joined up, they had just lengthened the training procedure for Navy pilots. They sent me to three months of preflight training in Seattle. Then they sent me to three months of light-plane training in Spokane . . .

I could see endless training stretching far into the future. The war would be over by the time I reached the Pacific. Most of the 30 men in my group were equally upset. So I got together with Gordon Bennett, one of the trainees, to try to do something about it.

Our quarters were in the dorms of Gonzaga University in Spokane. Nearby was an Army base. Gordon and I decided, with the innocence of youth, to try to get out of the Navy Air Corps and try to get into the *Army* Air Corps. We had heard that getting your wings in the Army was a much faster process.

So we walked onto the Army base and tried to find an officer to talk to. We couldn't seem to find anyone. Finally, we found a captain in Recruiting who listened and made some notes.

"I'll look into it and get back to you," he promised. We told him where he could get in touch with us.

When we got back to our quarters, our base commander called us into his office. He looked a little angry.

"I understand you went over to the Army base and tried to leave us," he said.

"Yes, sir."

"Well," he said, his voice rising, "I wanted to let you know *you are herewith discharged from the Naval Air Corps.*"

"But—"

"*YOU'RE OUT OF HERE!*"

We went to his second-in-command and asked if there was anything we could do.

"Well, you could probably call up the Seattle Navy headquarters that runs this base and ask them."

So we called up there and they told us to come to Seattle for a hearing, and they put us up in a hotel for a couple of days. Then, bright and early one morning, we showed up for the hearing. We told them why we wanted to transfer—that we had heard about much faster training in the Army.

The naval officers were taken aback. They weren't used to this kind of bold thinking.

"You want to transfer out of the Navy and into the *Army*?"

"Yes, sir," I said.

We told them the training was endless and the war would be over by the time we saw the enemy.

The officers seemed impressed by our eagerness to get into action. They seemed to admire our grit and determination.

"Why don't you come back later today and we'll have a decision for you," said the admiral. We wandered around Seattle for a few hours and then returned.

"We're going to send you back to your unit," said the officer. No explanation, just a flat order. "Good luck."

The board reversed the order of our commander who wanted to boot us out of the corps. Gordon and I returned to our base, where word of our hearing had preceded us.

We were the heroes of the base.

My attempt to transfer from one branch of the service to another reveals another key aspect of the Bellows nature. I tend to challenge authority.

I don't do it in a bullying way, or in an overtly aggressive way. I am just extremely stubborn. Like the Chinese water torture, it's drip, drip,

drip. I never give up, never retreat from my position. Mind you, I don't challenge authority head-on. I just have a very clear idea of where I am going and what I want to do. If you stand up to me, I will not knock you down. I will figure a way around you. The publisher has the ultimate power move: he can fire me. But short of that, I am always pushing my program, always advancing my agenda.

But God knows, I don't always achieve my goal. Take the Navy. They were not to be hurried. It was an early lesson for me in top management's ability to ignore passion in the ranks. From Spokane I went to St. Mary's College near San Francisco for physical training and courses in meteorology. Then to Norman, Oklahoma, for bigger-plane training. Then I was given my wings in Jacksonville, Florida, and learned to fly the F6F Hellcat. Then we went to bases on Florida's west coast to practice field "carrier" landings, plus real carrier landings; then to Palm Springs for more training and simulated dogfights with other planes and shooting at sleeves; then to San Diego to practice landings at night (I am not making this up); then to a carrier that was a practice location for new pilots; then to a replacement squadron on Hawaii. Then the war was over and we were sent to replacement duty on a carrier in the Saipan and Guam area.

You see? I was right. They took so long with my training that I never got to the war.

But what a thrill it was. You're by yourself, only one seat in the plane—yet with a group of other planes making up the formation. Each individual in charge of his own plane, each formation a powerful unit. The perfect metaphor for life in a city room . . .

What an experience! You could really get to love it. The umbrella of sky. The limitless ocean. *And* I never got shot at! My toughest duty was one emergency landing when oil splattered my windshield. And those suspenseful, daunting night carrier landings.

This was the precursor of the way I practiced newspapering—my brand of "kamikaze journalism"—landing a speeding fighter plane on the truncated deck of an aircraft carrier at night. Aiming for a tiny target.

That's a big part of life. The excitement and fun that you get out of taking a risk—not being set in your ways and not worrying about security.

My motto has always been, "Have fun and find a way to stir the pot." Life is safe near the shore and dangerous on the open sea, where the waves are high and the carrier decks are small. But I've always felt that a man should set sail, not lie safe in the harbor.

Now I would be heading back to Kenyon College to finish my education. I had learned something about risk. And 20 years later, when I returned again to Kenyon to deliver the commencement address, I would talk about taking risks. By then I had honed my thoughts into a kind of philosophy, which I shared with the graduates:

> Security—that prized goal for some—helps us forget the reason for being. It is the fat insurance policy, the palatial home, the luxury car. It is the appearance. And it is the delusion. . . . There is the young graduate who walks in for the job interview and asks first about the pension plan. He's already worked out all his values, even at that young age. He's placed security first. And yet that kind of security will gain him nothing if he loses himself. . . . The essence of life is perpetual discovery.

I came back to Kenyon from the Navy to complete my graduation requirements. I had been majoring in economics, but shifted to philosophy. I thought it might teach me more about what life could hold for me. All those hours flying in the clouds had changed me, given me a deeper, broader, more questioning outlook. Of course, back at Kenyon after the war, it was more boys boys boys. First South Kent, then Kenyon College, then the Navy, then back to Kenyon. Boys boys boys. This succession of male environments may help explain why I have had a tough time mixing with the opposite sex. I didn't mix easily. My shyness kept me from approaching women.

I must admit that the "li'l ole country boy" was not the biggest joiner on the campus. But I was president of my fraternity, and also did a little work for the college paper. It turned out to be my first exposure to newsprint.

My departure from Kenyon and into the outside world started one spring day when I walked into the office of my philosophy professor,

Notice of Separation from the U.S. Naval Service

Serial No. 429754
Character of Separation: *Relieved from active duty under honorable conditions.*
Means of Entry: *Enlisted 10/8/42*   Commissioned: *12/6/44*
Qualifications: *Aviator*
Service: *Los Alomitas, Ca., Pearl Harbor, Hawaii, Saipan*
Remarks: *American Theater, Asia-Pacific, Victory WW2*
Job Preference: *Student*
Preference for Additional Training: *Economics*
Date of Separation: *11/26/45*

Dr. Philip Blair Rice. Rice had become a mentor in my life and now I really needed him. In two months I would be leaving the campus and I still didn't have the foggiest idea of what I wanted to do. I respected Professor Rice and had the feeling that his knowledge extended beyond the world of academe. And I needed some guidance. Have life, will travel.

Phil Rice had a sort of split personality. He was a scholar who also enjoyed the roar of the presses. He had written an esoteric book on ethics. But he also had a taste for journalism. He enjoyed telling people that he had been a newsman before he donned the robes of scholarship. He had tried out at the *Cincinnati Enquirer,* worked there a short time, written some editorials for them, and then had seen a bigger future in teaching. He was my father confessor on campus. But thank God for his fling with the newsroom. His flirtation would lead to my lifelong love affair.

Phil Rice was the cofounder, with John Crowe Ransom, of the *Kenyon Review,* one of the most respected literary quarterlies in the world. I guess Rice's respect for writing, reflected in the founding of this great magazine, was passed on to me, in his classes and in our talks.

When I was settled in Professor Rice's office, he asked:

"What are your plans, Jim?"

I made an attempt at wry humor.

■ The Rice Scholarship Fund at Kenyon College

James G. Bellows, '44	*John A. Goldsmith '42*
Carl Djerassi '43	*James D. Logan '42*
E. L. Doctorow, '52	*Robie Macauley '41*
Walter Elder '42	*Paul Newman '49*
Donald H. Gillis '51	

A group of Kenyon alumni established and endowed a scholarship fund honoring Philip Blair Rice. This list shows that Phil Rice mentored a lot of people who have achieved a measure of success. ■

"Well, since economics was my first major, I thought I might go into Merrill Lynch and make a lot of money."

He nodded soberly.

"That's all right," he said. "It just depends on what you do with it."

I still treasure that remark. I have mentioned it to thousands of people.

Rice's skepticism about the value of money as a primary goal has stayed with me. Let me say a word about money and work.

I have always been passionately in love with work. It has nothing to do with money. It has more to do with loving what I'm doing and wanting to do it well.

It also has something to do with wanting to make a difference. I have looked on journalism as a sort of quasi-public service that lets me make a contribution to society.

My mother remembers my talking to her during my college years about becoming a minister. Well, journalism for me became a kind of pulpit.

Lots of young people today don't have this kind of fervent relationship with their work. They see it as ancillary to their lives—a means to an end—even though they spend eight to ten hours almost every day of their lives doing it. Ancillary?? What they should be bringing to their work is *passion.*

Passion and attitude. I've always tried to maintain a positive, confident, upbeat, optimistic attitude. And that's very important to young people starting out their lives, whether it's in an interview or after you land the job. Attitude and passion are very important.

The Bellows Work Ethic, According to My Children

I would say that for all his children, his example of enjoying what you do, being proud of what you do, came through. His interest in everything we did gave us a sense of pride in our own efforts. All of us have that characteristic in common; we really enjoy our professional lives.

Amelia Bellows, graphic artist

What's really great about him and has helped me a lot is his curiosity. As a financial adviser, I've got to be a listener. Until I know about my clients, what makes them tick, I can't give them good investment advice. I don't find that men, in general, ask too many questions. But Jim is always interested in the other person, peppering them with questions like, "What are you going to do with the rest of your life?"

Priscilla Bellows, Merrill Lynch

He's a motivator, because he's a perfect example for me. I'm a managing director in Latin America for a Midwest utility. A lot of my work we call "pushing the rope." It's frustrating, but I have his drive and internal optimism that somehow things are going to work out. Unfortunately, I also have his aversion to company politics!

Felicia Bellows, Alliant Energy

What is really worth emulating in Jim is his real dedication to work. He has a very strong work ethic, but he strongly believes you should work at something you love. He was fortunate to find that in journalism, and he brought a great deal of talent and energy to it—and to his life! Knowing him has enriched and expanded my life immeasurably.

Michael Sohigian, lawyer

One time when I was in conflict about which one of two jobs to take, he told me it was a simple decision. I had given my word to one company, and he said, "This is about what kind of person you want to be. Your decision is indicative of how you want to lead your life." That's why he's definitely my hero in life. I asked him to write this book because I want my children to know who he is and why what he did was so important. I want them to know they come from someone unique and special.

Justine Bellows, residential contractor, Ryan Associates

My kind of passion has attracted some of the best people to me. Some exceptional journalists who could easily have worked for the big paper in town have been willing to take a chance with me.

I think I've had the kind of career I've had—bringing excitement to underdog newspapers—because I've had this enthusiasm. Though, frankly, sometimes I might have been too optimistic for my own good.

My work in newspapers has never brought me a lot of money. (That didn't arrive, ironically, till I went to work on the Internet.) But my life in newspapers would bring me something better than money: the joy of the journey and the knowledge that I was doing something that had intrinsic value.

Okay, end of commercial.

"What about going to work for a newspaper?" said Professor Rice. I considered.

"You know, I used to write editorials for a Cincinnati paper," said Rice. "It didn't work for me, but I had more fun in failing than a lot of my successes have brought me."

Newspapers, I thought. What did I know about newspapers? Well, I had pulled a red wagon along the sidewalks of Shaker Heights, tossing the Cleveland *Press* onto doorsteps. I had written a sports story for the Kenyon college paper that won me no awards.

"I think you might be well suited to newspaper work," said Rice.

Why not? I thought. The world of journalism could be exciting.

Rice suggested I contact John Goldsmith, a recent graduate who was working for United Press. He might tell me how to get started.

Rice was a sage, knowledgeable guy. He had failed in journalism but his memory of the fun he'd had, plus some unfathomable instinct, had triggered his suggestion that I pursue such a career.

Now, after a lifetime of work in newsrooms across the country, from New York to Washington to Los Angeles, from Miami to Detroit to Atlanta, I look back on his suggestion with gratitude.

"You might be well suited to newspaper work."

I often ask myself: What if Professor Philip Blair Rice had been a failed veterinarian?

CHAPTER 5

---◆---

Early Mentors

"NO EXPERIENCE, COLLEGE GRAD, NAVY FLIER, LOOKING FOR A JOB IN JOURNALISM."

My ad in *Editor & Publisher* produced several replies. After culling them, I chose a $75 offer from the *Columbus Ledger,* an afternoon paper in the town of Columbus, Georgia.

Years later, John Goldsmith, the fellow college alumni who had suggested the *E&P* help-wanted ad, recalled: "Jim had the good sense to go South. He accepted a job in Georgia. He involved himself in the major story of the century—the struggle for civil rights." Well, no. I wasn't that prescient. I chose the *Ledger* because the other papers that answered my ad wanted to hire me under the G.I. Bill. The government would repay the publishers a portion of my salary for a year or so. Only the *Ledger* was ready to pay me real money of their own, without government involvement. I had heard that a lot of publishers, on hiring a veteran, would keep him in that entry-level job as long as they could keep getting government funds, rather than promoting him where his talents might lead. So you stayed a cub. It was less complicated, and cheaper, for the publisher. I didn't want to find myself in that dead-end situation.

So I wired my acceptance to the *Columbus Ledger,* packed my bag, and boarded a bus for the Deep South. The old country boy was off for the country.

Columbus was a town of about 100,000 on the Chattahoochee River, separating Georgia from Alabama. In 1492 Columbus discovered America;

Edwin Pope Remembers My Moneymaking Skills

I never met anyone to whom money mattered less than Jim Bellows, but sometimes principles came into play and he acted accordingly.

In the mid-1950s I was executive editor of sports and he was news editor of the Atlanta Journal, *which basically held a license to print money. Jim was making about $150 for working about a 60-hour week. One day he came out of the managing editor's office in a rage. He said he had been offered a $5 raise, which was so paltry percentagewise that he told the managing editor, "No thanks, you keep the money. If that's all you can afford, you need it more than I do."*

The m.e. was delighted to do just that.

in 1946 Bellows discovered Columbus. It was my first trip south except for when the Navy sent me to Jacksonville, Florida, as part of my endless flight training odyssey. I had to adjust to a different culture and a different time zone.

I rented a little room in the home of the superintendent of schools. Next day I reported to the *Columbus Ledger* and met Jim Fain, the city editor who was my new boss. He seemed a little chilly. I learned why.

Before my arrival, the *Ledger*'s editor, Bryan Collier, had told Fain, "I've hired this guy out of an ad in *Editor & Publisher*. He was a Navy lieutenant, no experience. I'm paying him seventy-five a week."

"Seventy-five!" Fain exploded. "I'm paying all my reporters a lot less than that!" Fain quit on the spot—but was prevailed upon to stay.

Jim Fain was to become a valued mentor, but his first look at me was not encouraging. "I was not well disposed to him at all. He arrived, sallow and skinny. He's talking the way he always talks. I couldn't hear the first two words of any of his sentences. And I was lucky if I picked up something in the middle so I could get the gist of it."

A couple of weeks after I started, Jim Fain chewed me out for coming in with a story that had a couple of holes in it.

"Don't *ever* bring in a story that doesn't have all the facts!" barked Fain.

Next day the town magnate died. He was a fellow named W. C. Bradley, and he owned one of the cotton mills that were the underpinning of the town's economy. Bradley had died in the morning. It was a must story for the Sunday paper, so Fain called me into his office.

"Bellows, go out to the Bradley house and get any pictures they have of him going back to infancy. And while you're there, get some details about the death."

About an hour later, the magnate's son-in-law calls up my city editor and he is boiling.

"Fain," he says, *"get this bastard out of here!"*

"What's wrong?" says Fain.

"He wants to know where he fell. . . . He wants to know where his arms were. . . . He wants to know if he was facing up or down. . . . He wants to know what sort of expression he had . . ."

I wasn't coming back with any holes.

The Deep South carried some culture shock for me. It seemed to me that the blacks in town deserved something better than they were getting. But there weren't many people who were hot on the subject in those days. And if the blacks were, they managed to conceal it. I remember telling some newsroom colleagues that when I saw a black man I saw him the same as I saw a white, because we were all grains of sand in the universe. I hadn't thought much about this subject until I found myself hurtling through the clouds for the Navy.

If Georgia was a new world for me, so was journalism. It was a few months before I learned how a newspaper story should be written.

The *Ledger* was a great kindergarten for a cub like me. Fain only had a few experienced reporters, so he had to throw me at some of the important stories that came up. I once covered a murder trial in Phenix City, the bower of corruption across the river in Alabama. The town was rich in learning experiences for an apprentice journalist. It was bristling with gambling, prostitution, murder, and other newsworthy vices. Phenix City was the playground for the foot soldiers who trained at nearby Fort Benning. It was their periodic mission to get to Phenix City and back without getting caught.

At the murder trial, the lawyer for the defense had succeeded in exposing the perjuries of a key witness during his cross-examination. As the witness floundered, the lawyer turned around, looked at me at the press table, and said, "Before God, anywhere but Phenix City I just won me a case!"

One of the things I learned is that everyone sees a car crash differently, each from a different angle. And everyone sees an event differently. Your experience, or lack of it, molds what you see. A good reporter tries to get the views of several witnesses to an occurrence. That lets you deliver an objective picture. One person may have an ax to grind. A few will give you objectivity and an approach to fairness. Columnists can be subjective, sounding off on just one side of an issue. Reporters can't. That is, they *can*, but they should *not*.

Columbus had a literary history. The fabled screenwriter Nunnally Johnson, who wrote the screen adaptations of *The Grapes of Wrath* and *Tobacco Road*, grew up there. Carson McCullers, one of the most talented literary artists of her generation, also came from Columbus. Most of her novels—*The Heart Is a Lonely Hunter, Ballad of the Sad Café, The Member of the Wedding*—were set in a little Georgia town that was Columbus in all but name.

One day, when I was working on the city desk, a little old lady came in collecting for the PTA. She was a former schoolteacher and she had a Carson McCullers novel in her hand. I remarked on it and she said:

"Oh my yes, I had little Carson in the fifth grade. She was a sweet little girl."

"You don't say."

"Yes. But I have no idea where she learned all those words!"

At the *Ledger* copy desk was an extraordinary young editor named Bruce Wilder. Bruce weighed 80 pounds and had muscular dystrophy. Each day he had to be lifted out of bed in the morning, and back into it at night. Each day his wheelchair was pushed from his hotel room to the *Ledger* office six blocks away. Bruce was a thin, frail, extremely intelligent young guy of 28 who had grown up in Royston, Georgia. From his wheelchair he spread cheer throughout the newsroom. Most days when we had put the paper to bed, I would walk to Bruce's hotel and spend an hour talking shop. Bruce was the most courageous young man I've ever known. I didn't want you to think Columbus was filled with nothing but craven publishers, deceitful lawyers, and hooded bigots.

There was a woman who worked at the Veterans Administration in town, which was on my beat. She had a boyfriend and she had a girl-friend and one day she suggested that I make it a foursome. Bear in mind that I had just come out of three successive all-male institutions. The double date sounded fine. That's when I met Marian Raines. Raised in Columbus, she was a real Georgia peach. Six months later Marian and I were married. Besides the bride, groom, and minister, Marian's friend and my city editor were the only ones present for the ceremony.

As I was writing this chapter, my wife, Keven, leaned over and said with some surprise:

"Jim, you didn't invite your parents to your first wedding!"

"No."

"And you didn't invite them to your *second* wedding, to Maggie."

"Well, no."

"And you didn't invite your parents to *our* wedding."

"No, I didn't."

"I think your readers will wonder about that."

"Well, with Marian, I had never been married before and I just wanted to get it over with."

"Very romantic. And the second time around?"

"Well, that was a scandal. I had left Marian to marry a woman who was a divorcée. There had been no divorces in my family."

"And why didn't you invite them to *our* wedding?"

I didn't have a good answer. After all, my parents and I were very close, I loved them and they loved me. Keven is much more analytical than I am, and she believes my parents had a lot to do with making me a maverick.

"They made you that way," she says. "Inadvertently, they sort of set you on your own path at a young age. I don't think you felt rejected. You knew your mother had a lot on her plate and didn't want to be a burden to her. And that's one of your strongest personality traits. You don't want to be a bother to anyone. So, you developed this independent streak. If anyone disapproved of your wife, you didn't want to hear about it. You believe in yourself and you know what is right in any situation. Basically, you are not terribly interested in what anyone else thinks. And that includes the publishers you've worked for and—"

"Okay, Keven. Thank you."

"Listen, it's your book."

After my marriage, in 1946, I wrote my parents to let them know about the wedding. "I have just married a long-nosed Episcopalian," I announced. My parents were Episcopalians and this was my way of currying favor.

Marian was the daughter of an architect in town. Since he was conservative and I was not, and he was somewhat anti-Semitic and I was not, he and I did not hit it off especially well. He was also vocal on racial issues. And he wasn't fond of journalists. Marian didn't get along that well with newspaper people either.

Of course, Marian had a significant rival. I had just met my lifelong love, and each year she grew more alluring. You guessed it—her name was Journalism. There's no question that journalism ran my life. I was working like crazy, trying to learn my trade, trying to learn how a newspaper gets put together, and devouring papers from all over.

After the Klan brushup and being hung out to dry by the *Ledger* publishers, I was eager to see the little town of Columbus in my rearview mirror. Jim Fain had moved on to the *Atlanta Journal* and in 1950 he helped me aboard. It was a bigger paper with a broader horizon.

When Marian and I arrived in Atlanta, we moved into a garage apartment connected to an old mansion on Peachtree Street. I started on the copy desk at the *Journal* and learned all about editing copy and writing headlines and the makeup of pages in the composing room.

I was then promoted to news editor to replace Jim Fain, who had been made the editor of the *Dayton (Ohio) Journal*. The news editor is the person in charge of laying out the pages and deciding what stories and pictures go where. He puts the paper together page by page.

You may think you have the paper very neatly arranged through one edition, only to be shocked the next moment with the news that a group of Puerto Ricans have shot up the House of Representatives. You have to stop the presses and rearrange things to include the breaking news. Then there was the day, after two editions, when the Supreme Court ruled on school segregation—not an unimportant story to Atlanta, Georgia. Again, you stop the presses, remake the paper, and print as many copies as you can.

Atlanta was my first two-newspaper town. One reason I like two-newspaper towns—along with giving people two voices on controversial issues—is the fun that can erupt from the competition. Take the Great Atlanta Elephant Caper.

The *Atlanta Journal* and the *Atlanta Constitution* pursued one of the great rivalries of American journalism (that is, until they merged in 1953). There was a guy named Asa Candler who was part of the Coca-Cola dynasty, a company whose roots are deep in Atlanta. Asa Candler had a big estate in the northeastern part of the city, where he kept a private zoo. The animals used to get out occasionally, but the police would never make a fuss until they had checked with Candler. We are talking lions and tigers here.

At one point he decided to give away all his animals, and he gave two baby elephants to the Atlanta Zoo. Their names, inevitably, were Coca and Cola. Coca developed a knee ailment and this became a problem that captured the attention of the public. The city followed the progress of the elephant's medical condition on a day-to-day, hour-to-hour basis. And Coca finally died. At this point, the *Journal's* resourceful city editor, Bob Collins, started a fund to replace Coca. Atlanta's schoolchildren deserved no less. Next morning, the *Constitution* started their own fund. It was quite a race. The *Journal's* elephant fund grew more quickly because we had a bigger circulation. It was clear we were going to win the elephant war.

So the *Constitution* acted. They sent their columnist Celestine Sibley to ingratiate herself with Asa Candler. (In the *Journal* newsroom we called her Celestine Sob-ley.) By then Asa Candler had moved into a retirement home outside of town and Celestine's stories had a high butter-fat content. She would sit for hours with Asa Candler as the eccentric millionaire played his accordion. She flattered him so well that he came through and gave the *Constitution* enough money to buy an elephant. So the *Constitution* came out the next day and trumpeted victory.

The *Journal* promptly put its own spin on the story: a nasty old millionaire's elephant is one thing, but Atlanta's schoolchildren need their *own* elephant. A populist argument. Soon the *Journal* had reached its financial goal.

Now the problem, for both papers, was to find an elephant. It was winter. The *Constitution* found an elephant up in New Hampshire. The *Journal* found one at a circus's winter quarters in South Carolina. So Collins sent a reporter to escort our elephant into town. It seemed important to beat the *Constitution*'s elephant into town—and we did.

A few years later the *Journal* took over the *Constitution*—the papers merged, with the *Constitution* bowing to the *Journal* for a chunk of *Journal* stock. *Time* magazine reported the event and, recalling the war of pachyderms, headlined the story "Merger of the Elephants."

Ralph McGill was an icon. He was the editor of the *Constitution* and wrote a daily column for the paper. His memory is sainted in the civil rights movement, and for good reason. During a Georgia gubernatorial campaign, Ralph McGill wrote a column on the corruption of politics. His imagination transported him back to ancient Greece and he brought forth a colorful analogy: "I am Diogenes, sitting in front of my tent with a lantern, looking for an honest politician." In other words, there were no honest politicians, and it didn't really matter whom you endorsed.

Well, the sports editor of the *Journal* was a guy named Ed Danforth. At that time, Atlanta had a minor league baseball team called the Atlanta Crackers. And Danforth wrote a column in which he said: "I am Diogenes, sitting in front of my tent with a lantern, looking for a left-handed pitcher with some control."

Atlanta columnists could really throw the high hard one.

Another fine journalist I first ran into on the *Journal* was Agnes Ash, who impressed the hell out of me. She was to join me later at the *Miami News*. But before I moved to Miami, there was Motown.

It was 1957. After the buyout in Atlanta I missed working in a city with two newspaper owners. The two Atlanta papers had become a morning-evening newspaper combination with one owner and one voice.

Besides, I'd been in the same position at the *Journal* for quite a while, and I thought there might be more excitement down the road. So I called Lee Hills, who was editorial chief at the Knight newspaper chain (it later became Knight-Ridder). I told him I was looking for a little more challenge and he said he'd like to get me into the fold. So he sent me to Charlotte, North Carolina, for some tests and to the *Detroit Free Press* for some interviews. Shortly thereafter I went to work in the motor city.

Detroit was interesting because it was my first exposure to journalism in a big northern city; the unions and car industry battles made it very different from Atlanta and Columbus.

In Detroit I discovered that whether you are a newspaperman, a carmaker, or a stock broker, you can learn from the other fellow. (In this case, the other fellow was the *Detroit News*.) But you've still got to put out the best mousetrap with your own trappings.

I accepted a job as assistant Sunday editor with the *Free Press* and in the first year I also spent some time as assistant city editor on the night shift. By the time I completed my two-year stint on the *Free Press,* I had honed my skills on the copy and city desks and in the arts and magazine departments.

In 1958, Marian and I went through Atlanta on a vacation trip south with our kids to see my wife's relatives and I dropped by to see my friends at the *Journal*. Gene Patterson, the editor, said, "Jim, are you all that happy up there?"

"Yeah," I said, "but I wouldn't mind getting closer to running a paper." He said I should talk to Bill Baggs down in Miami. "He's looking for a managing editor at the *Miami News*." I called Baggs, flew down to visit him, and accepted my first major position in the newspaper business.

Bill Baggs was a prince among men. He was loved by the people of Miami, who stopped him on the street to talk all the time, and it was always a pleasure for us to walk through the town to lunch. Bill was a dedicated liberal, populist, and environmentalist. He taught me an awful lot about how to deal with people, how to keep tabs on things, how to stay positive. He also taught me about two-martini lunches, a tradition shared by thousands of newsroom colleagues in big cities across the United States. I called Baggs a "sidewalk editor," someone who brought a great practical experience to the job. He was a wonderful writer, too, turning out three or four columns a week for the editorial page. He wrote in a pleasant, soothing way, but always made his point. He once described the Washington statesman Chester Bowles (who was in Miami on a visit), as "a fellow who resembled an amiable moose who had lost his antlers."

Miami was a two-paper town, the *News* sharing the pond with the big-fish *Miami Herald*. Baggs felt that our staff needed encouragement to keep them energized when they knew their *Herald* counterparts were better paid, and more fully staffed—when we sent one reporter on a big story, the *Herald* sent three.

Baggs taught me that we had to make more noise at the *Miami News* to be heard above the competition. When we had a story that the *Herald* didn't, we played the hell out of it, to make the point of our exclusivity.

Howard Kleinberg, the *News* sports editor who later became the paper's managing editor, recalled Bill Baggs after his death in 1968: "He was an enigma. Bill operated in mysterious ways. As a working editor on a failing newspaper, battling against a competitor three times its size, he had almost unfathomable connections with some of the most important people in the world. Few of us accepted those ties as fact until after Baggs died—and Ted Kennedy showed up to be a pallbearer at Bill's funeral, and when Hubert Humphrey sent a letter of condolence, as did Averill Harriman and William Fulbright. The *Washington Post* editorialized: 'He was a man for all underdogs, everywhere, and against the venal and the repressive and the bigoted.'"

The *Miami News* was an underdog paper. It was struggling to survive, to hold its head above water. It was the habit for most struggling

Bill Baggs and the Bull-in-the-Newsroom Incident

It was sometime around 1962. Joe Tanenbaum was publicity director for Gulf-stream Park. Annually, the Florida Derby was a pre-runner to the Kentucky Derby. As part of the extravaganza, and prior to the start of the regular races, they were going to ride ten Brahma bulls down the straightaway for the fun of it.

A few days before the race, Tanenbaum called me seeking publicity for the Brahma race. He said he was going to bring one of the bulls down to the newsroom. I went into Baggs's office to warn him. He was most unhappy and told me to get Tanenbaum on the phone and tell him that the bull was not going to be allowed in our newsroom.

Several hours later, Baggs and I were having lunch in the paper's cafeteria, when his secretary, Myrtle Rathner, charged in in a panic. "Bill," she screamed, "there's a bull in the newsroom. In fact it's in the women's department. And, Bill, it shit all over the floor!"

Baggs rushed up to the newsroom, blaming me all the way, and into the women's department. Most of the staffers were hiding in the ladies' rest room. One had passed out, and some were standing on top of their desks in panic.

Baggs was enraged. I'd never seen him that angry. He stared down at the awful pile on the floor, turned to me and told me to get someone from jani-torial service. Eventually a black janitor known only as L.B. arrived with a straw broom and a dust pan. He looked at his task, then at Baggs. "Mister Bill," he lamented, "things around here are getting worser and worser."

Howard Kleinberg

"second" papers to try to match the giant competitor in coverage, which was bound to fail, because of the giant's far greater resources. So in Miami, we took a different tack. We went after the best people, paid them more, encouraged them more, and pared our staff to fit in the new people at the same overall cost. We didn't try to match the giant story for story. We *did* try to find the best editors who would exercise the best judgment on what stories to cover.

Jim Head was one of the journalists to leave the fat-cat *Herald* and join me at the *News*. I had worked with him at the *Detroit Free Press,* and would later bring him to the *Trib*. Jim Head recalls his—and other journalists'—switch to the *Miami News*:

"Soon enough the *Miami Herald* found that Jim had come to play. At the *Herald* one of my copy editors left to go to work for him. Several months later I had a call and found myself looking at the man across his desk. Within 30 minutes I was out of his office with a raise and a new job at the *News*. In the next few months half a dozen *Herald* editors jumped ship to swim upstream to the *News*."

It required a continuing passion for the best on our part; it required ideas, and the courage to try something new. In the process, I think we put some poetry and artistry into the paper that wasn't there before. For example, we retraced one of Florida's hurricanes several weeks after it hit, and created an eight-page special section to tell the story in human, personal terms. We were trying, in a very small way, to do what John Hersey had done in *The New Yorker* on the Hiroshima bombing.

The *Miami News* was really my first rescue mission. John McMullan, one of the *Herald's* top editors, recalled that I had inherited an "absolute disaster." The once nimble *Miami News* had tried, without success, to become the *New York Times* of the South. "Few newspapers could lose as many readers as the *News* managed to do in such a brief time," said McMullan. "That's why they brought in Bellows."

I tried to capture the tempo and attitude of the seaside city with its lavish hotels and ocean breezes. Bill Baggs nicknamed me Sunny Jim, a tribute to my dour demeanor.

Gene Patterson recently reminded me of another nickname I attracted: "At the *Miami News* you earned Baggs's label as 'the Blue Darter' when you would hurry across the newsroom in a blue suit. You did some really good things with that expiring paper while Baggs played whimsical oracle and one-club golfer."

In the interests of historical accuracy, I should say that the "Blue Darter" label was first pinned on me by Jack Tarver, the fellow who ran the Cox newspaper chain in Atlanta. But I did play golf with Baggs several times—me with a full complement of clubs, he with one club, a four-iron, I believe. He was quite a spectacle on the course.

When the Miami hurricanes weren't spawning special sections, they were providing life lessons for my six-year-old daughter, Amelia. She remembers what it was like when one violent storm swept in on the city: "We were in the eye of the hurricane. And there had been all these preparations. And when the storm arrived, I remember my father took me out on the porch in the middle of it all. It was very still. And he said it was wonderful to be able to see this. He had this sense of wonder that was communicated to me as a child. I think that quality has been special in his professional life. He said, 'We're right in the middle of it now.' And later on when I was a little older, he would say, 'Always remember, you've got to retain that sense of wonder at what the world is like. It's endlessly fascinating.'"

Miami was really my first opportunity to work with a staff. And the joy of it was in learning that people gain the greatest feeling of well-being if they know that their ideas, their work, their heart is wanted

---

■ Do They Teach This at Journalism School?

Jim liked to count football scores. It helped make him appear to be a perfectionist. Each Sunday morning during the football season, he would arise and count the number of college football scores in the Miami News. *Then he counted the* Herald's. *If the* Herald *had more, he would call me at about 8 A.M. Usually I had returned home not much earlier from a night out with my wife and other* Miami News *people.*

He would upbraid me if the Herald *had more college football scores, which it almost always did. Finally, I used a trick similar to that which someone did to the* Herald Tribune *years later: A caller would contact the* Trib *to report scores of a fictional New Jersey college and an equally fictional running back who was setting all sorts of fictional records—which the* Trib *duly reported. In my case I had a clerk inventing colleges, thus more scores. I soon caught up with the* Herald.

Howard Kleinberg ■

and needed! This is not the same as belonging to a club or organization. It is personalized inspiration that is needed. I learned that what might seem to be the easiest management "gift" of all is also the most rewarding. I don't think you should ever—in an insurance office, law firm, or newsroom—concede automatically to conformity. You should never fail to give full credit for ideas, or work or effort, even where maybe only partial credit is due. You should try to build on the strengths, and seal off the weaknesses, of your people. You should aim high enough to meet almost-impossible expectations and keep aiming higher every time achievement is near. You should never fail to answer with decisions, especially the right "no" at the right time. And of course, you should always praise in public but criticize in private.

You will get help because you've told people you *need* help. No man has ever climbed a mountain by himself—it takes a helper or two. And if you try to stand on a mountaintop alone, you're likely to fall off, or worse yet, be pushed off.

After that solemn advice, let me recount one of the lighter moments from my days at the *Miami News*. My propensity for dashing across the newsroom has been noted. On one occasion, we had learned from the Associated Press ticker of a "talking dog" that had been reported in

---

Joy in the Newsroom

Miami News *editor Bill Baggs had a daily ritual. When he arrived shortly after 6 A.M.,tousled and sleepy-eyed, he'd stand in his office door and look out at the newsroom. "Hey, fellers," he'd shout, "ain't newspaperin' fun?" Then he'd rip a mad cackle and dart into his burrow.*

He was every bit as shrewd as Walt Kelly made him out to be in "Pogo." For all his dash, though, he was remote while Bellows was the quarterback and catalyst. Jim wanted a lean and hungry team, which he assembled. Some of us would have damn near worked for free just to be a part of that— and some of us damn near did, but I heard no one complain. The reward was in what we did.

Jim Head, copy desk chief, *Miami News*

London. As I was dashing across the newsroom, a reporter tried to flag me. "Jim, what do I do about this talking dog story?" he said. I didn't break stride. "Call him," I said.

As managing editor of the *Miami News*, I had to give some speeches to professional groups, and I was hampered by my shyness. In Atlanta I had attended Toastmasters, a club whose purpose is to help members learn to be more comfortable with public speaking. When I later moved to New York to edit the *Herald Tribune* and started to get a little national publicity, the managing editor of the *Miami News*, Ed Pierce, invited me down to speak to the Florida Press Association. My voice was okay, but I was still nervous and insecure before an audience. And Pierce's introduction went like this: "Jim Bellows is a very distinguished newspaperman, nationally recognized, but he's a little unpredictable. I don't know what he will speak to you about tonight. The only thing I can tell you about him is that *he is the funniest man on earth!*" And he sat down, leaving me with something of a problem. I think I survived . . . barely.

The plaque read:

GRAND BOSS AWARD
TO JAMES G. BELLOWS
FROM THE WOMEN'S DEPARTMENT
THE MIAMI NEWS

The ceremony in the women's department of the *Miami News* was not as formal as the signing of a peace treaty. Just very sincere. They seemed to appreciate the support I gave the women in the newsroom, the recognition and the promotion. Jean Wilson ran the women's section of the paper, and she was first-rate, as was the crew around her. Aggie Ash, whom I had first known on the Atlanta *Journal,* pulled a heavy load as business editor. I suspect she was the only woman business editor in journalism at the time. And Rollene Saal, the women's feature writer, was top-notch too. She was one of the writers who helped present the plaque. Rollene recalls, "Back then we were Jim Bellows's gals, the women lined up, desk after desk, in one big room adjacent to but separate from the city room where the guys were. Jim was tall, handsome

Agnes Ash's Hidden Story

I learned how passionately Jim Bellows felt about making the most of break-ing news when he persuaded the Atlanta Journal's *city editor, Don Carter, to confront me about a story I had hidden in the overset drawers of the joint composing room that the* Atlanta Journal *shared with the* Constitution.

Through luck and feminine guile, I had managed to obtain an eyewitness story to a double murder in Milledgeville, Georgia. I was saving the exclusive for the Monday Constitution, *aware that my paper would need a strong second-day piece.*

Bellows, as news editor, must have been informed about my holdout by a Journal *reporter on the scene. He insisted on running the story in Sunday's joint edition. Bellows was right, of course. I saw the impact a strong sidebar feature added to breaking news. Bellows, already developing a flair for drama-tizing a story with illustrations, had illustrated the story with a map tracing the perp's footsteps through the dusty streets of Milledgeville right over the carpet in the victim's law offices. Color wasn't available to the news pages in those days, or I am positive the footprints would have been as red as Georgia clay.*

in that loose-limbed Gregory Peck way. Every one of us in the Women's Department was a little in love with him.

"We had really talented women in the section. I can recall the portly food editor, Bertha Hahn, who knew hundreds of ways to use a mango; the society editor, Myrna Odell, who peeked over the closed wall of the elite Bath Club and married a Palm Beach Firestone; and others. . . . Jim hired these women, was able to give us space to stretch in, and admired and encouraged our work."

Rollene Saal went on to become editorial director of the Literary Guild and editor-in-chief of Bantam Books.

Bill Baggs, the editor of the *Miami News*, was a good friend of John Denson's, the editor of the *New York Herald Tribune*. Denson was looking for somebody to run the *Trib*'s newsroom. Baggs knew that I was out-growing the job in Miami and would probably be lured away soon anyway. So, as a favor to both Denson and me, he told Denson, "You could do worse than talking with Bellows."

Thus, educated in Columbus, Atlanta, Detroit, and Miami, I finally journeyed to New York late in 1961 to work as an executive editor under John Denson, who as editor had reshaped the daily paper with its publisher, John Hay Whitney. It was the top journalistic challenge in the country. It meant competing with the biggest giant of them all, the *New York Times.*

When Bill Baggs died in January 1968, I wrote a letter to Jack Tarver, who ran all the Cox newspapers, including the *Miami News:*

> We'll miss Baggs. The whole damn world will. We all know
> that. But that's not what I'm writing you about. I want to
> talk about the Baggs legacy. For many, many years the
> *Miami News* has existed and survived with bailing wire
> AND Bill Baggs. The paper stayed alive because Bill Baggs
> was there, the people stayed there because Bill Baggs was
> there. But now Baggs is gone. What about the *Miami
> News,* which Bill cared about so much? It is not going to
> be *easy* to keep that paper alive and vital without him.

I Send a Woman to Cover the 1959 Patterson-Johansson Fight

Most revealing of Jim's ingenuity, prescience, or plain audacity was when he sent me to the World Heavyweight Championship fight in Miami between Floyd Patterson and the blond Swede, Ingemar Johansson. Jim just thought it would be a good idea for me to get as close as I could to ringside and write about what I saw. That turned out to be Patterson's devout mother, her lips moving in prayer for her son, and then the Big Swede himself, handsome in his satin robe, who brushed so close that I could not only smell his sweat but I also saw the color of his fear.

Rollene Saal, women's department feature writer

Somehow, you, Jim Cox, or someone has to instill a new spirit and aura of confidence in that small hardy band who have to carry on without Baggs. You've got to realize that without Baggs there you've got to reward that hardy band more than you people have in the past. They now have an immense burden and responsibility that they didn't have before. They can do the job pretty well IF they are given some indication the owners care.

The *Miami News* persevered for another 20 years and closed its doors on December 31, 1988.

■ Agnes Ash Tells How We Won "Dear Abby" Back

While I was on maternity leave, Bellows asked me to help him resolve a situation he had with the column "Dear Abby," a circulation keystone. In 1959, Abigail Van Buren wanted to pull her column from the Miami News, *preferring to run in the* Miami Herald, *side by side with that of her sister, Ann Landers.*

Bellows had a plan. The News *would print a local advice column and it would be so good, it could eventually be in syndicate competition with both sisters. He asked me to write it. He even had a pseudonym in mind. "We'll call it Jane Dare," he said, twisting his copy pencil to contain his excitement.*

It sounded a little off the wall, even for Bellows. I told him I'd think it over and come in to talk about it the next day. The idea was so ridiculous, it appealed to my sense of humor. Arriving at the Miami News *offices the following day, I spotted the circulation trucks rumbling out of the garage. They carried promotional boards announcing next Sunday's introduction of a "Jane Dare" column.*

All I could say when I went into Bellows's office was, "I wanted to tell you that Jane Dare is the name of an applesauce cake sold by the A&P."

"I thought the name was a little familiar," he replied, unconcerned about a confrontation with A&P.

Within three months, before grocery chain lawyers got wind of the piracy, "Dear Abby" had capitulated. She was back exclusively with the Miami News.

■

CHAPTER 6

◆

The Shining Moment

Those were exciting times.

Tom Wolfe sparking the New Journalism.

Jimmy Breslin showing the *New York Times* how to do "local."

Clay Felker putting his stamp on the new *Sunday* magazine.

An irreverent ad campaign needling the competition.

President Kennedy canceling his subscription.

My wife attacking me with a candy jar at the office.

I was overwhelmed. The big, big city—New York, New York. The legendary newspaper, the *New York Herald Tribune;* the famous publisher, Jock Whitney; writers like Walter Lippmann, Joe Alsop, Art Buchwald, Walter Kerr, Red Smith. And the "li'l ole country boy" now the number two man, reporting to a brilliant, tempestuous editor, John Denson.

It was the best of all possible worlds. Two years before, in 1959, Bill Baggs had hired me as his managing editor at the *Miami News*. Now he had recommended me for a better job in the city that never sleeps. Onward and upward.

Baggs sent me to New York to see his friend John Denson. The crotchety *Trib* chief needed what he called an "executive editor of news operations." Denson outlined the job, the hours, and the focus, and it sounded fine to me.

Denson impressed me as a wild, angry genius. His words would bounce around surrealistically, his thoughts flying in various directions. The

Art Buchwald's Indifference to Money

I didn't have too much direct contact with Bellows because he thought I was working on the European edition of the Herald Tribune. *I told the European edition I was working for Bellows. Neither of them could lay a hand on me.*

If there was any correspondence it was with Jimmy Breslin. I once wrote to Jimmy that Jock Whitney had given me an airplane for a Christmas gift. He wrote back that Whitney had given him a stable of horses, one of which was later to win the Kentucky Derby. This started a long list of "letters."

Jim Bellows was always surprised that I could get my copy in on time. I obviously had the answer. I didn't hang out with the despicable crew that he did. Bellows was a kind man. And he never saw any reason to give me a raise. He and Dick Wald made sure that I was never responsible for breaking the Trib's *bank account. Whenever the subject of money came up the two of them took me downstairs to Bleeck's and explained to me that money wasn't everything.*

job? Well, he would direct things, and I would make sure the job was done right. Easier said than done.

I signed on at the start of 1961, just as a lanky Bostonian was starting a new job at the White House. The paper's offices were on West 41st Street, and the *Trib* rented me a small apartment on East 38th Street—near enough to the paper since most nights I'd be working late. Meanwhile, Marian was looking for a house we could rent for ourselves and our two daughters in Connecticut. Till then, she had never been north of the Mason-Dixon Line. From Old South to Old Greenwich in one step.

Here's how my schedule at the paper shaped up: Arrive for work at 9 A.M. Leave the office at 8:30 P.M. when the next day's first edition was locked up. The first paper would be delivered to me at the apartment, or wherever I happened to be, at about 9 P.M. I looked over the "early bird," read some of it, called the news desk to check on late news, and changed whatever was necessary in story placement or headlines.

We had a daunting task—to make the *Trib* a strong competitor against the monster *New York Times*.

The next six years were Camelot.

John Denson was the front page. He spent a lot of time fashioning its look, because that was crucial in getting us a big newsstand sale and luring new readers. Denson designed the look and shaped the writing of the front-page stories. Then he tinkered with the stories till he got what he wanted. He laid out the front page—what went where, what size pictures, the crop of the pictures, the size of the headlines. And then he wrote the headlines. Then he *rewrote* the headlines. And rewrote them again. And he *still* wanted to rewrite them, even when it was time to print the paper!

Gail Sheehy Remembers Her Days on the Women's Page

"Bellows wants to see you."

This did not sound good. Not to a rookie reporter at the Herald Tribune *who happened to be a girl and pregnant. It was 1964, when "girls" hired by big city dailies were routinely tucked away on the women's page and exercised their reproductive functions only at the peril of career advancement. What's more, in my first months at the paper I had been turning in the kinds of stories that my immediate boss, Eugenia Sheppard, an epic figure among women's editors, considered unsightly at best—about poor women, pregnant women, addicts in the prison system, Harlem women on rent strike—and radical at worst. "Bellows wants to see you" could only mean one thing. An editor-in-chief who would growl something like "Whaddye thing you're doing, sister?" and tell me to stick to the soft stuff or get lost.*

But Bellows was misnamed. He spoke only inaudibly. "Are these yours?" he asked, holding up several of my stories. I 'fessed up.

"I like this sort of gritty stuff," Bellows said, "in the middle of all the fluff. Keep it up."

Bellows was the radical. He was always ahead of the times and ready to stick his neck out to back writers or editors who challenged the status quo. Over the years whenever I saw him socially, I would run past him my latest book idea and listen very very carefully for his few words of reaction. I would know I was on the right track when I saw his devilish twinkle and heard the words, "Keep it up."

Letter to me, April 8, 2001

I was learning the ropes under a brilliant, difficult man who had the rare ability to make the news more fascinating. What I learned by watching John Denson would prove invaluable to me when I later took the reins. Headlines, layout, connecting things, deciding what stories to run, how to show the conflict and the human part of the story.

Denson had come to the *Trib* from his post as editor of *Newsweek*. Coming from a weekly to a daily produced a problem—*Newsweek* had a week to get it right; on a daily you can't always get it right that night, and that was agony to Denson.

This was in the days of hot type. The Linotype machine contained thousands of little pieces of metal from which you would create newspaper pages. New York publishers were married to this quaint technology, which had not changed a lot since the Civil War.

The composing room was where the Linotype machines crouched in subterranean darkness. It was where the front page came together. The editor had to see that everything fit: Was the headline too long? Do we have to cut a paragraph? How did the picture look there? Sometimes Denson's rasping voice rang out: *"This isn't what I wanted!"*

I remember the evening when, just before press time, the hot type for the whole front page spilled on the floor. We scrambled frantically to put everything back in place.

John Denson would drive management crazy. As he sought perfection, the paper's closing would be delayed and production costs would rise. So would the temper of Walter Thayer, the handsome, impeccable, wealthy Wasp attorney who was president of Jock Whitney's company, Whitney Communications. He was not a man of feelings or much aware of those of others. The staff called him North Wind because he could chill the bones. "He lives in Whitney's pocket," someone observed, and this was a good place to keep an eye on Whitney's change. His major interest was money—how the paper spent it and how the paper lost it. But he never thought deeply about human consequences—hence his readiness to cut the staff.

Need I say there was tension between Denson and Thayer? My job was to make things work. Denson would tinker while Thayer burned. And Bellows would grind his teeth as he tried to move text and layouts

John Denson vs. the <u>Trib</u>'s Sports Editor, Stanley Woodward

When [Denson] failed to grant Woodward's claim that he had the same right to express himself freely in the paper as Walter Lippmann . . . the sports editor gave a year's notice of his retirement. Denson replied that if Woodward felt that way, he ought to leave at his earliest convenience. So Woodward left the paper he loved in disappointment and rage. In his book Paper Tiger, *Woodward put his finger on the source of Denson's chief shortcoming of character: "Denson once said to me, 'Everybody on this damn sheet thinks he has a proprietary interest in it.' His attitude was that people employed by the* Herald Tribune *should work there for the money he paid them, do what they're told, and shut up." But it was precisely that proprietary interest that was the true strength of the paper, Woodward argued, and in refusing to cultivate it, in riding roughshod over it to impose his will, Denson defeated himself.*

Richard Kluger in *The Paper*, 1986

■ John Denson fired Stanley Woodward, but the sports editor eventually returned to the *Herald Tribune*. And when he did, his first column began, "As I was saying before I was so rudely interrupted . . ."

into production. I would be down in the composing room trying to put the paper together, while Denson was upstairs, still changing things.

Bellows on the phone: "We're getting late, John. . . . You've got to decide, John. . . . We've only got ten minutes, John. . . . Is this absolutely necessary, John? . . . We're gonna be in trouble, John . . ."

In the depths of the composing room, I hovered over "the chase"— the portable metal frame that held the type for the front page, thinking, "There's no way we can get a different crop on that photo."

But, hell! John Denson was making the *Trib* a better paper.

I was trapped between these two men, Denson and Thayer—the artist and the autocrat.

On one occasion the trap was sprung when Denson was away at his Vermont retreat and Thayer summoned me to his office.

"Bellows, I want you to put together a list of all editorial personnel in priority order. Who are the most *indispensable,* down to the most *dispensable.* All the way through the staff."

What a rotten thing to do. Well, I put Denson at the top of the list. The most indispensable. I figured if I did that, Thayer would know I was not going to play his game. When Denson got back, Thayer reviewed my list with him. Denson erupted out of the meeting like a gas main explosion. He headed for my office and started yelling at me at the top of his lungs.

"What the hell were you doing! You put up that goddamned list!"

He was really furious that Thayer had put me up to it. But he took it out on me.

"What the hell was I supposed to do, John?" I asked. "Tell the president of the company to fuck off?"

Thayer Alerts Whitney That Breslin
Has Offended Mr. Nixon

Confidential Memo

FROM: Walter Thayer
TO: Mr. Whitney and Mr. Bellows

Dick Nixon telephoned this morning before 9:30. He said he had had a number of calls today about Breslin's appearance last night on the Tonight *show. Apparently Breslin was pretty rough on Nixon. . . . Nixon said the show has been described to him as "antagonistic and vicious." Nixon relates Breslin's so-called antagonism to the fact that Breslin called Rosemary Wood, Nixon's secretary, a short time ago asking for an appointment to see Nixon. He was told that his name would be added to the list and that Mr. Nixon would see him sometime in the future. . . . According to Nixon's secretary, Breslin's comment was, "All right. Take my name off the list."*

■ Thayer was Nixon's protector and was touting him for president. When Jimmy Breslin in his column mentioned Nixon's use of profanity, Thayer complained to me, "Nixon never uses profanity!"

John Denson had done a hell of a job at *Newsweek*. In the nine years he was editor there, circulation rose 50 percent. He was a native of the Louisiana hill country and the prejudices of his early years had stayed with him. He saw events in terms of heroes and villains, and he thought most politicians fell into the latter category. They were a bunch of frauds and rogues, particularly JFK.

Under Denson, the *Trib* was engaged in an anti-Kennedy vendetta. President Kennedy knew that Denson was not his friend. David Wise, our White House correspondent, recalled the situation:

> Covering a young, aggressive Democratic administration for the nation's leading Republican paper was not always an easy matter. At times it required some of the skill of a high wire act. On May 19, 1962, I was in New York on one of my occasional trips to confer with the editors and publisher when the phone rang in my hotel room around 7 A.M. Groggily, only half awake, I answered. It was Pierre Salinger, the president's press secretary. There were no pleasantries; he got right to the point. "I thought you'd like to know the president's reaction to this morning's *Herald Tribune*," Salinger barked. Uh, well, yes, go ahead, I replied. "The president said, *'The fucking Herald Tribune is at it again!'*" Salinger would appreciate it, he added—and apparently President Kennedy would appreciate it very much as well—if I would pass that message on verbatim to Jock Whitney. I said I would. . . .
>
> Jock Whitney had invited me to join him and top editors for lunch that day in the paper's executive dining room. I was seated across the table from the publisher. After the main course, Jock leaned back expansively, looked directly at me, and asked, "Well, David, how are you doing in Washington?" I waited until the waitress had finished clearing the plates and left the room—it was 1962, after all, and males still held to the now-quaint idea that women should be shielded from locker-room language.

■ Judith Crist Remembers the Critical Years

Fresh winds were ablowing when in 1960 I became editor for the arts [at the Trib]. Jock Whitney bought the paper and not too long thereafter Jim Bellows became his top editor. . . . Toward the end of March, Whitney and Bellows asked me to meet with them. They told me that I would be their movie critic. Six weeks later I wrote a scathing review of Spencer's Mountain *which was at the Radio City Music Hall. On Monday Warner Bros. barred me from its screenings, and the Music Hall withdrew their advertising from the* Trib.

Was I fired? The Herald Tribune, *courtesy of Whitney and Bellows, simply ran an editorial decrying my nemeses as childish and declaring that the* Tribune's *critic, right or wrong, had the right of free speech. The wire services carried this "news" coast to coast and a landmark was set for critical writing.*

Warners and the Music Hall returned. . . . The next month my damnation of the 40-million-dollar Cleopatra *("a monumental mouse") earned me more national notoriety, a compliment from Whitney, a Newswoman's Club prize and, later, a warm friendship with Joseph L. Mankiewicz, its writer-director. Also to come was a Press-section piece in* Time, *in which an unnamed Hollywood bigshot gave me a triple-S rating—"snide, sarcastic, supercilious"—and Billy Wilder said inviting me to review a movie was akin to asking the Boston Strangler for a neck massage . . .*

I learned early on that it isn't the critics who are "courageous" or "outspoken" but the editors and publishers who give them their voice, in my case Whitney and Bellows. ■

"I'm glad you asked that question," I replied. "Only this morning I got a message from the president, which I was asked to pass on to you." Well well, the president had sent him a personal message. Jock leaned forward in eager anticipation. What had the president said? he asked.

"He said, '*The fucking* Herald Tribune *is at it again!*'"

Whitney gave me a quizzical look, then turned the conversation elsewhere. For some reason, I wasn't fired. Maybe only the ancient Greeks shot the messenger.

On another occasion, Kennedy's anger with the *Trib* showed itself in a different way. The Soviets had menaced one of our "weather" planes that had "wandered" into their air space. David Wise reported the real story. It was actually an American spy plane on a mission to check Russian missile sites. Kennedy was furious. Pierre Salinger promptly announced that Kennedy had canceled all White House subscriptions to the *New York Herald Tribune*! You can't buy that kind of publicity. (When a copy of the *Trib* was used to line a box for newborn puppies in the White House, JFK reportedly commented, "It's finally found its proper use.")

Denson and Thayer continued to pull in opposite directions—Thayer devoted to efficiency, Denson to perfection. Finally, Thayer found what seemed a way out of the Denson problem: Just take the paper's nightly lockup out of Denson's hands and give it to me.

Denson shrieked it was a scheme to lock *him* up.

Dick Kluger described the end of the Denson era in two crisp sentences in his book about the *Trib, The Paper:* "Denson went charging through the interconnecting door between his office and Whitney's and demanded to know who was running the paper. Whitney told him."

Denson resigned on October 11, 1962. Stirring times were ahead. (In more ways than one. Five days later JFK was staring at pictures of missile sites in Cuba.) Whitney posted a statement on the bulletin board: "The management has found it desirable to propose certain organizational changes in order to meet the editorial and mechanical needs of publishing. . . . The proposals were rejected by Mr. Denson and he is no longer with the *Herald Tribune*." Period.

Jock decided, Lord love him, not to bring in an outsider to replace John Denson. He changed my title to managing editor and put me in charge.

Shortly thereafter, he removed the word "managing" and I was editor in title as well as function. Word that I was the new editor of the *Trib* reached me when I was out having dinner with two editors out of my past, Bill Baggs of the *Miami News,* who had first recommended me to Denson, and Ralph McGill, of the *Atlanta Constitution.* Our meal turned into a quiet celebration.

The great New York newspaper strike of 1962–63 began in December.

Bert Powers was the 41-year-old head of the printers union, and he was well named. He represented 3,800 printers and he had an intractable agenda: better hours, better wages, a cut of anything the publishers saved from better technology, and a single expiration date for all union contracts.

Powers told his printers to prepare for a lengthy strike. And New York's publishers were ready. A formula for a long struggle.

And so the strike began. And as the two sides wrangled, our readers were finding other things to do with their time.

Jock Whitney tried to turn lemons into lemonade.

"Heaven forbid that I would say anything good about the strike," said Jock, "but it did give us time."

It gave us time to redesign the paper.

Most of the staff was out, all except for a small group of executives. And as the strike wound through its 114 days, we set to work making the *Herald Tribune* more exciting to look at and to read. Several of us worked on redesigning the Sunday paper, others on the daily.

When the marathon strike finally ended and the paper reappeared, it smashed some traditional attitudes of what a newspaper should be. For one thing, it didn't look like the newspapers that people were accustomed to seeing. Take our new Sunday edition. It looked different. It read different. It contained four news sections—general, women, sports, business. Each was dramatically set off with a six-column photo on the outside and lots of white space on the inside.

We also offered a sparkling new book section called *Book Week,* whose editor was Dick Kluger. For as long as anybody could remember, *The New York Times Book Review* had been on top of the field. We gave them a rival. We also had a new Sunday magazine, called *New York,* that had the city buzzing. Tom Wolfe later wrote:

> In an incredibly short time, *New York* revolutionized the Sunday supplement field. It had never occurred to anyone that a Sunday supplement could be high quality. That was precisely it. Nobody ever thought of it before. In

no time, *New York* had influenced practically every good young journalist starting out. *New York* was like a manifesto: There are no more limits to nonfiction . . . if you have the stamina and the courage to do the reporting and the skill to put it together.

So the *Trib* resumed publication after the strike with me at the helm. I had a lot in common with John Denson—we both wanted a brighter, livelier paper. We both loved bold graphics and a clean look. And we both muttered unintelligibly under stress. But there were personal differences. Richard Kluger described them in *The Paper:*

> Secure in his own gifts and limitations, Bellows was unthreatened by the talents of others, readily encouraged them, and knew how to delegate to those whose skills and character he trusted. Also unlike Denson, he hated confrontations yet managed to leave no one around him in any doubt about who was in charge. His style of leadership was an amalgam of authentic shyness, projected humility, and studied inarticulation. . . . What was unmistakable in his manner was that beneath those vaporous words, behind that steel-edge look, a very private, very self-contained man of mystery cared deeply about his mission and was waging war with a combative tension coiled just below the surface. If you did not share his purpose, his body English made plain, you had no business being here. He inspired, then, not by dread, as Denson had, but by letting the staff know it was needed.

Yes, and I would focus utterly on the paper, without a backward glance at ego or fraternal acceptance. I was 41, with no major metropolitan experience. And I was up against the great gray lady, the *Times*, nose to nose, and I was determined not to play it safe. Being typecast as an outsider, as I was, can definitely be a blessing in disguise as long as you have the nerve.

Brouhaha with Jock, Ike, and Bill Buckley

John Hay Whitney ruled the content of the paper with a light hand, delegating almost all newsside decisions to his editors. But he had one blind spot: Dwight D. Eisenhower.

As editor of the Tribune*'s Book Week, I had the responsibility for selecting the reviewer when the first volume of Eisenhower's presidential memoirs,* Mandate for Change, *was published. Plainly I was not going to risk professional suicide by picking an outspokenly liberal critic likely to hatchet Ike. Nor would I opt for a copout valentine by someone of Ike's own political stripe. But what about turning to an outspokenly conservative reviewer— someone from Ike's own party but to his right politically (same church, different pew), like, say, the acerbic but reliably readable William F. Buckley, Jr.? Buckley agreed to the assignment with an alacrity that should have tipped me off.*

The opening line of his review, when it hit my desk, read, "Why this book?" And it proceeded, in crisp, curled-lip fashion, to take our war hero ex-president to the cleaners. . . . I was summoned to the publisher's office. "Why," he asked me, "should we run this review?" Doing my best not to gulp audibly, I said something on the order of, "Well—um—Buckley is a well-respected commentator, and—and—well, we asked him to review it, and I think we should stand by our choice—it's the honorable thing to do."

Whitney, at least as honorable as I was and with a billion or two more in the bank, was not buying it. "I know Bill Buckley," said Whitney, "and he's a smart-ass. I don't feel that we're obliged to run his piece—it's disrespectful to Eisenhower."

Our solution was to treat Ike's volume as if it were the just exhumed sixth book of the Torah. We quickly enlisted three additional reviewers from different perspectives. Democratic Senator Hubert H. Humphrey from the political left, an Eisenhower administrative insider who was suitably admiring, and an eminent historian, Henry Steele Commager. I'm sure Jock was not thrilled by this clumsy solution, but I took no more flak on the matter.

Richard Kluger, editor of *Book Week*, in letter to me, 2001

"It was a wonderful time. Everyone was slightly insane. We were young and we were all crazy, and Jim was crazier than anybody else, except that he didn't look it."

Those were Richard Wald's words in recalling the wonder and the madness of those days. Dick was 32 and he was my main man. I'd made him my national news editor, to replace Freeman Fulbright, Denson's shadow, who had fallen on his sword when Denson resigned.

Dick Wald had just been fired by Denson. He was in charge of the *Trib*'s London bureau and was back in New York on home leave when the ax fell. Wald remembered those hectic days:

> Denson told me he'd give me a couple of months to find another job, but I had to be out by the end of the year. That was the first time I had met Jim [Bellows]. And I'd been in the office getting to know him. Denson didn't like me and he wanted me out. My wife and I were scheduled to sail back to London. So that morning I'm on my way to the pier. And Buddy Weiss, Jim's managing editor, phones me and says, "Come in to the office and say goodbye." And I come in, and Jim says, "Would you like to be the national editor?" And I said, "What the hell are you talking about?" And he tells me that Denson was fired last night and they need a national editor.

Tom Wolfe Remembers Malcolm X

At the desk behind mine in the Herald Tribune *city room sat Charles Portis, who later wrote* True Grit. *Portis was the original laconic cutup. At one point he was asked onto a kind of* Meet the Press *show with Malcolm X, and Malcolm X made the mistake of giving the reporters a little lecture before they went on, about how he didn't want to hear anybody calling him "Malcolm," because he was not a dining car waiter—his name happened to be "Malcolm X." By the end of the show Malcolm X was furious. He was climbing the goddamned acoustical tiles. The original laconic cutup, Portis, had invariably and continually addressed him as Mr. X . . . "Now, Mr. X, let me ask you this . . ."*

New York *magazine, 1972*

Years ago, Betty Rollin wrote a book about her career in journalism, and called it *Am I Getting Paid for This?* My feelings exactly. Those were heady days. I spent most of my time at my desk in the heart of the newsroom, little time in my office in the executive suite.

Every day I met with my top editors at 4 P.M. for the "page one meeting." Three or four of us were regulars. The assistant editors who had any story prospects for page one would come in with their reports—city, business, national, foreign, sports, science, education, women's. And it would boil down to one man's decision as to what was going to go on the front page. That's the way it had to be. You couldn't let it turn into a shouting contest. You had to keep moving along and get it done. I loved it! And I loved the authority that came with the job.

Each day we would struggle to get a handle on the torrent of news. Our reporters and editors had a formidable job—to relate the news, from Bonn to the Bronx, to the interests of our readers. I prodded them to get behind the bare facts and search out the intimate *details* of a story, put it in perspective. I continued to remind them that a good reporter-writer is a sorcerer at commanding seemingly incidental details to serve him or her.

I was looking for fresh ideas. And I was looking for young people who had them. If I heard a good idea in a job interview on Monday, the kid who articulated it could be on the paper on Wednesday, and the idea in type on Friday.

A lot of exceptional people were attracted to the ferment. There was a Brit named David English. He was the New York correspondent for the *London Express*. And one day he called me out of the blue and said he'd like to help. Because he was impressed with what we were trying to do. David English came in with some great ideas and some great headlines.

Sometimes there was too much Fleet Street in his approach. The Brits have a competitive fever—each London paper has a special flavor. Once David put a headline on a Walter Kerr review that the critic hated. Usually the headline for his review mentioned Walter and the name of the play. David was more inventive. He dipped into the review for his headline. That wasn't how Kerr wanted it handled. He wanted to stick

Jim Flanigan Remembers Bill Safire

The Trib's *business department was in an older building joined to the Tribune Building on West 40th Street. The Tribune Building wasn't so new, but it was newer than the old annex that housed business news. The Fire Department decreed that nobody could smoke in those surroundings, but of course in those days most people continued to smoke.*

Sid Gordon was a wire-haired, wiry veteran deskman of few words but unquestioned authority. Sid governed the small personnel announcements that were life and death matters for the public relations companies. You know the items, "Mr. Galahad named President of Megacorp," etc. So the PR men used to bring Sid a bottle of liquor to curry his benevolent graces. William Safire, later presidential speechwriter and New York Times *columnist, was a liquor-toting PR man in those days.*

Sid put the liquor in an Army surplus wall locker. Then every night, after first edition copy had gone along, Sid would open the padlock on the wall locker, take out a bottle of whiskey and place it opened on his desk. And every member of the business staff was entitled to take a paper cup and pour a shot of the graft booze. It made a novice reporter feel like a grown-up to be included in such a ritual.

with the old style, where the headline just said, "Theatre Review: [name of show] Walter Kerr." Then you read the story to find out what Walter Kerr wanted to say. You don't put the substance of the review in the headline so people don't have to read the review if they don't want to! Yes, Walter Kerr even reviewed the *headline*!

I learned a lot about the Brits from David English. He was to become the editor of the *London Daily Mail* and would be knighted by the Queen. And when he died ten years ago at 68 he was still on the job.

I tried to edit with a light touch, making my wishes known in an oblique and often opaque manner. But one time with our Washington bureau chief, David Wise, I was uncharacteristically blunt on the phone: "We won't attend any more backgrounders in Washington," I decreed. "Don't send any more reporters to backgrounders. If government officials don't have the courage to speak on the record, they

---

■ Dave Laventhol on Foreign News: Who Says a Good Foreign Correspondent Has to be Dull?

While I was on the Trib's *foreign desk, Jim's instructions were to make the international news interesting, in line with the paper's slogan, "Who says a good newspaper has to be dull?" Not everyone agreed with that philosophy, particularly some of our few remaining foreign correspondents.*

I would take the clips, wires, and our own correspondents' files and put together a story. The old Tribune *way was to gauge the political and diplomatic impact. The new way was to find some salacious quotes deep in the wire file and lead the story with the precise details. Of course, the correspondent's byline—in this case Tom Lambert's—was amply displayed.*

Needless to say, Lambert wasn't enthused and left shortly thereafter for a distinguished career at the Los Angeles Times. *It didn't seem to bother Bellows, who knew we couldn't afford the foreign correspondents anyway.*

Dave Laventhol is now publisher and editor
of the *Columbia Journalism Review.* ■

---

won't be in the *Herald Tribune.*" This meant trouble. David pleaded that backgrounders were the lifeblood of Washington reporting. "Senior administration officials," "a White House source," "a presidential aide" were the time-honored ways that officials floated out news while preserving their anonymity and their options. David Wise recalled my edict:

> Bellows is right. It was a disgraceful practice, but his order was a problem. Gently, I pointed out what would happen. "The secretary of state will have a few reporters in for drinks," I explained. "He'll make news, the AP will move the story, the *Times* will put it on page one. Then I'll get a call from you asking why in hell we got beat on the story." The only way to change the system, I suggested, was if every news outlet boycotted backgrounders. And that wasn't going to happen. Grumbling, but seeing the wisdom of my words, Bellows dropped his diktat. He could be stubborn but he was always fair.

Drew Pearson and Jack Anderson wrote a widely syndicated column that spawned an idea for our own column pairing two journalists. Rowland Evans worked for the *Trib* at our Washington bureau. Robert Novak wrote for the *Wall Street Journal*. They seemed an odd couple—Evans was debonair and dined with Bobby and Ethel; Novak was the black knight of whom it was said, "A day without Novak is like a day without darkness." But it might just work, I thought. I proposed a double-byline political column to Evans; he liked the idea. I then approached Bob Novak and managed to convince him to give it a try. Evans and Novak's Inside Report started out with a bizarre forecast—that a dark horse named Barry Goldwater would win the GOP nomination in '64. And they were right. When Rowland Evans died last year, they had become the longest-running tandem in newspaper history.

My main effort to brighten the *Trib* was in taking chances on new writers and letting them write in whatever style made them most comfortable. When a reporter started banging out a story, besides telling him to type faster, I'd say: "Just spread your wings and try to do a thousand things!" I'd urge writers to open their eyes, to seek the new and different. Because news is what is *unusual*. We think it's just *recording* things that take place. But it isn't. You've got to decide, with intuition and instinct, what is unusual here. That's why whatever success I've

---

Harry Rosenfeld Remembers the Exuberance and Struggle

At the Trib *we put it together with spit and paste and a paper clip. We used the library, we used our Washington bureau, we had a guy at the UN, and we cooked up a foreign report that we basically wrote from all the wire services.*

It was just a wonderful experience, and I'm glad it happened to me while I was young. I don't know that I would have had the legs for it when I was old.

It was exuberant, it was exciting. We were fighting the New York Times, *we were fighting for our existence, and we fought for a good long time, courtesy of Jock Whitney, bless his soul.*

■ Harry Rosenfeld was the *Trib*'s foreign news editor and later played an important role at the *Washington Post* in the Watergate story.

David Wise: Washington, D.C., November 1963

You called and asked me to take over as chief of the Washington bureau. I began work on Monday, November 18, 1963, hoping for a quiet week while I got my sea legs. On Friday, the president was assassinated.

On November 25 I wrote the story of Kennedy's funeral and burial at Arlington National Cemetery. I usually write fast. But that day the words came slowly. Near the top of the story, I wrote that when the lone bugler played taps at Arlington, the high, sixth note had cracked. I told how John-John had saluted as the caisson bearing his father left the church, of Mrs. Kennedy at Arlington, the folded flag, the 50 Air Force jets thundering overhead, Robert Kennedy crying at graveside. Deadline was fast approaching and I didn't know how to end the story. Then it came to me. I wrote:

"And then, it was over . . . the three volleys of muskets, and the solitary bugler who could not quite bring himself to play the high, sixth note of taps, the note that, like the heart of a nation, had broken . . ."

Damn, that was right, I knew it was right.

The next day Breslin called me.

"You son a bitch," he said. "I saw that last line."

It was the greatest compliment I had ever received in the newspaper business.

had as an editor comes from a catholic interest in things, and the tendency to say, "Hey, I haven't heard of *that* before—wouldn't *that* make a great story."

I've already talked about the special brilliance of Tom Wolfe and Jimmy Breslin. They appealed to two different kinds of New Yorker—Tom reached the avant garde and the sophisticates, Jimmy reached the middle class and the people who didn't have representation.

Jimmy's was visceral writing, with a wealth of gritty detail. Some attacked his "fictionalized journalism." Some yelled, "That's a lie!" Some said his characters weren't real. Well, I met a lot of crazy characters that Jimmy spent time with and they seemed real enough to me. I never objected to Jimmy's colorful inventions, if that's what they were, so long as the essential point of the story was true.

For example, Jimmy wrote a classic piece on the Kennedy assassination called "A Death in Emergency Room One." Jimmy was not inside that room, but he talked to people who were, and he used a wealth of detail to make the scene convincing and indelible.

"Who says a good newspaper has to be dull?"

At the point when readership and advertising were swelling, management decided to spend some money to promote the newly designed paper. So we hired a hot young ad agency, Papert, Koenig & Lois, to develop a campaign. They produced a series of newspaper and television ads with that provocative motto.

Sure, it was a bit of an overstatement. The *Times* wasn't always dull. Sometimes it was merely tedious. And overwritten. And the motto was meant to needle the ponderous *Times*.

The account executive on the *Trib* account was a young fellow named Paul Keye. Paul found the *Times* a sitting target for the ad campaign his agency was creating for us. "What a stupefyingly boring paper the *Times* was in those days," he recalls, "smug, changeless, compiled for posterity—conscientiously edited for some yet unborn archivist—with the editorial selectivity of a supermarket aisle camera." Paul recently reminisced about how Madison Avenue came to the *Trib*.

> Jock Whitney had serious reservations about the tone of the ads, but hotter heads prevailed. . . . Someone had thought of the idea of showing the next day's paper on the 11 P.M. television news on CBS. . . . This entailed having the agency send someone to the *Trib*'s editors conference, 4 P.M. convocation. . . . Then, someone had to write a spot around the agreed-to front page. . . . Then someone had to wait for the page proof, cab to the CBS studio, rehearse and record the announcer, tape the commercial and complete the spot so it could be reviewed by the CBS Censorship Department one hour before air. I followed that routine for 11 months. Your basic 9 A.M. to 11:30 P.M. job. It was, hands down, the best job I ever had. . . . I

remember a piece that Jock Whitney wrote for the kick-off of the campaign. It ran on the front page of the paper, and one line said, "News is more than what happens."

We dragged the *Times* into covering New York City, in addition to the rest of the world. We couldn't hope to match the *Times*'s massive coverage of national and foreign news. Yet we had to establish a niche for ourselves. The answer was to rediscover New York.

News of the city was the last thing a New Yorker could depend on finding in the daily paper. The *Times* usually relegated stories on life in the city to its back pages, along with the shipping news, and gave it cursory treatment. I was determined to focus attention on our hometown.

That's how local news took over the *Trib*'s front page. We dispatched reporters and columnists to track down their stories within the borders of the city, and kept them on top of New York's volatile fads and fancies.

The best thing we did was launch a daily series on the town's brutal big-city problems. We called it "City in Crisis." And in the process we helped make a young patrician named John Lindsay the mayor of New York.

The series said in effect: Sure, the *Times* does a swell job covering the world, keeping you abreast of what's happening in Borneo and Madagascar. But the *Trib* cares about the city. Subliminal translation: "We have a reason for being here." The series gave us something special to promote. And beyond that, it was important journalistically, because it waved a red flag concerning a lot of dangers that were in our future.

In addition, our approach was different from the *Times*'s. If they had done it at all, they would have run a hundred separate stories attacking the problems of the city from different perspectives. We wrapped everything up together. And we said: Here's the problem and here's what needs to be done about it.

Jock Whitney, like most men of immense wealth, was a Republican. So he viewed the series as a means to discredit Mayor Robert Wagner's Democratic administration and bring the GOP back to power—which it did.

Jimmy Breslin: "A Death in Emergency Room One"

The room is narrow and has gray-tiled walls and a cream-colored ceiling. In the middle of it, on an aluminum hospital cart, the President of the United States had been placed on his back and he was dying while a huge lamp glared in his face. John Kennedy already had been stripped of his jacket, shirt, and T-shirt, and a staff doctor was starting to place a tube called an endotracht down the throat. Oxygen would be forced down the endotracht. Breathing was the first thing to attack. The President was not breathing.

Dr. Malcolm Perry unbuttoned his dark blue glen-plaid jacket and threw it onto the floor. He held out his hands while the nurse helped him put on gloves. The President, Perry thought. He's bigger than I thought he was.

He noted the tall, dark-haired girl in the plum dress that had her husband's blood all over the front of the skirt. She was standing out of the way, over against the gray tile wall. Her face was tearless and it was set, and it was to stay that way because Jacqueline Kennedy, with a terrible discipline, was not going to take her eyes from her husband's face.

Then Malcolm Perry stepped up to the aluminum hospital cart and took charge of the hopeless job of trying to keep the thirty-fifth President of the United States from death. And now the enormousness came over him.

Here is the most important man in the world, Perry thought.

The chest was not moving. And there was no apparent heartbeat inside it. The wound in the throat was small and neat. Blood was running out of it. It was running out too fast . . .

New York Herald Tribune

I put Dick Schaap, then our city editor, in charge of "City in Crisis." He brought in his old *Newsweek* buddy Barry Gottehrer to head the task force producing the series. (Barry went on to become a member of Mayor Lindsay's staff.) We weren't after Mayor Wagner's scalp; we weren't trying to anoint John Lindsay. We just wanted to focus on the things that afflicted New York.

We discovered that New York's problem was not municipal vice, but smugness and indifference (pretty much what ailed the *Times*).

The series began on January 25, 1965, with the following indict-ment, written by Dick Schaap:

"New York is the greatest city in the world—and everything is wrong with it."

Then we reviewed some of the bruises on the Big Apple: One fifth of the people lived in poverty; half a million were on welfare; the schools were overcrowded and substandard; it took four years for a case to come to trial in court; public housing had created as many problems as it had solved. Years later, Tom Wolfe would fashion a sparkling novel out of these appalling urban problems: *The Bonfire of the Vanities.*

Throughout the life of the *Tribune,* New York had been a place where wealth and poverty elbowed each other. But the *Tribune* had seldom been the one to show the contrast to its affluent readers.

We had to hire extra telephone operators to handle the flood of calls that responded to the series.

"City in Crisis" gave John Lindsay a great platform in his race for mayor. "The weight of the articles was overwhelming," he said.

Our "City in Crisis" series was not without its light moments. On the fourth day, Barry Gottehrer got a call from a guy who said there was a teenage hangout in Brooklyn where drugs were being sold to teen-agers, and cops were participating in it. He told Barry that he was will-ing to talk and had the evidence. Barry recalls the meeting he set up with our very own Deep Throat: "He comes to have lunch with me at Bleeck's. I get a private table way in the back. The guy is wearing a long raincoat. He's nervous and very secretive, constantly looking over his shoulder. He had an envelope stuffed with papers. The guy is telling me there are a dozen cops on the take and the Mafia is involved. Finally I say: 'Aren't you concerned about your safety in opening up like this.' And he says: 'That's why I carry protection.' And he opens up his raincoat and reveals a plastic water pistol in a Gene Autry belt. This guy is a nut!"

Jimmy Breslin was the major factor in pulling the *New York Times* into local coverage. He did it with his down and dirty columns on the

Jock Whitney Can't Imagine Anyone Really Liking the <u>Times</u>

FROM: John Hay Whitney
TO: Messrs. Thayer and Bellows

I find myself coming back to the same conclusion every time I ask what there is about the Trib *that's so different that I would have to read it, if I had no connection with it. It is that the* Trib *is the only really interesting newspaper I know. Actually, I often think of it as fascinating. . . . On every page, almost every day, there's a story which, in the way it's written and presented, requires my attention—and rewards it . . .*

People—lots of people—tell me "I'm crazy about your paper—my wife is nuts about your paper—won't let me have it"—this kind of thing. Not just the routine compliment but a special enthusiasm.

This is what we must bottle because it is our unique appeal. Imagine anyone really liking the New York Times.

Memo in early 1962

underside of New York City life. When Jimmy set out to do a series of columns on Harlem, he wrote me a letter, and that letter is framed on a wall in my home, because it is such a terrific example of journalistic brains and zeal:

> Dear Jim:
>
> Tomorrow night I intend to move into somebody's apartment in Harlem. . . . What I intend to do there is simple. Build five parts, and build them on anything of this sort: small facts, gathered in many places and gathered in such numbers that the copy can be flat, understated and totally effective because of the facts. . . .
>
> You follow this theory with everything. With the schoolyards, which are crowded at 7:30 A.M. because parents have to leave early and the kids are locked out of the apartments and with nothing else to do they go to

school. And with the furniture repossessions and water and gas and electric shutoffs and the gas station habits— 50 cents worth of gas for the Cadillac. You do this with acts from small people. In the street and from merchants and bankers.

The entire story is based on one idea: These are people. They are bewildered, uncared about and angry. They have a right to anger because white people would prefer to speak to them in great generalities and do nothing about the housing or the type of food they have to eat because of the salaries they make. The question is, as this summer comes up, will their anger show in a legitimate drive or will it erupt? . . .

Now this is a nice, big statement. It is of the type I intend not to use. Not even once. But the small facts, gathered and put together, will say the things themselves.

Breslin

Tom Wolfe was called to my attention by Bob Donovan, head of our Washington bureau.

"The *Washington Post* has this marvelous young writer and they aren't using him very well," he said.

"Tell me about him."

"Well, he's good. *Newsweek* wanted to use him to do a column, but they don't have enough room for him—his pieces run a little long."

I hired Tom Wolfe. And so began Tom's years of breakthrough feature stories and a conversion to tailored white suits. In addition to writing for the daily paper, I wanted both Tom and Jimmy Breslin to write for the newly designed Sunday magazine. It made a great showcase for their gifts. With people like Tom and Jimmy we had an array of writers that the *New York Times* couldn't match. They had some gifted writers—like Gay Talese, Homer Bigart—but they didn't give them the showcase we gave ours. If we didn't have the *Times*'s sheer number of bodies, they didn't have our talent and a willingness to spotlight it.

The strike was finally behind us and we had used the time to make the paper livelier. Circulation was up. Whitney was delighted. *New York,* the Sunday magazine, was hot. People were talking about the *Trib.* We had brought aboard an extraordinarily talented group of youngsters—Wolfe, Breslin, Gail Sheehy, Clay Felker, Richard Reeves, Dave Laventhol. The "City in Crisis" series had been a journalistic coup. People were saying, "Who says a good newspaper has to be dull?"

But not all my memories of adventures at the *Trib* were editorial. Some of them, sadly, were conjugal.

CHAPTER 7

◆

Maggie Changed Me

My office at the *Trib* was on the third floor. One day in early May 1963, my wife, Marian, walked in downstairs, told the doorman who she was, and went up the elevator without waiting for permission. Just as the doorman was calling my secretary, Jane Maxwell, about the imminent stormy entrance, Marian burst into my office, slammed the door, and started shouting at me, calling me some very colorful names. She had picked up a candy jar from my secretary's desk and she hurled it at my head. Her aim was pretty good.

At this moment, Jane opened the door and later told Dick Wald she saw Marian brandishing a knife. But I was there, and though the candy jar scratched the side of my forehead, I never saw a knife. It was hard to blame her for her visit, though I wished we could have talked in private before the candy jar started flying.

I guess we need a little back story.

In January 1961 Marian first came up to New York to look for a place for us to live. This was shortly after I had started my new job as executive editor of news operations at the *Trib*. The day Marian arrived was also the day I met a woman who was to change my life.

Maggie Savoy was the women's page editor of the *Arizona Republic* in Phoenix. We had both been assigned to the same Associated Press managing editors' committee. She called when she was in town covering the annual designer fashion show to see if we could meet, and we made a lunch date. I made a reservation at a fancy place on 57th Street and got there a little early. Shortly, a tall—nearly six-foot—woman with a beautiful, strong, open face framed with dark hair came striding confidently toward me. I said to myself, "If that's her—wow!" She was truly the kind of woman who knocked your socks off.

There was instant rapport. Over a long two-drink lunch (I drank martinis, she drank bourbon—another wow!) we swapped stories. She had grown up in Omaha, married her football hero after they both graduated from the University of Southern California, and moved to Phoenix. They had one son and had divorced, and she had remarried, a banker named Rocky Pitts.

At the end of the lunch, I mentioned that my wife was at that very moment scouting houses in the Greenwich, Connecticut, area. I wanted to live in the area because it was where my wonderful Aunt Ada lived, who had helped my parents pay for my prep school years at South Kent. I had visited her often in those days and had grown to love the area. I knew my children would enjoy living there.

Maggie suggested that Marian and I stop by at the Pierre Hotel, where she was staying, for a drink after dinner. We were staying at a Holiday Inn. I told Marian that I had never met such a charming, larger-than-life woman, and that I wanted them to meet. Obviously, I in no way understood what was happening to me. We joined Maggie for a nightcap.

I didn't see her again until a year later, when the designer fashion shows came around again. We had corresponded a bit about committee matters, and I did keep thinking about this fascinating woman with whom I had made a deeper and faster connection in one lunch than I had with any other woman in my life. Of course, I hadn't known what I was missing till I met Maggie. You don't miss something that you don't know exists.

Soon Marian did find a place in Old Greenwich, and we moved in. During that year, my family and I began more and more to live separate lives—I in an apartment in New York City, Marian and the girls out in Connecticut. It seemed like the best way to meet the demands of my job and simultaneously create a great environment for the kids. It seemed to be working for a while. My career shot forward, and the girls were very happy. But the marriage was strained and weakened, though we were not aware that this was happening.

I spent more nights in Manhattan than at home, because the first edition of the *Trib* went to bed about 8 P.M. After that, I'd go out to a restaurant to relax and have dinner; someone would bring me the first paper to okay about 9 P.M.; and I would talk with the desk by phone or sometimes go back to the office. It was usually too late to take a train home, sleep, get up, and take an early train to reach the office by 9 A.M.

Another source of stress was Marian's reluctance to come into the city. She was a wonderful mother and good wife in many ways, but she wasn't much of a social butterfly, nor was she particularly fond of journalists. She had little in common with my colleagues. This had been true in Miami and was even more so in New York, where she had to make a real effort to go to dinner or a party with me. Unfortunately, my social obligations were increasing along with my job responsibilities.

I realize now that at the end of that year, when Maggie showed up again in January 1962, the marriage was fraying around the edges, as I led more and more of my life in New York, focused on my work, and

---

■ **The Maggie Phoenix Story**

A newcomer arrived in the Valley not long ago. He was a person of cosmopolitan consequence; had been everywhere and knew everybody. He had spent only a few hours . . . before he became aware of a subtle force which seemed to pervade the lives of people hereabouts . . .

"Wherever I went," he recalled the other day, "all I heard was 'Maggie, Maggie, Maggie.' It was damned annoying; all this Maggie business. When she finally called me for an interview I already detested her and I told her so. She came anyhow. Now. like everybody else, I love her dearly."

Not every influential newcomer finds Margaret Ann Case Savoy, woman's editor of The Arizona Republican, *an annoyance. [They] sense in her a strange and mighty influence. They feel that behind her shiny-bright and beauteous face, her glowing smile . . . that among all women in the Valley she is not just a key figure, but the key figure.*

Dickson Hartwell in the *Arizonian*, January 3, 1963 ■

Marian stayed in the country, focused on the children. With the 20/20 hindsight that all of us are cursed with, I see that Marian and I were probably not a good fit in a lot of ways, but we were young, eager to get on with our lives, and probably eager to go to bed with each other—which many of us didn't do with serious girlfriends till we were married. Both of us were pretty inexperienced, but when we met back in 1949, we were both old to still be single: I was 27, she was 25. So the time was right, and she was the gal. She was as good a wife as she knew how to be—certainly as good as I was as a husband—and I am eternally grateful to her for my three wonderful daughters. I deeply regret having caused her so much pain.

A Maggie Column on Women's Lib

I'm one women's libber weary of big, strong, handsome, successful, intelligent, tycoon-type males who approach me at parties (of all times!) and—instead of a healthy oblique pass—give me the puzzled hangdog question: "Maggie, what is this woman's lib thing all about?"

I'd show feminine compassion if they didn't invariably follow with a smirk of masculine wit, viz.:

"Why incinerate lingerie?"

"What more do they want?"

"I promise not to think of Betty Friedan as a sex object."

"Vive la différence."

At this point I look around for some wall-eyed ex-footballer. He's no threat to me. I don't want to play his game. I'm no threat to him.

Then I melt. Poor men. They're threatened, afraid. Lysistrata might strike again. They really need *reassurance.*

Depending on the inquisitor I answer variously.

If he's intellectual, I remind him: "Our brains weigh the same; it's our paychecks that are slim and unladylike."

If he's a politician, I simply remind him: "We outnumber you."

If he said—some still do—"Woman's place is in the home," I brighten. "It's so wonderful we want to share it. Here's my dishrag."

If he's a newspaper editor, I pay attention. Out of habit—I've been paying attention to them all my professional life. Out of habit—I'm married to one.

I was mostly living in the city, so meeting Maggie for dinner when she returned in January 1962 was not a problem. After dinner we took a very long walk. We were oblivious to the cold. By this time we had acknowledged the powerful attraction we felt. I knew I was falling in love with her; astonishingly, she felt the same. But what were we to do about it? The obstacles to our being together seemed insurmountable. After she went back to Phoenix we talked about it constantly, in letters and on the telephone.

A few months later, another bombshell hit. I was named editor of the *New York Herald Tribune* at the age of 40, and shortly thereafter I went to Paris to meet with the staff of the *International Herald Tribune,* based in the French capital. Between meetings I walked the streets of Paris, trying to calm down, slow down enough to think through what was happening to me. How could I be in love with another woman when I was married and the father of two children with another on the way? I was so high, so exhilarated by my feelings for Maggie, but at the same time I was so troubled by the thought of breaking up my home. But there was never the thought of trying to have both. An extended affair would have been intolerable for all of us.

Shortly after I flew back to New York, I realized that I had to spend some time with Maggie, talking to her and learning about her, to be absolutely sure that I wanted to turn my life and the lives of three other people upside down in order to be with her. I believed I had been in love with Marian when I married her, but this was much, much more. I was completely overwhelmed! And that this wondrous woman expressed the same feeling for me was, to me, unbelievable.

So when Maggie did a story on the Menninger Clinic, I took a few days off and flew to Topeka. We made love for the first time, and we knew without a shadow of a doubt that we had to be together, and that we would do whatever it took to make that happen. But what a mess! We were both married and lived on opposite sides of the country, and my third child was on the way.

A few days after I returned to New York, I got a phone call telling me that Maggie's husband, Rocky Pitts, had been killed in a car crash. I immediately wanted to be with Maggie, but I knew it would make things

A Maggie Column on Fashion

Fashion is Fun and Games, a great Spectator Sport that anybody can play.

The beautiful people play it passionately, train like it's an Olympic decathlon. The Jackies play it with intellectual detachment. The Twiggys, Barbaras, Penelopes and Chers play it with pure cool.

I play it like a born loser.

They have to drag me to the game, and I'm a poor sport about it.

Here I am, with a closetful of short skirts, summer coming, cringing once again as the midi casts its ominous shadow before me . . .

I've been caught in Fashion's Hammerlock so many times I'm losing my nerve.

Too tall when the boys dreamt about Janet Gaynor; too short now that Veruschka is Vogue's Darling, mouth too big when Betty Boop had men booping, too small now that Carol Burnett has all eyes.

Hair too short when Hedy was heady; too long when Twiggie was biggie. Nobody looked at me after Lana put on that cheap sweater; Paris copies make me look pouter-pigeon today. When I was skin-and-bones, Liz Taylor was zoftig; now that I'm zoftig Peggy Moffat is skin-and-bones.

worse if I went to Phoenix. I needed to be somewhere so that Maggie could reach me night or day when she needed to. So I flew to my friend Jim Fain's house in Dayton, Ohio, and huddled over the phone in a little basement room, trying to reach Maggie, support her, and assure her of my love and my eagerness to help in any way I could.

Rocky Pitts's violent death was horrible, but it did pave the way for Maggie and me. At least one of us was now free, although traumatized and badly shaken. After that I finally told my troubles to Walter Thayer, who was Jock Whitney's second in command. I didn't want the growing turmoil in my personal life to spill over into the paper. He sent me to a lawyer named Robert Young, who became a lifelong friend and counsel. I described the situation to him, concluding with the dramatic confluence of events—my wife was having a baby and Maggie's husband had just died in a car crash.

"Sounds like Kafka to me," said the lawyer.

I agreed. I barely recognized myself. I had never had an affair, never broken my vows before, and even before marriage I had had very few sexual encounters. But Maggie and I seemed destined to be together. We hadn't been looking for trouble. We were married and content when we met for professional reasons. We hadn't jumped into a relationship. Lots of time had passed, but I had never met anyone who found me so appealing, attractive, and interesting. With her I was all those things for the first time in my life. Because she believed in me with such joy and fervor, I began to believe in myself—maybe for the first time. This was the most powerful experience I had ever had. My first solo landing in a Navy Hellcat on an aircraft carrier paled in comparison. I had been blown totally off course by Maggie Savoy.

In June 1963 I left home, moving bag and baggage into my apartment in New York. In the days before, I had taken each of my two daughters aside and told them as honestly as I could that I was in love

A Maggie Column on Mothers

Hi, Mom. Why did you get gray? With all those . . .

Disappointments? Like you waited so long and lovingly for my first word. And it was "doggie."

Flaps? Like when Aunt Maud paid a call. Mustached, so huge her lapel watch just perched on her "shelves," she puffed, "Come, sit on my lap, pretty baby." "I don't see any lap," I scowled.

Crises? That first day of school, I was home early, front tooth missing. Second day, long curls dipped in green ink.

Shocks? That first day, second grade. Back door slams; icebox door slams. You ask, "What's your new teacher like?" "Middle-aged like you, Mom."

This is the first Mother's Day I can't reach Mom by any phone.

So you know why I flew mad at Daniel G. Baldyga when he told me: "To figure the compensation on a disabled housewife, you take the minimum wage for a 40-hour week."

Those are fightin' words, Dan.

A 40-hour week?

with another woman, and that I was leaving to be with her. I told them also how sorry I was to be doing this to them, but that we would continue to see each other regularly.

I have carried around a lot of guilt because of what I did to Marian and the girls, and it will never fully leave me. I have condemned myself for the pain I brought them. There were weeks of depression, visits to a therapist, feeling torn apart because I had betrayed my marriage vows and abandoned my family.

So many people have said to me over the years, "How could you do that?"

Back at the *Miami News* several years before, I had berated Milt Sosin, one of my best reporters, for doing the same thing.

"How can you leave your wife and two kids for another woman? How *could* you?!" I had badmouthed him all over the newsroom.

So, how *did* the Anglican acolyte from Cleveland, schooled by ministers, raised in a strict middle-class family, turn into an adulterer? Nothing I can say can adequately explain it, certainly not excuse it. All I know is that I was in a big new world—the biggest city in the country, at the helm of the hallowed *Herald Tribune,* in the limelight that shone on the youngest editor in the history of a historic New York paper. And I had been swept off my feet by a beautiful woman who boosted my confidence and improved my skills to live life to the fullest.

If making a life with her meant turning my principles inside out, then that was the price I had to pay. The cost also included my daughters for a very long time. Marian rarely let me see them, until we had an agreement covering visits.

After what seemed like a long time, the divorce was final and Maggie and I could be together.

A few weeks later, Maggie caught a flight to New York to be with me. We got a new apartment and got married there, in May 1964, with Jimmy Breslin serving as best man.

It was a Saturday afternoon and Jimmy's duties included bringing a judge to perform the ceremony. The unmistakable Breslin prose captured the moment:

I asked a close friend, a New York City judge, Louis Wallich, to officiate. Judge Wallich at this time had jurisdiction over everything but his own marriage; he was divorced from his wife, Millie, and also was calling her up and asking her for dates.

When we arrived at the apartment, people were sitting around on the couches and one of them said to my wife, "What's going to happen today?" and my wife said, "Gee, I think Maggie and Jim are going to be married."

"Oh," the people said.

When Judge Louis heard this, he put his drink down. He went into the bedroom and began going over all the papers necessary for people to become married in New York. He was busy squinting at the record papers. The number of names Maggie had fascinated Judge Louis. Her name was Margaret Ann Case Savoy Pitts Bellows.

[Maggie's birth certificate name was Margaret Ann Case, and the marriage to me was to be her third.]

"This reminds me of the aliases they put down on the criminal sheet," the judge said.

Judge Louis told me to shut the bedroom door.

"Is this thing all right?" he asked me.

"Of course," I said. . . .

Out in the living room, Maggie's big-eyed, wide style of life caused Louis to perform the warmest ceremony he says he ever has done. . . .

Maggie really hit New York. As editor of the *Trib,* on occasion I had to entertain people at the apartment. Tom Wolfe described Maggie's impact:

The thing was that New York, in the circles Maggie and Jim moved in, is supposed to have a certain sophistication; but if so, it seldom reaches the personal level. The town is actually composed of several million people in black raincoats. . . . With the coming of Maggie, however, all that changed, and I imagine that several thousand people in New York are still wondering what in the hell ever happened to them. At a party at Maggie and Jim's the usual parochial knots never had a chance to form. Maggie would move from group to group and fix them with those incredible 150-watt eyes and cut loose with her marvelous laugh. . . . Then, shaken loose, everybody found themselves for one weird moment afloat in the main channel of life.

Seven months after our wedding, in December 1964, Maggie was diagnosed with uterine cancer. She began chemotherapy, and the disease went into remission, but we lived the next five years in its shadow.

Most every Sunday at noon I would drive out to Greenwich and pick up the girls for the visiting time Marian and I had agreed on, returning them later in the afternoon. Maggie and I took my two older daughters, Amelia and Priscilla, on a European tour the following summer. Felicia, the youngest, joined later in the weekly visits, but it was many, many years before we bonded, as I strove to show her my better side. She turned out to be the most like me—smaller when young, feisty, focused, stubborn, and determined.

I am very happy that given the events at the time of her arrival in the world, I was able to restore a close relationship with Felicia—and with my other wonderful daughters.

CHAPTER 8

◆

Decline and Fall

Jock Whitney was married to Betsey Whitney. She was beautiful, intelligent, funny, and—more importantly to her fame—one of the three Cushing sisters. They were the children of a prominent Boston neurosurgeon who, with his wife, did something right in bringing up the girls, because they all married well a couple of times. The most famous of the sisters was Babe, the woman who is said to have coined the phrase "You can't be too rich or too thin."

Babe was married to Bill Paley, the man who started with a couple of radio stations and built CBS into what was known, during his lifetime, as the Tiffany Network. He was a giant of the broadcasting business and a great friend of Jock's. (They had nearby estates in Manhasset, on Long Island.) Where Jock went, Walter Thayer was close behind. Walter saw Paley a good deal and talked about him a good deal more. Occasionally, I gathered, he tried to out-order Paley from the wine list at "21."

In those early years I was worried about the future of the paper. Our circulation seemed to be stuck in low gear, no matter what interesting innovations we injected.

One day in 1965, Walter came to see me and Dick Wald and said, "You really ought to go see Bill Paley. I was talking to him and he has some great ideas about the *Trib*. He's always thinking about something new. And he really knows how to touch the popular mind. And he really wants to help us."

Jimmy Breslin Remembers His Trib Office

Right outside the door, Walter Kerr, the drama critic, would sit at the type-writer, coughing nervously, his hands moving back and forth while he tried to figure out which keys he wanted to hit. He had an hour and 10 minutes to make the paper. His wife, Jean Kerr, would sit on the couch in my personal office. Jim Bellows would come in with my copy in his hands and say, "Now look, I don't want you to make yourself look bad by going off here." Always with class. He would take a chance that would raise your hair, too. It was a beautiful way to work . . .

Jock Whitney is the only millionaire I ever rooted for. The guy hired me while I was drunk at a bar. He seemed to think my conduct was a mark of excellent character. His behavior as an employer only improved from then on.

There was one day . . . when Whitney sat in an editorial conference and looked at a folder containing a large series of articles that were being worked up. The articles were about Republicans in New York State who were practicing the art of thievery while in office. Whitney looked through the copy. Names of people he knew . . . kept appearing in the copy. He shook his head. In virtually any newspaper in the country, the shake of a publisher's head while he's looking at this kind of copy means the stories are dead. But Jock Whitney put down the folder and stood up and said, "Well, battle stations, everybody." He walked out of the room and the series ran.

"A Struck Paper, Famous and Needed,
Goes Down," *Life,* August 16, 1966

I did not know Bill Paley, but secretary-to-secretary we set up an appointment to meet at his office, and I took Dick with me to the meeting.

CBS was in the so-called Black Rock, a very modern building on Sixth Avenue at 52nd Street, where all of the furnishings were carefully integrated. Paley had turned a ground-floor space into a wonderful restaurant. Paley liked to eat well.

Those were the days when I believed in preserving my options. So when Wald and I walked over from the *Tribune* building on 41st Street,

I carefully organized the walking so that we almost never stopped for a traffic light. I didn't know what I was going to say to Paley, or what he had in mind for us, so I spent my time trying to outwit the traffic by never crossing a street until it was absolutely necessary.

We got there on time and a little out of breath, and the first thing that hit me was that his office was even bigger than Jock's. It had a Picasso on one wall and I think a Matisse on another. And his desk was an old many-sided card table with holders for drinks in each corner.

He was very cordial. We shook hands all around and we looked at each other. His cuff links looked more expensive than my suit. Wald was probably wondering who his tailor was. And then he opened the conversation.

"What can I do for you?" he asked.

"Well," I said, "I think you know we're having a few problems with the paper."

He smiled.

"And we thought possibly you might have some ideas we could use to help out."

■ **Tom Wolfe Writes on <u>Tribune</u> Writers**

[Charlie] Portis had the desk behind. Down in a bullpen at a far end of the room was Jimmy Breslin. Over to one side sat Dick Schaap. We were all engaged in a form of newspaper competition that I have never known anybody to even talk about in public. Yet Schaap had quit as city editor of the Herald Tribune, *which was one of the legendary jobs in journalism—moved* down *the organizational chart in other words—just to get in this secret game . . .*

Here was half the future competition in New York, right in the same city room with me, because the Herald Tribune *was like the main Tijuana bull-ring for feature writers. . . . Portis, Breslin, Schaap . . . Schaap and Breslin had columns, which gave them more freedom, but I figured I could take the both of them.*

You had to be brave.

"The New Journalism," *New York* magazine, 1972 ■

He looked a little startled. "I don't know anything about newspapers," he said. "Why do you think I can help you?"

I looked to Wald. I figured he ought to do something. He didn't do anything.

"Well," I said, "Walter Thayer suggested that maybe you could help us with a few editorial ideas that would liven up the paper."

"I leave that sort of thing to the news guys," he said. "I'll be happy to have them see you and tell you what they think. I mainly get involved with the entertainment problems."

"We could use some of that, too," I said.

"Why did Walter think I could help you?" he said.

I looked at Wald. Wald looked at the Picasso.

"I thought you two had been talking about us," I said.

"Why?" he said.

I was stumped. I didn't know what to say next. Wald came to the rescue. He said, "Where did you get this desk?"

We talked about the desk for a few minutes, and then Paley said, "You know, there is one thing I would advise."

"What's that?" I said expectantly.

"You ought to make the paper so interesting that people demand to buy it."

"Uh-huh."

"I know you have production problems. Walter was telling me about them. But, it has been my experience that if you make something interesting enough, people will *demand* to get it. That usually solves all problems."

"Well, our problem," I said, "is in getting the word out that the paper is pretty interesting right now. It has a lot of good things in it, but we can't seem to get any boost in circulation."

"That's probably not right," said Bill Paley.

"Oh, our circulation is not growing the way we want it to," I said.

"No no," he said, "I mean you're probably not right about it being so interesting."

"We think it is," I said. I realized that he probably never read the *Trib*.

"That's your mistake," he said. "If it was as interesting as you say it is, people would be demanding it and your problems would go away.

JFK Had His Eye on My Job

Forty years ago, people used to wonder what John F. Kennedy was going to do once he wasn't President anymore. His circle gloated that he would be only fifty-one after his second term. His plans for the post–White House years were unfixed. He talked vaguely of going back to the Senate, or being president of Harvard or Yale, or getting his hands on a newspaper—the New York Herald Tribune, *perhaps.*

Hendrik Hertzberg in *The New Yorker,* August 20, 2001

It just isn't interesting enough. That's what I was telling Walter. You ought to make people *demand* it."

"How do we do that?" I asked.

"That's the trick," he said. "It's always the same, whether it's print or radio or television—getting them to want more of it. That's what I always tell my guys. And they agree."

"But you don't have any particular ideas about the *Herald Tribune*?" I said.

"Well, I'm not a print person, you see. You know much more about your business than I do. I wouldn't presume to get into details with you. Just get people to demand it. If you double your circulation, things will be a lot better," said Paley.

I thanked him for his time. He was quite gracious about wanting to help. As we were going out the door, he said: "Remember, all you have to do is double your circulation. Keep that in mind and it really will be okay."

When we got to the lobby, I asked Wald what he thought. Wald said he was glad Walter had set that up. It was nice to put things in perspective. Now all we had to do was to see if we could beat all the traffic lights on the walk back.

I was disappointed. We had gone to Bill Paley with high hopes—too high, for sure—and come away with zero. The oracular advice was not very helpful. Bill Paley was right, of course. If we could get the people of New York City to demand our paper, circulation would rise. I'm sure this advice worked with television. Get them so they are screaming for an entertainer and you're going to get higher ratings.

So I was still worried about the future of the paper.

At the *Trib,* an instant palliative for worry was downstairs at the rear of the building, on West 40th Street. It was a bar and restaurant called Bleeck's (pronounced Blake's). When the people who worked at the *Trib* said, "I'm going downstairs," it meant to Bleeck's.

Bleeck's, formerly the Artists & Writers Club, was one of the great saloons in the city. It started out in 1925 as a speakeasy disguised as a drugstore across the street from the old Metropolitan Opera House on Broadway at 39th Street. Middle-aged manufacturers and their young models would come over for lunch from the Garment District. They liked the food and the wood-paneled bar, which one writer called "Early Butte, Montana."

Reporters and critics from the paper would drink and chat with the creator of Pogo, Walt Kelly. And at night, the place became a cultural crossroads where opera singers, Broadway-musical stars, press agents, and writers like Arthur Miller, John O'Hara, and A. J. Liebling matched wits with the folks from the *Trib*.

Presiding over the place was its dapper co-owner, Ernie Hitz, an Austrian-born innkeeper who would cry whenever anybody sang "Edelweiss." Hitz was one of the numerous people that Jimmy Breslin put on his list of people he wasn't talking to for the next year in his annual New Year's Day column.

"I don't care that Jimmy's not talking to me," said Hitz. "I just want him to put my name on a check for the money he owes on his bar tab."

Some of our people felt that as long as Bleeck's continued to prosper, nothing too bad could happen to the *Trib*.

After Jock Whitney bought the *Herald Tribune,* in 1958, Red Smith, the paper's legendary sportswriter, who knew Jock Whitney from the racetrack, brought him to Bleeck's after he had been shown around the premises for the first time—the city room, the composing room, the shipping dock, and the executive offices. Red then told Jock he wanted to show him the home of *Trib* personnel in their leisure moments, and they had repaired to Bleeck's.

Jock Whitney and Red Smith entered the crowded bar, which was buzzing with the conversation of reporters and columnists.

"Well, what do you think?" asked Red.

Whitney frowned.

"I should have bought the bar," said Jock.

It was at Bleeck's where Dick Schaap was once interviewing Norman Mailer, as he recounted in his memoir *Flashing Before My Eyes*. They were talking about Mailer's new novel, *An American Dream*.

"Who's reviewing it for the paper?" asked the novelist.

"Tom Wolfe," said Schaap.

"What does he say?"

"I don't know, but I do know that he compares the book to *Crime and Punishment* and you to Dostoevsky."

"Guess who wins that match," growled Mailer.

The first time around, when the *Trib* fell into the black hole of the great strike of 1962–63, there was at least an ancillary virtue. The 114-day strike gave us the time to redesign the newspaper. This time, in 1965, there would be no benefits and no reprieve. For me it seemed like a case of strike two and you're out.

And this time around we would be without the fraternal muscle of the *New York Times* in our struggle with the printers, for the *Times* said that it was "not ready to take a strike." And so as the printers' contract approached expiration, the Gray Lady of Times Square surrendered to

---

Mr. and Mrs. Reid and the Hoovers

There are many anecdotes about the old saloon . . .

There is this apocryphal story. At one time in the Prohibition era, Helen Reid became annoyed because Ogden was spending so much time at Bleeck's. So she called the FBI's J. Edgar Hoover to ask him to shut down the illegal place. But Mr. Reid got wind of this and got in touch with a higher ranking Hoover in the White House Oval Office. Bleeck's stayed open.

Frank Waters, National Desk at the *Trib*

Dick Schaap on Journalistic Principles

The journalistic principles are the same for covering a pennant race or a race riot. You use your eyes, your ears, and, as Jimmy Breslin has always preached, your legs. You go to the scene. You talk to the people involved. You ask questions. You look for the small details that illuminate the larger story and reinforce credibility, and then, using those details, using quotes, using the richness of the English language, you tell the story as vividly, as honestly, as compellingly as you can. Your story has a beginning, a middle, and an end, and each leads seamlessly to the next. But the beginning, the lead, and the ending, the denouement, must be especially strong.

Flashing Before My Eyes, 2001

Bert Powers and his printers. She gave them the wages, benefits, and the veto on equipment changes they wanted.

Some observers had the unworthy thought that the *Times*'s softness was attributable to a desire to bring the *Tribune* down. They knew we could not survive another strike. So the *Times* accepted the contract, it was said, because it would be fatal to the *Trib*.

I am even told by heads more sober than mine that it is quite normal for a competitor to use his strength to his advantage. Hey, baby, that's why they call it free enterprise.

When the *Tribune* suspended publication before the first long strike, we lost 18 months of momentum and growth. Now, as we were just starting to regain momentum, another strike threatened.

By February 1966, Whitney and Thayer were negotiating for our survival. The survival of a couple of other papers in town was also very much in doubt.

When the negotiations stalemated, Thayer started secret discussions with Hearst's *Journal-American* and Scripps Howard's *World-Telegram* about a merger.

I feared that the *Trib* would not survive. What a tragedy if the legendary paper that had a history of a hundred years, had sent Stanley to find Livingston, had fought off the *New York Times*, would expire.

Horace Greeley had started the paper back in 1841. There was a time when there were splendid and colorful papers in New York, and none sparkled as brightly as the *Trib*. The *Times* and the *Trib* jousted for the loyalties of the affluent set. And they battled for decades. The Reid family owned the paper through three generations.

By 1958 the *Trib* was close to breakdown. That was when President Eisenhower prevailed on his friend Jock Whitney to buy the paper and preserve the voice of modern Republicanism.

Whitney's arrival had begun a renaissance. But now, as the whispers of Thayer's negotiations with the *Journal-American* and the *World-Telegram* for a merger became audible, I began to feel that I was working under a death sentence. Down at Bleeck's, we didn't want to believe that the paper could ever disappear. (In 1981, Bleeck's itself was reduced to a pile of ashes after a fire.)

But sometimes good newspapers, even great newspapers, die. Even papers that can boast writers like Horace Greeley, Walter Lippmann, Jimmy Breslin, and Tom Wolfe.

There may have been solutions to the *Trib*'s terminal decline. Perhaps the answer was to become an afternoon daily. But Walter Thayer ruled out that idea. Thayer was not really a newspaper person. He was a dealmaker. If there wasn't a deal to be made, he was not much interested. And the solution for the *Trib* lay in the possibility of finding new ways to do things.

Hence, Walter Thayer made a deal with the Hearsts and with Scripps Howard, the respective owners of the New York *Journal-American* and the New York *World-Telegram*, to join in a venture that would create a new paper—the *World-Journal-Tribune*.

The unions were furious because this obviously would mean a loss of jobs. The overall editor of the new hybrid would be a Hearst man. The *Trib* had stopped publishing. There was not a hell of a lot for me to do.

Dick Wald, a few others, and I left 41st Street and moved down to the *World-Telegram* building and began to seek distraction from our forced inactivity. We even took a crack at running the elevator.

During this period, Walter Thayer and I were barely speaking. Dick Wald became our representative to the committee that was organizing

Art Buchwald's Epitaph for the <u>Trib</u>

"No, Virginia, There Is No *Herald Tribune*"

When President Kennedy canceled his subscription to the New York Herald Tribune, *I wrote a letter to my little friend Virginia, assuring her that, although the paper wasn't read in the White House, it was still very much alive and would remain alive as long as there were Presidents in the White House to cancel their subscriptions to it.*

The other day I received another letter from Virginia. It read: "Dear Sir: I am seven years old and all my friends tell me there is no New York Herald Tribune. *I won't believe it's so until I read it in your column. Are they lying again?"*

"Dear Virginia:

Unfortunately, this time your friends are telling the truth. . . . No, Virginia, there is no Herald Tribune *. . .*

"Everyone loved the Herald Tribune, *even the competitors, but that did not prevent it from dying. Alas, Virginia, how dreary New York will be without the* Trib, *as dreary as many other cities where newspapers have died and none have come to take their place.*

"A newspaper is not like Santa Claus. You don't have to see Santa Claus to know he exists, but you have to see a newspaper. You have to touch it and feel it and read it and, what's more, believe in it.

"A newspaper cannot be published on faith alone. It needs editors, advertisers, and distributors, and readers, and if you can't have all of these, you can't have a paper, at least not for very long.

"No Herald Tribune. *It's true, Virginia. Those of us who worked for it thought it would live for a thousand, ten thousand years, from now. We thought it would gladden the hearts of Virginias for generations to come. We didn't believe it would disappear until it happened, and some of us can't believe it still.*

"I'm sorry to break the news to you in this way, but, although your friends were right, tell them not to gloat when a newspaper dies. A little of the truth, beauty, romance, love, faith, and fancy that the world is so short of dies with it.

"Sincerely, A.B."

Boston Globe, August 23, 1966

the new staff. We were deciding who would go and who would stay. Paul Schoenstein, who had been the managing editor of the *Journal-American,* was touting his own people and denigrating ours.

"Listen, kid," he said to Dick, "just because they can write doesn't mean we want them. I got guys who don't know a verb from a noun, but they're terrific."

"What are they terrific at?" asked Wald.

Schoenstein was too angry to tell him.

By August, with the strike dragging on, Jock Whitney decided that he could not afford to put out a separate *Herald Tribune*, which he had been weighing. It was over. No more *Herald Tribune*.

Jock called a press conference. Sitting at a walnut table 40 stories above Sixth Avenue he read a statement: "I have never been involved in a more difficult or painful decision. The *Herald Tribune* had a voice, a presence, a liveliness of thought and distinction of style that many have appreciated."

He paused a moment and then continued to read the statement, which had been neatly typed on *Tribune* stationery on an IBM Executive typewriter. The IBM would soon be a relic, along with the *Herald Tribune*.

"It is an attempt I am glad to have made—one that did succeed in bringing together men and women of great talent and sensibility. They had a newspaper to be proud of."

The day Jock Whitney read his solemn announcement, Jimmy Breslin filed the following report:

> The *New York Herald Tribune,* after publishing 131 years, Monday went the way they all go out, in an office full of lawyers and businessmen and publishers sitting at a walnut table and looking at a statement neatly typed by secretaries on electric typewriters. It's funny about newspapers. When they are printing, the biggest stories they have are written by somebody who types with only two fingers on flimsy copy paper and he crosses out a lot of lines with the X key and then words are penciled in all over the copy and it winds up a sloppy-looking sheet of paper and it is very important.

The *World-Journal-Tribune* began publishing in September 1966 from the *Telegram* Building. The new venture had the oldest staff ever assembled for a daily newspaper, since it was entirely chosen by seniority. Dick Wald was part of the new team.

I stayed uptown at the *Trib* building.

In October 1966 a funny thing happened to Dick Wald on the way to the composing room. He was running the Sunday paper and he went down to find out how many Linotype operators were there, so he could estimate how much copy he'd be receiving. The printers went wild. Counting compositors was against the agreement. No one could know how many union people were working.

Dick came uptown to sit with me in the *Trib*'s big, empty editorial floor on 41st Street. Walter Thayer had forgotten to turn the phones off, so we were able to call all over the country and give recommendations for the *Trib* people who were looking for jobs. One guy at a midwestern college said he wanted to hire one of our reporters as an example of why his students shouldn't study journalism.

On our final day there—the building had been sold, and next day the movers were coming to take the furniture—Dick Wald and I were the only ones in the newsroom.

The phone rang. It was Jock Whitney.

Dick and I had been snipping Jimmy Breslin's columns for an

anthology that Viking Press was bringing out. I chose the columns, Dick wrote the introductions to the columns. Viking had agreed to accept it in lieu of a book that Jimmy had promised and never delivered.

"How are you feeling, Jim?" asked Whitney.

"Fine, Jock, fine."

"What are you doing?"

I told him we were assembling a collection of Breslin's columns.

We chatted, and then Jock said good-bye and Dick and I took a break from the book.

We stepped around the battered furniture that would soon be under the auctioneer's gavel, and spent a few minutes improvising a game of baseball. Dick pitched, I hit. My bat was a 20-inch cardboard tube from the inside of a paper roll. The balls were wadded up newsprint. As usual, I swung for the fences. I think I hit three desks.

■ The Cartoonist Stan Mack Recalls the <u>Trib</u> Spirit

I remember the first time I saw Jim Bellows. I knew he was some kind of boss of bosses, but I was a young, callow graphic designer new to the world of newspapers. Now here he was, trim, quick, cocky, in shirt sleeves, doing pushups in the Sunday editor's cubby. It was the sheer exuberance of energetic, ambitious people who knew they were astride something tremendous.

I'd fallen into the job at the Trib, with its innovative Sunday design format. I showed Peter Palazzo, the new and beleaguered design director, my portfolio. Palazzo threw pad and pencil at me and said you're hired, start doing layouts! And they're late! Editors, snorting and stamping their feet, were lined up outside his office. The new rules said the "art department" had to do all the layouts . . .

There was a great pride and camaraderie among the staff, because the Trib was making waves. Along with the recognition its writers and editors were getting, the Trib's designers and illustrators became major award winners.

When the Trib folded, I moved on to the New York Times . . . then the Village Voice as a kind of cartooning new journalist. I created a weekly column called "Stan Mack's Real Life Funnies," which reported on life up close and off beat, Jimmy Breslin style. ■

A Telegram from Richard Burton
to Jimmy Breslin's Publisher

PARIS TELEXE DE NICE
THE VIKING PRESS 625 MADISON AVENUE NEW YORK

*THANK YOU ENORMOUSLY FOR THE BRESLIN BOOK STOP I AM A FANATI-
CAL ADMIRER OF HIS AND SINCE HIS ARTICLES APPEAR ALL TOO RARELY IN
EUROPE THIS BOOK HAS FILLED A BIG GAP STOP HE IS IN THE GREAT LINE
OF MODERN AMERICAN JOURNALISTS RING LARDNER RUNYON ETC WHO
BEAR CONTINUAL REREADNG STOP HIS HUMOR DELIGHTS AND HIS COM-
PASSION IS MOVING AND UNSENTIMENTAL THANK YOU AGAIN*

RICHARD BURTON

April 8, 1965

As the *Trib* joined hands with the *Journal* and the *Telegram* in their descent into oblivion, there was no role for me. I was not very interested in this new hybrid anyway. Editing it would not have been a great career move, even had the job been offered to me. After a medley of struggling papers, I set out to find a prosperous one. I had heard that Otis Chandler, the golden boy of California publishing, had set out to transform the *Los Angeles Times*. So I wrote to Nick Williams, that paper's editor, to tell him I was at liberty. "Have pencil, will travel."

The new composite *World-Journal-Tribune* that hit the newsstands in early 1967 was not a badly written paper. But, as Dick Kluger, the *Trib*'s historian, observed with some sadness: "It was a misbegotten thing, a patchwork paper, soulless and joyless."

Soon the money ran out and the *World-Journal-Tribune* closed its doors in 1968. But of course the real *Tribune* had died in 1966.

In 1900 there were 25 dailies in New York. By 1923 the number was down to 17. As I write this, there are 3—the *New York Times,* the *Post,* and the *Daily News.* There is no longer a New York edition of *Newsday;* it only serves Long Island. The city has suffered from the decline.

After the *Tribune* folded, Dick Wald went out to visit Jock Whitney at his home. Jock had a bad cold. He was in bed. He had a bad heart and poor circulation. It was the beginning of a serious decline in his health.

With them was a man named Sam Mark. Sam was the man who handled Whitney's personal finances—he dealt with the money for the Whitney family and arranged the trusts.

"How much money did it cost me in the last years of the *Trib*?" Jock asked Sam.

And Sam Mark said, "Oh, it was averaging about three million dollars a year." That was net loss to Whitney. And Whitney looked at his friend and said:

"Hell, I could only have kept it going for a hundred years."

David Burgin with Red Smith at the Trib

I stood there, disbelieving at the suddenness of the impending catastrophe. I was rigid with fear, as my boss, Tom "the Holy Terror" Turley, blasted me with invective. Good God, would this ever end!

The New York Herald Tribune *newsroom had come to a stop to watch the drama.*

Standing right next to me through all this was my hero sports columnist, the Great Red Smith. Turley was in charge of the Herald Tribune News Service, which sent out Trib *stuff to 50 client papers around the country. I was the glorified copy boy. Turley allowed me to "edit" the Great Red Smith for our client papers, which meant I got to put paragraph marks on the copy, and maybe catch a rare typo.*

Red Smith had been in Philly the day before and had seen his column in a Philadelphia paper. The first and third takes had been transposed as it went out on our wire, so that his lead paragraph was in the middle of the column.

Now here he was back in New York the next day, calmly asking Turley how it was that his column had been changed. I heard it all and froze. Turley lit into me. Mr. Smith and I just stood there.

"I'm truly sorry, Red," said Turley, "I promise you this will never happen again."

"Well, Tom," said Smith, "all I wanted to say is that I thought the transposition made the column read much, much better."

Dick Schaap Remembers the Trib

The city room of the Herald Tribune . . . *was a wonderful place to work. Perhaps because we all realized the paper's chances for survival were slim, there were no petty intrigues, no jockeying for position, no infighting, no sniping. We might have been going down, but we knew we were going down in good company.*

The rising star of my cityside staff was Tom Wolfe. . . . He was, obviously, a stylist—but he was also a magnificent reporter, painstaking and perceptive, with a dazzling eye and ear . . .

The editors of the Herald Tribune *were as diverse and talented as the reporters, starting at the top with Jim Bellows, who mumbled every word he spoke yet managed to communicate perfectly. Bellows had an instinct for a story, and loved good writing, which meant that good writers loved him . . .*

Flashing Before My Eyes, 2001

■ Dick Schaap was 67 when he died on December 21, 2001, from complications following hip replacement surgery.

CHAPTER 9

◆

East Is East and West Is West

When I met Nick Williams in Washington in 1966 to seal the deal for my move to his paper, he frowned and said: "Try to get your arms around *West* magazine."

West was the new Sunday supplement that the *Los Angeles Times* had just introduced. I think *Times* editor Nick Williams and *Times* publisher Otis Chandler were looking for the same kind of edgy quality in *West* that I had brought to *New York*, the *Herald Tribune*'s successful Sunday magazine. So who better than me to turn *West* into something hot?

What had worked in New York could work in L.A. Right? Wrong.

Los Angeles was not New York.

L.A., as is well known to mapmakers, is a very spread out city. New York is a very *compressed* city. People in Los Angeles don't have much in common with one another. New Yorkers have similar frames of reference. In L.A. the range of interests is broad. So it would be hard to find topics for *West* that would ring a bell for a million different readers. As Peter Bunzel, the editor of *West,* noted: "*New York* magazine was primarily aimed at Manhattan. There is no Manhattan in Los Angeles."

Though we had some good staff writers, like Art Seidenbaum and Digby Diehl, who both made books out of the fine things they wrote for *West*, we never managed to find any stars outside the paper. The closest we came was a guy who walked in one day and launched a career in novels and movies. Bunzel recalls:

"He walks into my secretary's office and tells her he has a manuscript, but he wants to watch me read it. I said not on your life. But I went out to meet him, and here was this ornery-looking gangster type named Eddie Bunker who had spent most of his life in jail. And he had become self-educated there. And the article he gave me was called 'A Day in the Life at County Jail.' And I thought it was extremely well done. So we ran it in *West*."

Eddie Bunker went on to write several best-sellers, including a prison novel that Dustin Hoffman made into a movie, *Hard Time*. Bunker's latest book is called *Education of a Felon*.

We never quite found another Clay Felker either. Clay was one-of-a-kind—a young man with verve and varied interests. He was brilliant at conceiving a story and handing it to the ideal writer. Mind you, writer

---

The First Editor of <u>West</u> Recalls Admen in the Asylum

It seems to me I was trapped in one of those Allan Berg concertos where you have the sensation of having been in an insane asylum.

In 17 years in the magazine trade, I had seldom encountered an advertising man. Now I found myself in meetings with packs of them at the end of the 1960s. Not only did they demand to know what I was going to put in the magazine, they also had their own agenda, which I was clearly expected to heed.

Enter Jim Bellows. It's not an exaggeration to say that Bellows saved West *at this point by giving it new life and direction. . . . He presided over all this in his own kinetic style. The hallways became his personal wind tunnels. In meetings he always seemed impatient to get on to his next appointment, certainly more important, it appeared, than the one he was presently in. He communicated in bursts of words and phrases, which, when interpreted, were actually clues to complete ideas. You found that a conversation was a little like doing the* London Sunday Times *crossword puzzle on the run.*

The magazine went on for several years [with Peter Bunzel as editor] until the Times *finally pulled the plug on it. . . . Jim Bellows charged back to the East Coast on another rescue job.*

Marshall Lumsden was the original editor
of *West*, which started up in October 1966

■ Humorist Burt Prelutsky Discusses
Our Love/Hate Relationship

*Looking back on our 11-year professional relationship, I would have to say
that James Bellows and I had a love/hate relationship. He loved him and I
hated him. Well, perhaps hate is too strong a word. The truth is that I did
feel underappreciated. I felt, as a humorist, that Jim was the audience who
never quite got the joke. From the beginning, he made it clear that the writers
he truly admired were those he had left behind in New York. It was constantly Jimmy Breslin this, and Tom Wolfe that and Dick Schaap the other
thing. If you were writing west of the Hudson, Jim's attitude strongly suggested that you weren't quite cutting it. And if, God forbid, you were writing humor, you really were wasting time and paper, unless your name was
Buchwald.*

*For the record, I appreciate the shot that Bellows gave me. But he never
made writing for him a very joyful experience. . . . To be fair, I should say
that once, when I was complaining about Bellows, my old friend Rubin
Carson, who rarely has a good word to say about anybody, sprang to his
defense. I can only suggest that Bellows must be diamondlike. To one person,
the facets appear hard and icy; to another, warm and sparkling . . .*

Burt Prelutsky wrote a satiric column for *West* magazine. ■

Larry Deitz and designer Mike Salisbury came up with some wonderful
ideas, like rediscovering the architecture of Los Angeles that was described in Raymond Chandler's Philip Marlowe novels. And Burt Prelutsky wrote some witty columns.

But it was frustrating to see that the sort of ideas that had flourished
in New York City didn't strike a chord in the sunny city. New York was
a more intellectual place. L.A. was relaxed, laid back, horizontal in
topography and posture.

Of course, New York intellectuals have been taking pot shots at Los
Angeles for years, but they still adore the climate and the income.
Woody Allen famously observed, "The only cultural advantage [to L.A.]
is that you can make a right turn on a red light." Fred Allen said, "It's
a great place to live if you're an orange." And Neil Simon said, "When

it's 100 degrees in New York, it's 72 in Los Angeles; when it's 30 degrees in New York, it's 72 in Los Angeles; but there are 6 million interesting people in New York, and 72 in Los Angeles." My experience has been that there are plenty of interesting people in L.A., but their interests are very *diverse*. So when Nick Williams said, "Try to get your arms around *West*," it called for a very big reach.

The competitive climate was very different, too. When I was editing the *Herald Tribune* and trying to put the new Sunday edition together, there were seven dailies elbowing one another on the newsstands. In Los Angeles the *Times* was the monster paper, and the competition was weak.

Sure, I had been brought in to make *West* exciting, to get people talking. But the *Los Angeles Times* didn't really need to get people talking. They had everyone in town *buying* the paper. All they really wanted was to keep making money and wheeling it to the bank.

West was supposed to be the male-oriented equivalent of the hugely successful *Home*, the *Times*'s Sunday supplement aimed at women. *Home* was the signature of the Sunday paper. It dealt with living rooms, kitchens, beds, baths, and beyond. But selling a home magazine to California women was not exactly rocket science. Home is the consummate interest in California. Along with a nice tan.

But *West*? Now what was *West* all about? No one seemed to know what to do with it.

Before I arrived, *West* had talked about sports, automobiles, and pretty women, the big three of male interests. But Otis and Nick felt that there was something missing. Meanwhile, *Home* had a wealth of advertising. Members of the *Times* ad department didn't have to sell very hard to get orders for *Home*, but this could not be said for *West*.

Though the *Home* supplement was under my control, it didn't need me. It was as controversial as blueberry pie; it was much admired, and it was a cash cow. *West,* on the other hand, was the mutt of the litter.

The *Los Angeles Times* had been successful with everything they had done and they expected that somehow *West* would also be successful.

And what about writers? Well, New York is the media and publishing capital of America. So you can throw a rock and hit three good writers. (Many editors do this for fun.) But in Los Angeles, there are 8,000 members of the Writers Guild and they are all writing episodes of *Friends.* The printed word is not quite the tradition in L.A. that it is in New York, as William Faulkner discovered when he couldn't get a table in the MGM commissary.

Another problem was Dorothy "Buff" Chandler, the queen of the Chandler clan. I don't think she really liked *West.* She adored *Home,* because she liked the idea of sheets and gardens, and that's what *Home* was about. She liked the theater, too, which is why she raised $18 million to build the Los Angeles Music Center and bring culture to the wasteland. She liked music, which is why she saved the Hollywood Bowl when it threatened to become a parking lot. But she didn't care for what I was doing with *West*—the quasi-investigations, the edgy "sophistication." Another part of the *West* dilemma was that the Chandlers thought of themselves as icons of Los Angeles. So their newspaper had to be above reproach. It had to be . . . important.

With dominating papers, affluence breeds sobriety. I saw it at the *New York Times* and at the *Washington Post.* Abundance breeds dullness in a newspaper.

I have always been wary of prosperity. When I chose journalism as a career, a college classmate said, "Jim is just afraid to make money."

A Letter from Charles Champlin to
Jim Bellows About the Los Angeles Times

Otis Chandler was the real miracle of the paper. Nothing in his muscle-building, surfing background began to suggest the publisher he would become . . .

My favorite illuminating anecdote from my early days there in the 1960s was when I was sent back to New York to persuade Martin Bernheimer to become the music critic. But Bernheimer was reluctant to come because he assumed Buff Chandler would be pulling his puppet strings. But they passed along Nick Williams's words to Martin: "You tell him that he should protect Beethoven and we'll protect Bernheimer." That was the way it worked out.

Nick and Otis Chandler himself ran interference and Martin never fully appreciated how much Buff wanted him fired.

And when I recently ran into Otis Chandler, he recalled the day I came to his office to say good-bye: "You were the only one who ever told me you were leaving the paper because it was too prosperous for you."

Otis wanted to shake up the paper and make it better.

But he found that a vibrant newspaper—and an emboldened *West*—would also shake up a lot of the people who were the paper's basic constituency. And it would also offend members of the Chandler family, who were not exactly on the cutting edge of change. And, most perilous of all, it would shake up the paper's advertisers. They wanted an atmosphere of serenity in which to sell their wares. Ed Carter, who ran the Broadway Stores, one of the city's biggest retail chains, once told my wife: "I think of the *Los Angeles Times* as a *religious* newspaper." (Ed and the Broadway Stores would be the *Los Angeles Herald-Examiner*'s biggest supporters when I took over that paper in 1978.)

Nick Williams was in a tough spot. Yes, he had brought me to the *Times* in the hope that I could cure it of its stodginess. But every time I reached for the fire and brimstone, every time I tried something different, one of Nick's memos would hit my desk:

> Let's take another very hard look at *West*. . . .
>
> There is too much of a tendency toward the put-on and the put-down in *West*'s articles. Much of it can be construed . . . to be deflating important people and important segments of L.A. and the Southland. . . . Sure it amuses any group or individual to see somebody else's ox gored, but in time too many oxes are gored, too many people are alienated, too many segments of our middle-class audience are offended. We have GOT to watch the mix. We have GOT to avoid over-sophistication. . . . This is NOT a national mag. . . . It's a mag with a huge and concentrated audience, and its appeal therefore MUST BE BROAD, broad enough to appeal to MOST of the *Times'* Sunday audience.

Advertisers were the golden goose, and some of Nick's most concerned memos were about them. We had published a sparkling article

> ## To Otis Chandler's Home for Dinner
>
> *Otis was to the manor born. The first shock when you entered Otis's home was the animals. You had to get past the antelopes and bison and elephant tusks in the libary. Otis was a big-game hunter. I remember going to dinner there one evening.*
>
> *And after dinner the women retired to his wife Missy's boudoir to patch up their makeup, which I thought was hilarious. Then the ladies rejoined the gentlemen in the library. And I said, "It's hard for me to believe this. I have never been to a party in my entire life where the men and women separated after dinner." And Joe Alsop was sitting on the ottoman, and he looked at me and he said, "Well, my dear, I have never been to a party where they did not."*
>
> Keven Bellows, 1971

about crazy places to shop in L.A. Deep in the piece, the author mentioned that there seemed to be little difference in the prices at various supermarkets. Nick wrote me:

"The author . . . had to take a backhand to Safeway, Ralph's and A&P. . . . One thing you've got to hammer into the heads of ALL *West* staffers—never KNOCK an advertiser, even gently."

I guess I would have gotten along a little bit better at the *Times* if I had known how to play the game. Unfortunately I have the personality of a maverick, a firebrand, a bomb thrower. I rub some people the wrong way. I can be a little brash. And I don't fall back gracefully.

West magazine needed plenty of work, better subjects, more golden writers, and more *conflict*.

It also needed good design. Design had helped me make *New York* a success, so I knew we needed someone to jazz up the look of *West*. I had gotten to know Ralph Carson and Jack Roberts, who ran Carson Roberts, the biggest ad agency west of the Mississippi. I asked them to help me find a good graphic artist. And they came through.

They sent me a young fellow—23 years young. His name was Mike Salisbury, and he was as talented as he was temperamental. He gave the magazine a bold graphic flavor. His covers were every bit as fresh as the ones Peter Palazzo designed for *New York,* and maybe more edgy and off the wall.

Some of Mike's art was too smart for the room. "I never got any feedback," he recalls. "So in frustration, once I ran the hokiest cover I could think of. It featured every cliché in the book, and I picked the most rotten typeface. And the day it came out, some guy from the advertising department came running downstairs, waving it in his hand, and says: 'Finally, finally, you did a cover that works for us!'"

The stories were as hot as the graphics. One of them was about white country club discrimination, a gentlemen's agreement that kept Jews and actors out of the prestigious Los Angeles Country Club. It caused some clenched teeth in the Chandler clan.

Jimmy Breslin wrote a piece for us about Robert Kennedy, who happened to be a backpacking buddy of Otis Chandler. And Tom Wolfe wrote a delicious article in which he presented Las Vegas as a baroque sample of Americana. We had such exemplary writers as Budd Schulberg, Ray Bradbury, Herbert Gold, and Rex Reed. And it was on our pages that Dr. Laurence Peter gave America its first look at the Peter Principle—the thesis that everyone rises to his level of incompetence.

Nothing seemed to help. We just were not getting much advertising. While *Home* magazine was running to 120 pages at times, *West* rarely got above 40 and sometimes sank to 30.

It was a painful experience when they finally pulled the plug on *West.* I took it as a personal affront.

The readers of Los Angeles were the principal losers. When *West* went under there was no longer a local source of bold, sophisticated writing or brash content.

Consider the facts. I had spent years trailing the *New York Times.* Playing the role of underdog. Fearing that bankruptcy beckoned. Working with battered furniture in an ancient newsroom. Wreckage and exposed water pipes. Sluggish circulation and advertising. Living with stress and uncertainty.

I should have known it was too good to last.

Then the sudden reversal of fortune . . .

Prosperity!

When I moved to the *Los Angeles Times* it was culture shock. The place was like a bank or an insurance company. I called it "the velvet coffin." I mean, you felt you were taken *care* of. There was the pension, the benefits, the executive stock plan, the Picasso Room for special luncheons. Very different from the struggling second paper I was used to. Where you had to keep proving yourself every minute of the day to show that you were really *contributing.* At the *Los Angeles Times* the attitude was: Don't rock the boat. We're making a lot of money. Everything's going well. Another nice day at the office. Very relaxing.

That wasn't quite me. I wanted to roll the bowling balls, heat things up, get people talking. They wanted to proceed according to plan. Not an atmosphere to fire up the spirit, bring out the best in you, build innovation. But they took care of you all right.

Otis Chandler, the publisher of the *Times,* was the golden boy of the Chandler dynasty. Affluence was a natural condition. The Chandler clan had sort of invented Southern California, and there was money in that.

When Otis's parents, Norman and Buff Chandler, made their handsome son publisher, a lot of eyebrows went up at the *Times.*

West's Designer Takes the Job in 1968

When I first heard about the job, West *was a year old. The covers were basically hokey stock pictures of Los Angeles, and the magazine was put together with no concern for pacing.*

People said to me, "You can't go to work for that place—it's a conservative Republican newspaper." This was the sixties, and everyone was a radical hippie. But I thought to myself: If it's so rotten, the only thing I can do is make it better . . .

Once we did a heroin article, so on the cover I had a skull with lips on it, and the headline was "SMACK." And I got letters: How could you do this on Sunday, when our kids can see it, when we're all sitting down to dinner or coming back from church. And you have this horrible cover! So the next time I ran a cartoon cover, charming and innocent. So people wrote: How could you not be more serious? So there was no winning.

Mike Salisbury

"Oh, my God, another Chandler," they said. "And a bodybuilder and a surfer to boot!"

Not quite.

Otis, just 32, vowed with every drop of blue blood in his veins to make it the best newspaper in America. And he very nearly did it.

Back in the forties the *Los Angeles Times* was not exactly the greatest paper in the world. David Halberstam recounted how S. J. Perelman, on his way to Hollywood, once said, "When the train stopped in Albuquerque, I asked the porter to get me a newspaper, and unfortunately, the poor man, hard of hearing, brought me the *Los Angeles Times*."

But Otis Chandler shook things up. Here's how *Newsweek* described his arrival in a cover story on the Chandler publishing empire:

> As a schoolboy at Andover and Stanford University, Otis Chandler seemed more interested in lifting weights than in picking up books. He concentrated on bar bells and the shot-put, with minors in surfing and waterskiing. Blond, broad-shouldered and handsome, Chandler seemed the typical young southern Californian.
>
> Chandler has started one of the most remarkable revolutions in U.S. journalism. . . . He has hired some of the top newspaper talent in the business and transformed the once backward *Times* into easily the best paper west of the Mississippi. . . .
>
> To improve *West* magazine Chandler brought in James G. Bellows, the *New York Herald Tribune*'s last editor, as the *Times'* associate editor. This move left several noses out of joint but is likely to help the paper. Bellows is expected to supply the kind of bite to the *Times'* Sunday features that he helped give *New York,* the *Trib*'s brightly written, with-it Sunday magazine.

Otis Chandler and his brilliant editor, Nick Williams, had not been idle. First they hired Bob Donovan, the *Trib*'s elegant Washington bureau chief. Then they hired Paul Conrad, one of the best political cartoonists in the country. Nick warned his boss that Conrad's liberal instincts might be trouble. "Get him," said Otis. Top of that, they hired a lot of very good writers for their foreign posts. And then, late in the renaissance process, they hired me.

Of course, making Nick Williams his editor-in-chief was Otis's best move. Nick was a cultured, erudite man, the most shrewd and intelligent editor I've ever worked for. He played the chess game of personnel, handling his people very well indeed. And he knew the sociology of Los Angeles. He moved the *Times* from the nineteenth century to the twentieth, and yet nobody knew his name.

If Nick Williams had worked in New York or Washington, the press would have given him more of the kind of treatment they gave Ben Bradlee and me. But on the lost continent of California, Nick was just a quiet guy who got the job done. A tree falling in the forest.

I was pleased to be a part of the paper's renewal as associate editor. I was in charge of "soft news"—the sections on entertainment, real estate, and travel; *Home* magazine, the Sunday TV magazine, the daily women's pages, plus *West*.

When I moved west to go to work at the velvet coffin, my wife, Maggie, left the Associated Press and, switching wire services, got a job at United Press, a few smoggy blocks from the *Los Angeles Times* Building.

At the end of my first year at the *Times*, Nick Williams invited Maggie to lunch. He wanted to ask her to take over the *Times*'s women's pages.

He thought it was stuck in another century and needed modernizing. He later recalled the lunch:

> I went to meet Maggie at Cook's restaurant to try persuading her to join the staff as society editor. As usual, the downtown traffic was bad and I was late, and she'd got there before me and found a table and was sitting there, looking cool and pleasant, and I rushed over guiltily to the opposite chair and she held out her hand to me.
>
> And her finger caught the tip of a water glass and I got all of it, the ice, the water and the glass, about where no

standing man would wish a glass of water to land. It was cold as hell, going right through the sharkskin, and I gasped and grabbed a napkin and started foolishly mopping, flustered by all the attention I was getting, and nobody laughed except Maggie. Who, damn it, did.

Maggie took the job, but she balked at the label "society editor." She put up with it for a while, until what she was doing for the paper made the label seem absurd, and she had her way and became the paper's women's editor.

There was some rumbling because the *Times*'s rules forbade married couples from working in the same section of the paper. Evidently the *Times* disapproved of nepotism. . . . Otis Chandler, his parents, Norman and Buff Chandler, and the entire Chandler family probably disapproved of nepotism. But they decided to hire Maggie anyhow.

At night, when we returned to our house in the Hollywood hills, Maggie and I would divide up the dining-room table and work at our respective jobs. But shortly after Maggie was hired, in 1968, I got her into a little trouble. That was the evening of the dinner party the Chandlers were giving for Richard Nixon. I have never been a big fan of Richard Nixon, nor have I ever voted for him. But I did want to see

<u>West</u>'s Editor Talks About Designer Mike Salisbury

Jim Bellows was convinced that the important thing was the look of the magazine. To get people to read it, it had to really stand out, particularly as part of the huge Sunday newspaper.

In Mike Salisbury we had a guy who was absolutely his own man. He wouldn't take advice from anybody. He was extremely talented. He didn't give a damn about what an article said, and often designed layouts that were contrary to the theme of the article it was illustrating.

Yet I have to say he was a genius. I don't think the magazine would have had anything like the readership it did without Mike's art direction.

His covers were spectacular!

Peter Bunzel

what was going on at the party. So when Nick passed along to us the Chandlers' invitation, I attended. Maggie was told to cover the event. Now, you must understand that the Chandler family helped to create Dick Nixon—they supported him during all of his campaigns, groomed him for the presidency. In fact, when he lost to Jack Kennedy, they felt personally betrayed.

The Nixon affair was formal. The men wore white tie and tails. I bought the uniform myself. There were some twenty right-wing, deep-pocket supporters in attendance, cheering Nixon on. When we got home, Maggie started writing the story for the next day's paper.

"Jim," she said, "should I mention that the Chandlers were the hosts?"

I made the mistake of thinking of eastern journalistic propriety, not western.

"I don't think so," I said. "The Chandlers wouldn't want their names that prominently played up in the story."

Bad call. Very bad. I should only have a dollar for how much Buff and Norman Chandler wanted their names played up in that story. They were furious. They horsewhipped Nick Williams for letting it happen. We worked out a small story the next day mentioning the Chandler hosts. It was a black mark against me.

Then there was the parking lot caper. I had a spot in the executive parking lot and Maggie didn't. One morning I drove Maggie to work and parked in my appointed slot. Later, Maggie had to go to an appointment and used the car. When she returned, Buff Chandler saw her parking in the executive parking lot. She complained to Nick. After that we drove separate cars. Every day.

When I had been at the *Times* for six months, Nick and I talked about starting a Hollywood gossip column. One of the candidates to write it was Joyce Haber, a young woman on the staff who had been a *Time* magazine correspondent. Joyce could write with sophistication and style. The only other person in real competition was Rona Barrett, who did a radio spot on the movies. But we finally decided to go with Joyce. Her daily columns turned out to be easy to read and much more literate than Louella or Hedda had ever been.

I was trying to restore gossip to the *Los Angeles Times*. We needed a way to get at that inside information and what was going on, not just in the movie business, but in social circles as well. The column was well read, but even so, wherever I went I got beaten up:

"Why do you have that woman on your paper writing all that dirty gossip?"

"How could she say what she did about so-and-so?"

And the attacks would continue.

People would recite chapter and verse from Joyce's column. So these angry people were clearly reading Joyce religiously. And then they attacked me for running her. Why didn't they just turn the page?

Actually, Joyce's columns were pretty tame. Yet I was constantly fielding calls from the Hollywood community. It was probably the most fun I had at the *Times*, because I love to get people talking.

But times can change things . . .

It was 1970. American kids were dying in Vietnam. A lot of Americans were marching against the war. And a black militant group called the Black Panthers was protesting the war and preaching black power.

And now J. Edgar Hoover, who had been so sympathetic when the Klan manhandled me, was devoting a lot of time to discrediting the people who opposed the war, and especially the Black Panthers.

Mr. Hoover mounted a counterintelligence program (COINTELPRO) to discredit black nationalists and the antiwar movement. A man named Richard Wallace Held was the head of the L.A. section of COINTELPRO, and he had a talent for phony letters and fantasized rumors. He launched a scheme with a sexual twist against the actress Jean Seberg, a supporter of the Black Panthers. He used the *Los Angeles Times* to stir the pot.

Jean Seberg was married to the French novelist Romain Gary. In April 1970, Seberg, 32, was in her fourth month of pregnancy. The FBI decided to turn Ms. Seberg into a cautionary lesson for any other bleeding-heart celebrities who might be planning to support the Panthers. On May 27 Richard Wallace Held sent a memo from Los Angeles to FBI headquarters in Washington asking for approval to plant a story with Hollywood gossip columnists that Jean Seberg was pregnant not by her husband but by a Black Panther. Held's idea was

■ **The Decline and Fall of West**

Though it might provoke regret and even anger, the death of a newspaper or magazine is hardly big news in the United States anymore, for journalistic burial notices have become almost commonplace.

Look is dead. The Saturday Evening Post is gone. Several New York dailies have gone under, as have papers in other big cities . . .

Nevertheless, when West, the flashy color Sunday magazine section of the Los Angeles Times, recently announced it is ceasing publication, it was a surprise.

It was a surprise because the demise of West represented the first major failure of the Times' baron, Otis Chandler. After assuming leadership of the mediocre and reactionary Times from his parents, Chandler began to improve the quality of the newspaper tremendously . . .

Communication Arts, September 1972 ■

approved by Hoover, though he suggested that Held wait a couple of months, until the actress's "pregnancy would be more visible."

Your FBI in action. Held sent a registered letter to Hoover spelling out the scam. He proposed that the following note be sent to local columnists over the signature of a fictitious person:

"I was just thinking about you and remembered I still owe you a favor. So—I was in Paris last week and ran into Jean Seberg, who was heavy with baby. I thought she and Romain had gotten together again, but she confided the child belongs to [name] of the Black Panthers. . . . The dear girl is getting around!"

Hoover approved the letter. Held sent his poisonous tip to a member of the *Los Angeles Times* news staff. The desk editor passed the story along to Joyce Haber with the observation that it was "a good source"! She put it in her column, not mentioning Seberg's name specifically, but using language indicating that the pregnant actress might be Seberg. This is what Joyce wrote:

> Let us call her Miss A. . . . She is beautiful and she is blonde. . . . A handsome European picked her for his wife.

. . . Recently she burst forth as the star of a multimillion dollar musical. [Seberg had just starred in *Paint Your Wagon*.] Meanwhile, the outgoing Miss A was pursuing a number of free-spirited causes, among them the black revolution. . . . And now, according to all those really "in" international sources, Topic A is the baby Miss A is expecting, and its father. Papa's said to be a rather prominent Black Panther.

Several weeks later, in its August 23, 1970, issue, *Newsweek* went even further. It ran the story and named Jean Seberg as the actress in question. The international press picked up the story.

Jean Seberg responded to the "disclosure" by attempting suicide with an overdose of sleeping pills. This precipitated the premature delivery of her baby. It died two days later. The child's funeral was held with an open casket—the lie stood revealed, the baby was white. After that, Jean Seberg, her baby dead and her career shattered, regularly attempted suicide on the anniversary of her baby's death. On the night of August 30, 1979, nine years after her pregnancy, she was successful. She was found naked and dead in the backseat of a parked car in Paris.

On September 14, 1979, the FBI publicly admitted that it had indeed fabricated the pregnancy story to discredit Seberg. The *Los Angeles Times,* which had been the key mechanism of Jean Seberg's misery, issued an FBI statement: "The days when the FBI used derogatory information to combat advocates of unpopular causes have long since passed. We are out of that business forever."

On December 2, 1979, Romain Gary shot himself to death.

In 1990 Ward Churchill and Jim Vandeer Wall documented in chilling detail the FBI's various schemes against dissent in the United States in their book *The COINTELPRO Papers.* "There is no indication," they concluded dryly, "that Richard Wallace Held ever considered [the Seberg scam] to be anything other than an extremely successful COINTELPRO operation."

A committee of the U.S. Senate looked into COINTELPRO and did not hold as sanguine a view that the FBI's bad old days were passed.

"Cointelpro activities," said the Senate report, "may continue today under the rubric of 'investigation.'"

A few years later, Bill Thomas, the editor of the *Los Angeles Times,* said that he never did like gossip columnists anyway, and ended Joyce Haber's column. After that Joyce spent her time writing a best-selling novel about Hollywood called *The Users.* Joyce died in 1983, having learned to her regret that one of the users in Hollywood was the FBI, and that she and the *Times* were among the used.

Success can be stifling.

The *Los Angeles Times* didn't have any strong competition at home. It didn't have to worry about its readers, because its readers generally didn't get any other paper. Anyone who had any standing or wealth or power in town read the *Times.* Power corrupts, and it also can lead to lassitude.

The *Times* had always had a wealth of advertising and strong circulation. It just wasn't fired up by competition as the newspapers were in Washington and New York. The eastern press—the *New York Times,* the *Herald Tribune,* the *Washington Post,* the *Daily News* in New York, the *Washington Star*—were oriented to breaking big stories. This was the world that Otis Chandler was trying to enter. He had brought in Ed Guthman for hard news and me for soft, and he added a lot of excellent reporters to their Washington bureau.

That's why it was ironic when the *Los Angeles Times* dropped the ball on the story of the century—Watergate—which would have given the paper the prestige Chandler coveted. But the paper was still fighting to free itself from its history. The plain fact was, the *Los Angeles Times* could have had the jump on the Watergate story, but their conditioning got in the way. Ed Guthman, our national news editor, had picked up the story. The *Times* had a prime source for it. We did a number of stories and put them on the *Los Angeles Times–Washington Post* wire, the syndicated service we had formed.

The *Washington Post* was unhindered by its past. At about the same time, they got a tip that one of the Watergate burglars had a White House connection. Ben Bradlee assigned Bob Woodward and Carl

Bernstein to check it out. And once the *Post* had it, Ben Bradlee didn't let go. Trying to catch up on something like that is damn tough. There is a saying at the *Los Angeles Times* Washington bureau today that is a hangover from the days when Woodward and Bernstein were beating us on the story: GOYAKOD. It derives from an order that Ed Guthman gave the bureau: "Get off your asses and knock on doors!" The *Times's* Washington reporters checked by phone and dropped by offices; Woodward and Bernstein knocked on each and every door.

The break-in at the Democratic Party headquarters at the Watergate complex took place on June 17, 1972. Nixon shrugged it off, saying that "overzealous" people sometimes did bad things in a campaign.

In July, a few weeks after the burglary, with no one in the media paying attention to that "bizarre incident," the GOP held their convention in Miami and Ed Guthman smelled a story:

"We saw security around Nixon's White House staff that we had never seen before. One of our reporters, John Lawrence, had an appointment to interview John Ehrlichman, and Lawrence is waiting in the hotel lobby, and he has to go to the can. So he goes to the front desk and says, 'Where's the men's room?' And the guy says, 'Just a minute,' and he gets an armed guard to take him there."

Guthman and the *Times* reporters would meet each morning for a brainstorming session and they would each describe the unprecedented security. Guards were protecting the Nixon staff like they were protecting the president himself. The reporters batted it around. What's this all about? Has there been a bomb threat? And finally they reached a conclusion: It had to be Watergate—that "fifth-rate burglary," that blip on the screen that the entire press is ignoring. *That* was causing the siege atmosphere.

When Guthman got back to L.A., he found that his bosses didn't exactly like his coverage of the GOP convention. It was too strident.

Nonetheless, he directed our Washington bureau to dig into Watergate. Jack Nelson, the bureau chief, came up with a good source. He persuaded Al Baldwin, who had been the Watergate burglars' lookout, stationed in the Howard Johnson motel across the street from the Watergate, to tell his story. Then Bob Jackson, a reporter at our bureau, found another good lead. He had a contact named James McCord, a Watergate burglar and chief of security for CREEP, the Committee to Reelect the President. Jackson had a deaf daughter and so did McCord, and the girls went to the same school. McCord confided in the reporter and Bob turned in a good story.

Ed Guthman went to the managing editor, Frank Haven, and urged him not to put the Jackson story on the wire service that we shared with the *Washington Post*. This was the kind of story you share with *nobody*. When you have that big a story, you don't let it leak. Whether it's a Klan meeting or a fifth-rate burglary. Frank Haven was a blunt editor. David Halberstam called him "a man with knowledge but with no vision." He also said that there had been "a constant underlying tension . . . between Haven and Guthman." Haven resented his lack of influence on the Washington bureau and felt "snubbed and ignored." He insisted on putting the Watergate story on the wire.

"It's my duty," he said.

Halberstam shrewdly observes the difference between the *Los Angeles Times* and the *Washington Post*. The *Times* had a lot of fine investigative talent in its Washington bureau, said Halberstam. "Woodward and Bernstein of the *Post* were less established. . . . They were simply more willing to put in longer hours." The *Los Angeles Times* reporters, on the other hand, "were not as young, and they were no longer police reporters, they had done *that*. . . .

"On a story like this," said Halberstam, "Ben Bradlee's adrenaline was running, this was war, and he was not about to give the *Times* even a tiny hold in his own domain."

But listen! You have to understand. A western newspaper didn't *break* stories. They didn't take risks either—whether it was running edgy articles in their Sunday supplement or taking on a sitting president. They had had things their own way for too long, in advertising and circulation. It said something about just how little the paper had actually grown, despite the vigor and good intentions of Otis Chandler and Nick Williams.

Maybe it was all that sunshine. L.A. was a continent away from Washington and "the locale of the *Times* did not produce much urgency in general, nor did the general style of the paper," said Halberstam. The *Los Angeles Times* "was more like a magazine in tempo, events could wait, Southern California readers were in no rush."

The *Los Angeles Times* endorsed Nixon for reelection in the year of Watergate. The Nixon saga was traumatic. The paper hasn't endorsed a presidential candidate since.

CHAPTER 10

◆

Good Times, Bad Times

Maggie had a recurrence of her cancer in 1970. This time it was in her esophagus. She wanted to write about it to help others. A lot of people have written about cancer, but no one as far as Maggie knew had written of "The Second Time Around." Surgery and chemotherapy had stilled it for five and a half years, but now it was back.

So Maggie sat down and wrote some rambling notes about her new ordeal and sent them off to a New York friend and literary agent, Sterling Lord.

The following notes are not edited, and she probably wouldn't have wanted them published in this form. But they say a great deal about a great woman.

Sterling:

I'm doing as you said—leaning on you. At least until I get my mind into concentration-shape again. (That's part of it—it blows your mind.)

I can write lots better. But for now, I'm just putting down thoughts as they come.

There's something in the day-to-day bit of it anyway.

Basically, I see this as a light, happy book. I've learned a lot—practically all of it the hard way—about life and living. I've learned a lot more about dying.

So it will be a How-To book. I do believe the book-glutted market needs one. First time around I couldn't find any help.

As an outline, one does go through certain steps. They overlap, and not necessarily in order: Disbelief (it can't happen to me), calm, then rage and fury and debilitating feeling SORRY for yourself.

Somewhere in there comes a heightened sense of ME, and another rage that there will be no ME.

I am an entirely different person than I was 5½ years ago. Politically, emotionally, lovingly—every way.

I was lucky I faced my own death, for I have lived more, loved more, accomplished more, *been* more these last 5½ years than all the other years put together.

That is what I want to write about.

For the next six weeks I'll be batted around by the cobalt. So DON'T worry if the writing is sloppy and harebrained. I'll just keep it coming.

With any luck, I'll have time and feel much better afterwards. With fantabulous luck I'll die of a heart attack at 93. Meantime, with your help we'll produce a really helpful book.

Because, Sterling, if I'd known all my life what I learned when I faced my own death, I'd have been one helluva better dame.

One thing: I'm NOT scared. That's odd. I DON'T know why. I'm sad: I love Jim so, and the life we have.

Okay, Sterling: As I said before, I'm sorry the first time we get to work together it has to be THIS ONE!

Maggie

The book was in diary form. In the first entry she introduced herself to her reader:

"My name is Maggie Savoy. I'm gratefully Mrs. James G. Bellows, a newspaperwoman married to a top-notch newspaperman, a sensitive, compassionate man. He will, of course, edit this as he edited my life.

For once, I'll be helpless to fight back. . . . I can only trust him, as I trusted him when I got on a plane at midnight six years ago and gave him my life 'Longer than Forever.'"

Maggie Bellows died of cancer on December 19, 1970. When she died, Norman Corwin was one of the friends who paid a condolence call. He suggested that I publish a book about Maggie. That memorial book was one of the best things I've ever done. I had 200 copies printed for friends and family. The cover was a reproduction of a sign that my friend Art Seidenbaum hung on our front door the day after she died. It was a brightly colored children's drawing of a smiling woman next to the sentence: "Anyone Who Enters Here Must Celebrate Maggie." And they did.

The book contained essays about Maggie by 19 friends. I've reproduced some of them on these pages. It also contained some of Maggie's newspaper columns, as well as her notes on life and cancer and death.

I remember Maggie saying to me, "One thing I guarantee you. I am not going to be one of those people who say: 'Why me? Why me?'"

From the Book About Maggie

The sign on the door required that all who enter celebrate Maggie.

But Jim was asking a hard thing, not only because it took all the muscles of the heart and head to fly level in a cold downdraft, but because celebrating Maggie is a deep action, like Shelley apostrophizing a cloud or Blake a tiger. You don't do it with just a couple of drinks and a reminiscence.

Maggie had the kind of amperage and amplitude found in very special, terribly rare people. If you have never met her, just one look would do it, just one beam out of those warmly intelligent, fun-bright, compassionate eyes, and you knew she was one of the chosen. Even before a flash of the authentic Savoy smile. Even before she spoke a word. And of course when she did speak it only got better.

All praise Maggie. All praise. And damn it, you are missed.

Damn.

Norman Corwin

Maggie and I had taken several trips abroad in our brief time together, and I decided shortly after her death to take a whirlwind trip to some of our favorite places—sort of soaking up our memories and making them permanent. It was my way of grieving and honoring our wonderful life together at the same time.

I took her son, Billy Savoy, and his wife, Peggy, with me. They had never been abroad. I wanted to do something for them and I knew they would be great company. We went to Paris and stayed at the Bristol, Maggie's favorite hotel. I walked the streets that I had walked years before when I was trying to figure out what to do, just after we had fallen in love. I strolled down the Champs Elysées in the winter cold, stepping into shops and cafés we had loved.

We also spent a few days at the Savoy Hotel in London, in a suite Maggie and I had stayed in overlooking the park, now barren in December. Though being there without her forced me to experience her loss very deeply, the trip also confirmed for me what a lucky guy I was to have had such a wonderful, painful, rich, stressful, exciting, life-

---

From the Book About Maggie

I spoke to Maggie Savoy Bellows less than a week before she died. It is typical of her that she did not at any time in that brief conversation speak of anything save the future. She let me believe that we would get together after the first of the year. In my ignorance, I went along with her kind deception.

I said goodbye to her without knowing I was truly saying goodbye. . . . I will not try to overstate the case for Maggie, or she will start hooting at me from the shadows off-stage.

Yes, since she was larger than life, a Dickensian woman in all the best senses of the term, it would be a terrible disservice if I tried to cut her down in size from what she truly was. She was a tall woman, with a soul to match. . . . But the main element that recurs to me is her all-embracing warmth that moved with her, if you will, like an invisible cloud, a presence. I do not, believe me, overstate.

Ray Bradbury

altering relationship—if only for eight too-brief years. Most people don't have that in a lifetime!

Shortly after I returned from my European pilgrimage, my old friends Pauline and Leonard Buck invited me to dinner along with Rod Serling and several others. And we got to talking about Maggie and how I would work out a single life.

"We have to live forwards and understand backwards," Pauline said. "You know about that, don't you, Jim?"

Well, even though I had majored in philosophy at Kenyon, I had never heard that insight of the Danish philosopher Søren Kierkegaard before. It was right on the mark. I've always felt that perhaps Rod Serling was there to ease me into the surreal world of life without my beloved partner; but it was Pauline who gave me the key, and that philosophy has helped me ever since. I also pass it on every chance I get.

Charles Champlin Writes About Maggie

I wonder if Maggie ever fully comprehended the extent of the influence she had on me, on all of us who knew her. Not simply the influence of that vigorous, urgent prose or that exhilirating, indefatigable conversation. I mean the influence she exerted simply by conducting her life in the only way she could imagine conducting her life.

She saw that we are defined by our affirmations, not by our cautions and skepticism—that if "Yes" is perhaps the most dangerous word in the language, "No" is certainly the drabbest and most draining.

And maybe if you're living forwards and bounding down the street with perfect timing, you'll meet your next soulmate, as I did. As a single man, you're invited to a lot of dinner parties, and I was on my way to another one in Beverly Hills when I noticed a very attractive stranger walking toward me on the street. Surprise! We turned up the same walkway at the same time, smiling a bit awkwardly as we got to the door. Our hostess then introduced me to Keven Ryan Sohigian, a divorced mother of a five-year-old boy who was in the public relations business—a field of work we editor types frown on unless the "flacks," as we call them, have brought us gifts of newsy material, instead of a dull pitch for their latest client.

Slowly but surely we started to spend time together, and I was able to shoo her younger suitors away. We had a lot in common, as we had been brought up in traditional middle-class homes by conservative church-going parents. I have come to appreciate how much more agreeable it is if a couple's pre-wed culture is not markedly different. We were both passionate about our work, and moved easily together in different social settings. We became good friends before love developed.

I must say, there were plenty of reasons I thought we would fit together perfectly. Keven was a lot of fun. She's very smart—a Wellesley girl—a good cook and a great mother, and she wasn't too critical of my flaws. She also didn't seem to be a big spender, like yours truly.

Although she was young—33 at the time—she was very mature, having lost both her parents in her twenties, gone through a hair-raising divorce, and faced down the demons of alcoholism that plagued her family. And that was another thing that made us sort of an odd couple, since I was very much a two-martini-lunch man at the time, though I've cut back considerably—no doubt her good influence!

Clare Booth Luce Writes About Maggie

I have just returned from a brief visit to Phoenix, the city that Maggie called home for 20 years. There she has left an indelible impression, not only on a host of friends, but on the very landscape itself!

For Maggie is certainly the only woman in America of whom it may be said that she left a beautiful mountain—and a mountain beautiful—as a bequest to all her fellow citizens. If majestic Camelback Mountain stands today, it is largely because of Maggie Savoy's efforts to save it from the despoliation that suddenly threatened it in the Phoenix building boom.

My husband was a faithful reader of Maggie's interviews and articles and once said of her, "She is a good writer and an accurate reporter." And that was the highest praise he knew.

And what lingers in my mind, or rather my heart, was Maggie's loveliness and her lovableness. She seemed to "grock" everyone and everything. Her intelligence was illuminated with rare compassion. Dear Maggie . . .

■ Art Seidenbaum Writes About Maggie

Maggie Savoy Bellows had a brimming smile and a joyous bearhug on humanity. She changed the world.

Maggie took that patronizing title, women's editor, and squeezed every cuteness, every tea sandwich, every simper out of it. She was a society editor in the most embracing sense, taking on the whole community instead of the few fashionable creatures who live on guest lists.

Maggie wrote about women and about men, in a real world where women and men scuffle, bleed, beg, and once in a while behave like heroes. ■

Shortly before we met, Keven was arrested for drunk driving, which finally convinced her that she couldn't handle liquor. She joined A.A. and has been sober for 32 years (so far) and attends meetings every week. The point is, she got a second chance, as the Bible says we all get, and she made good on it. And it was clear that Keven was *my* second chance, not only to form a stable, loving partnership, but also perhaps to help my three daughters bond with me again.

We moved in together and finally I was able to convince her to marry me. It took a little doing. She was smarter than me, more outgoing, more talkative and 15 years my junior, which would keep me hopping. Hey, I'm no dummy, so I kept proposing. Keven felt it was all happening too fast.

She had some misgivings about having any kind of relationship with me. Maggie's "were pretty big shoes to fill," she said. She felt inadequate, not with me one-on-one, but with others who had strong feelings about Maggie and me. She thought it would be difficult. Maggie was so big in every way, and she had fought such a valiant struggle with cancer that her fight had become legendary in Los Angeles. That was a time when no once ever survived cancer—you got it and you died. But Maggie had beaten it five years before, and had kept going. So Keven had her doubts.

"Besides," said Keven, "I figured I would just be somebody that he got over his grief with."

But finally she said yes.

Joan Luther Remembers a Party at Jim and Maggie's

I was included in many of Jim and Maggie's "at home" evenings, but one was indeed extraterrestrial.

Free-flowing drinks, great food, lounging on the floor. . . . It was a good thing that I was sitting on the floor, otherwise I would have fallen on it. People sauntered in all night long, and every time the door opened, in came a surprise.

Thrills galore—Jimmy Breslin, Tom Wolfe, Abe Rosenthal, Charles Champlin, Art Seidenbaum, Joyce Haber, David Murdoch. But the highlight of the soirée was Jim giving one of his "Sermons on the Mount" about L.A.'s racial problems (the riots had just exploded) and Maggie bellowed, "Goddamn it, Bellows, you have never even been to Watts!"

There was one more acid test to come. Before she died, Maggie, who knew me very well, worried that I'd fall for some bimbo and be stupid enough to marry her. She made me promise that when I fell in love again, I would introduce the woman to Maggie's best friend, Reva Tooley, and if Reva gave the okay, I could proceed.

I couldn't very well tell Keven the reason I wanted her to meet Reva (I knew she wouldn't take kindly to being "reviewed"), but I had promised Maggie. So I set up a lunch for the three of us. Only Keven didn't know that I would find some excuse not to come. She was puzzled about why she had to have lunch alone with a perfect stranger, but she gamely went ahead with only minimal protest. Obviously, she passed inspection, and I could almost hear Maggie breathe a sigh of relief. Reva and Keven became friends that day, too.

Keven finally overcame her reservations, because I had the clincher argument. I told her that we couldn't live together because my first wife, Marian, would use our unmarried status as a reason to keep my three girls from continuing their summer visits with me in California. They lived in Georgia, and I was sure that she could find a Georgia judge to agree that the children should not be around me if I was "living in sin."

"I wasn't going to get married again," said Keven. "I'd had a horrible marriage. I was really frightened about marriage because I had had a bad one. And it had been as much my fault as anybody's. I had really not been a good wife, or any kind of a wife. And I said to Jim: 'You don't want to marry me. I don't know the first thing about how to be married.' And he said: 'Well, I've had a good marriage, and I'll teach you how it's done.'"

I must have been pretty convincing because we were married on a rock in the Pacific Ocean on July 1, 1971. (Hey, it was the seventies!) Chuck Doak, a Presbyterian minister friend of Art Seidenbaum's, officiated, with my two older daughters, Maggie's son Billy, and his family, and young Michael Ryan Sohigian standing up for us.

That day marked the beginning of putting my family back together again. My children looked on Maggie as the home wrecker. And Maggie, who didn't give parenting much time, thought, or respect, never got close to them on their visits. Keven gave her heart to my children as she had given her heart to me—God bless her!

Over the years we have added another daughter, Justine, to my three girls; her son, Michael; Billy Savoy; Billy's four children; and several granddaughters! And we have a big extended family with my sister's children and her grandchildren and the cast of thousands in the many generations of the Ryan clan. Various combinations and permutations of us get together often for birthday and anniversary celebrations on long weekends in faraway places, which we all thoroughly enjoy.

Despite all our kids and demanding work, Keven and I also work at keeping our marriage interesting and strong to help us get through the rough patches. When the children were younger, we would take a weekend away nearby at least four or five times a year to focus totally on each other and preserve the romance we both cherish.

Another gift we give to our marriage about every month or so is a sort of "time-out" that was suggested to us by a therapist-friend. On long road trips, or on a sunny afternoon on the patio, we take turns talking to each other. For about 15 or 20 minutes one of us talks—about ourself, our marriage, our kids, our work, our home, our money or lack of it—and the other one listens. No interruptions. Then it's the other's turn. It's a chance to really communicate openly and honestly in a safe space, and you feel good inside yourself after your own soliloquy. And after a while your listening really improves, because you're not thinking about what you're going to say in response. Responses are not allowed. Not even eye rolling. When it's your turn, you talk about yourself, what's on your mind and heart and soul—not about the other person. We highly recommend it as a great exercise for your marriage muscles.

I can't imagine how I got so lucky as to have two exceptional women fall in love with me. I thank God every day for Keven, whom I love so much for caring for me, helping me, supporting me, cheering for me, always being honest with me, and yes, criticizing me when I require it.

It hasn't always been easy for her, keeping up with the frantic pace of changing jobs. But she has made it work every time—keeping the home fires burning brightly, while restarting her own exciting and demanding career, landing her most recently in work for Dr. Laura Schlessinger as general manager of the radio show.

I joined the *Los Angeles Times* in December 1966. The following years were an explosive era. The *Times* supported the Vietnam War; Paul Conrad and I, and a few others, including Ed Guthman, questioned it. Otis Chandler had brought in Ed in May 1965 to build a national staff, which consisted of reporters in Washington, San Francisco, and Atlanta. Ed opened bureaus in New York, Chicago, and Houston as well.

Ed Guthman had a sparkling résumé. He had won a Pulitzer Prize for stories he'd written for the *Seattle Times* on the eve of the Joe McCarthy period. Ed's stories had cleared a University of Washington professor of charges by the state legislature's Un-American Activities Committee that he had attended a secret Communist training school in 1938. Ed found that the committee had subverted the evidence against him.

Guthman had captured the attention of Bobby Kennedy, who brought him to the Justice Department as his press chief.

Nick Williams was nearing retirement and the word was that either Ed or I would succeed him, with Bill Thomas, the metropolitan editor, the outside choice.

In his book *The Powers That Be,* about the *Los Angeles Times* and other

Cartoonist Paul Conrad Remembers

About 10:30 Jim would show up at my office, and then Ed Guthman would show up. The marvelous thing was, we never talked about cartoons, ever. We just discussed issues—What does this mean? What happened? What are the facts? And it was great to have someone to lean on, particularly on lean days—when you can't think of your own name.

I try hard to make the message in my cartoon quick! But sometimes something is perfectly clear to me, and I get letters: "What the hell are you trying to say??" And I figure, if they don't know, fuck 'em . . .

The first day I was at the Times, *in 1964, I went to the editorial conference. All they did was talk about "What should Conrad draw tomorrow?" "We gotta think of a cartoon for Con." I told them, if you guys don't mind, this is the last goddamn conference I'll ever come to. You do your job and I'll do mine . . .*

The move to the Times *was the best thing I ever did. It really was a nothing paper for far too long.*

■ Paul Conrad has won three Pulitizer Prizes.

publishing dynasties, David Halberstam reviewed the odds on who would become editor: "Bellows was a man of very special editorial skills, creative, imaginative, he loved to venture into areas where journalists had never been before. He was a man of great energy, and for a major editor, of little caution."

Ed Guthman: "He was the paper's most prestigious editor. But Guthman was never in the running. Perhaps if Robert Kennedy had not been assassinated it might have been different. . . . Guthman had come along at an important moment for the *Times*. . . . He had lent it instant credibility. . . . He had built a great staff . . . but his value to the Chandlers was declining."

Then there was Bill Thomas, the paper's metropolitan editor. Wrote Halberstam: "He was the best and most modern of the California group, a good editor, serious, very good on soft news . . . very smart and very ambitious and yet he was never contentious."

Halberstam added that I, on the other hand, "was not a particularly good careerist."

My chances were undermined at the daily editorial board meetings at which the paper's policy on the war was discussed. Otis, Nick, Guthman, Thomas, me, the editorial page editor, and editorial writers attended. I was constantly getting into arguments about the war. I was questioning the government handouts that said things were going fine, and questioning the paper's support of the war. Guthman took his name off the list of people to attend the meeting when the paper supported Nixon in the 1972 election. A few others were taken off the list. Finally, Nick Williams scratched my name off too. It was a clear sign that I was also off the track to the editor's chair.

Bill Thomas was the outside choice for the editor's job, the dark horse.

■ Martin Bernheimer, <u>Times</u> Music Critic, on Buff Chandler

Dorothy Buffum Chandler wasn't just the formidable matriarch of the Los Angeles Times. *She was the all-powerful matriarch of Los Angeles culture in general, music in particular. Rallying her troops of society ladies, raising vast funds, she saved the Hollywood Bowl, built the Music Center complex, and helped make the Los Angeles Philharmonic a major—though not altogether first-rate—American orchestra. She had no reason to like me, a snippy young music critic from New York who sometimes suggested that the esthetic emperors in the land of the plastic lotus were less than fully attired.*

Jim Bellows and his colleagues no doubt had their hands full protecting me. One day, Otis Chandler asked if I would visit his mother and clear the air. She invited me to tea. The initial small talk was cordial. But before it was time for me to leave, Mrs. C smiled as she first asked, then answered, a fateful question.

"Why is it, Martin, that you're so superior, so difficult, so intent on tearing down everything I've tried so hard to build up?" She paused. "You know, I think it's because you're Jewish." I thanked her for the diagnosis. "Don't get me wrong," she added. "Some of my best friends are . . ."

Bellows must have exchanged further words with her about standards of criticism at the Times. *Mrs. C and I never had another confrontation.* ■

All you Agatha Christie fans will know who got the job. Bill Thomas was acceptable to the Chandler family.

"He had none of the hard, unyielding drive of Guthman, nor the creative flair of Bellows . . . but he was sound and smart and he was not going to get anyone in a lot of trouble," wrote Halberstam.

Otis Chandler was surprised when I told him, in 1974, that I was leaving the safe waters of the *Los Angeles Times* to take over as editor of the financially distressed *Washington Star*. But the kamikaze journalist smelled another suicide mission, and nothing could dissuade me. Of course, when a married man with a family makes a career decision like that, it affects a lot of lives. On that note, I should turn the page over to Keven.

"Jim stirs the pot professionally. But he also stirs it personally, if you happen to be married to him. I couldn't believe it. When I married him, I thought he was a normal person. But he was masquerading. The *Washington Star* beckoned. We had just bought a house. We had just had a baby. I had just opened my own office. Huh? What?"

Thank you, Keven—

"I'm not through. He looks like a nice Midwestern guy. But oh no, he might as well be a Martian! He has a very clear vision about the kind of journalism he wants to practice. And it's true in his personal life too. He really is a visionary. When he talked me into having a baby, he had this crystal clear notion that what the family needed was a child to bind us all together, me and my son, he and his daughters. And he was absolutely right. Justine's life, her person, her presence in everyone's life, was just miraculous in terms of knitting us together. He saw that before I ever got pregnant. And I was not eager to get pregnant again. But he was persuasive. And he was right. I refer to Justine as 'Jim's best idea.' He's had a lot of good ideas—that was absolutely the best one he's had. He has a sense of what it's going to be like—personally or professionally—and then he's completely dedicated to it. And you just can't stand in his way, because it's going to happen."

Nick Williams, the editor of the *Los Angeles Times,* had reined in my exuberance at *West* magazine, but he applauded it once I moved on to the *Washington Star*.

Dorothy Chandler, 96, Dies; Arts Patron in Los Angeles

Dorothy Buffum Chandler, whose vision and fund-raising fervor helped transform modern Los Angeles and who, as the wife and mother of successor publishers, helped turn the Los Angeles Times *into one of the nation's great newspapers, died on Sunday at a rest home in Hollywood. She was 96.*

Mrs. Chandler's greatest single achievement was probably her nine-year drive to finance and build the Music Center of Los Angeles County, which revitalized the city's downtown district and fused old-line society with the newer wealth of Hollywood.

"She was really a ball of fire with whatever she set her mind to, whatever she wanted to get done," said James Bellows, a former editor of the New York Herald Tribune *and the* Washington Star *who was associate editor of the* Los Angeles Times. . . . *Mr. Bellows said he found Mrs. Chandler to be someone who knew her mind and was willing to debate and listen to argument and who eventually "usually got her way."*

New York Times, *July 8, 1997*

Nick is a wonderful editor, and when he was no longer responsible to the disparate middle-class audience of the *Los Angeles Times* and the strong opinions of its owners, he showed real excitement at the changes I was bringing to the staid Washington paper.

"It looks great!" wrote Nick, when I sent him some copies of the new *Star.* "The transformation, in so short a time, is incredible." Nick applauded when I tied down Pat Oliphant as our political cartoonist. "He's very, very good, moderately liberal but with solid humor."

"The *Star* as a whole," he said, "has taken on a very crisp, very carefully contrived appearance—a firm step away from the drabness of most American newspapers." I smiled when I remembered how often his memos on *West* had chided me for covers and headlines that were too bold.

Nick's praise meant a lot to me. So did the words of another interested party that he passed along: "Otis Chandler now expresses himself broadly on what you accomplished at the *Times.* He thinks you were a little quixotic to go galloping off in pursuit of a challenge at the *Star,* but he admires you for it."

The *Los Angeles Times* and I were never a good fit. I felt newspapering should be fun; the Chandlers thought it was work. Or duty.

I love good writing. I love talented people.

If observers thought I was a potential editor for the *Los Angeles Times,* then observers were wrong. Despite the fact that Otis Chandler was the best publisher I ever worked for, the Chandlers and I were on different wavelengths. As these pages may suggest, I am a man of inherent irreverence. And during the convulsive 1960s, conservative people were wary of irreverent ones. Perhaps they always are.

I don't think anyone—least of all Otis and Nick—doubted my professional ability. But my appearance and attitude suggested I was not sufficiently "serious."

David Halberstam put it best when he wrote, "Jim Bellows' problem was that he was a serious man who looked unserious, in a group of people who looked serious but weren't."

The *Los Angeles Times* has gone flat in recent years. It has lost the momentum it had with Otis Chandler, and compared with what he wanted to make the paper, it still has a way to go.

The *Times* has now gone through another change, with its acquisition by the *Chicago Tribune,* and it will be interesting to see what happens.

CHAPTER 11

◆

Joe Allbritton

Friday of the July Fourth weekend in 1976, Joe Allbritton, the publisher of the *Washington Star,* invited me and his other top editors to his home for hot dogs on Sunday.

"Oh Jim, by the way," he said, "I want you to reserve some space for me on the front page on Monday."

"What for?" I asked.

"I'm not going to tell you," said Joe. "You might talk me out of it." He laughed and disappeared into his office.

Now what was that all about? I wondered.

Why would Joe want space on the front page? He could be a little eccentric at times . . .

So at the paper that Friday, I asked Ed Yoder if he had any idea what the publisher had in mind. I had hired Ed, an erudite editor from North Carolina, to run the *Star's* editorial pages. George Will had passed on the job when I offered it to him. He said he couldn't handle it along with his regular column. That and scowling at Sam Donaldson on Sunday took most of his time. "But I've got the right person for you," he added, and suggested Ed Yoder, who was working as editorial-page editor for the *Richmond Times-Dispatch.* Ed would play a major role for me.

Yoder didn't have the foggiest idea why Joe Allbritton was cryptically reserving space on the front page.

I did not know that Joe and his wife, Barbie, had received the hottest ticket of the political season.

1976 was the Bicentennial year, America's two-hundredth birthday, and President Gerald Ford had invited Joe and his wife to join Betty Ford and the Nelson Rockefellers (Rocky was Ford's veep) to dine at the White House and then view the fireworks over the Washington Monument from the Truman Balcony on Sunday evening.

It must have been a stirring moment, sitting beside the president as the country celebrated its birthday.

Joe Allbritton was evidently moved by the experience. It must have confirmed a desire he had been weighing and that he had hinted to me over hot dogs. He hurried back to the *Star* offices and phoned his aide-de-camp, Steve Richard. He told him to write an editorial at once to endorse the nomination of his fireworks host, Jerry Ford, for the GOP presidential nomination over Ronald Reagan. He wanted the editorial taken immediately to the news desk. And he wanted it printed on page one.

■ Allbritton Resigns as Riggs CEO

Joe L. Allbritton stepped down as chairman and chief executive of Riggs National Corp. yesterday, handing the reins of the banking institution he has run for 20 years to his 32-year-old son Robert.

Allbritton came to Washington in 1974, when he bought the now-defunct Washington Star *newspaper for $20 million from the Kauffmann and Noyes families. Although well known in Texas as a Houston banker who made his first million by the time he was 33, Allbritton was a nobody in the establishment Washington hierarchy.*

The paper, and his channel 7 television station here that came with it, instantly gave him clout. By the early 1990s, Allbritton had parlayed his media investments into a $150 million fortune by selling the newspaper to Time Inc. . . . Most of all, he bought a 40.1 percent stake in Riggs, enabling him to take it over in 1981. . . . He's now worth an estimated $1 billion to $2 billion, a sum that has allowed him to indulge his love of art and horses.

WashingtonPost.com, Feb 15, 2001 ■

Ray Dick, the assistant news editor to whom Steve Richard gave the editorial, was the late-night man on the desk.

Ray called me at home. It was nearly midnight.

"Hi, Jim, this is Ray Dick. I got a problem."

"What's that?"

"Well, Steve Richard came running in with an editorial backing Ford. Allbritton wants it printed on page one. What should I do with it?"

Long pause.

"Why don't you just get it set and ready to run on the front page in a box above the fold. But hold on to it. And get *another* story ready that can go in the same place. I'll call the desk first thing in the morning before we go to press."

I got a few hours' sleep and then I called the publisher at about 7 A.M. I told him the night news editor had intercepted his front page editorial and called me about it.

"Joe," I said, "remember we had an agreement that you and I would discuss any important positions on issues before the paper took an editorial stand. You wouldn't do anything, and I wouldn't do anything until—"

"I remember," he said sourly.

"Well this is pretty important . . ."

Joe was fuming. He saw it as an obstruction of his right to say whatever he wanted in his own newspaper. He owned the *Star,* and damn it, he was going to endorse Ford for the GOP nomination.

But when I reminded Joe of our understanding, he backed off and agreed to talk to me later at the office.

I called the morning news editor and told him to use the substitute story we had prepared on the front page.

When I saw Joe later, I explained that it might be better to print the endorsement on the editorial page, and Joe and I agreed to meet with Yoder and discuss a decision at that time.

I *didn't* say that it was unprofessional and embarrassing to rush from the White House with a front-page endorsement of your host. I didn't say that the Beltway crowd and the Sunday morning prophets would eat us alive. I didn't say that this would revive the *Star*'s reputation as

Richard Nixon's patsy and keep us from widening our readership beyond Republican precincts. I didn't say that we were already fighting for our credibility and this would just about kill us.

A few days later, Joe Allbritton invited me, Ed Yoder, and Steve Richard to his home at 2400 N Street. We convened in the library, a high-ceilinged, book-lined room. Joe opened the conversation by addressing our editorial-page editor.

"Ed, I didn't want to bother you about this because the editorial page is not under my jurisdiction."

"Joe," Yoder replied, "*everything* is under your jurisdiction."

Ed Yoder then articulated for the publisher an expurgated version of why the front-page endorsement had been a bad idea.

"The front-page editorial is the nuclear weapon. Its connotation in journalism is altogether too heavy for this. The same purpose could be served by a regular editorial inside."

Joe nodded.

"Besides, the intervention of a newspaper in a primary fight is unusual and will raise the presumption that we will also support Ford in the fall election."

Joe nodded again. Good, a two-nod response.

"Finally, there is the risk that Ford might lose the nomination, and you should weigh what it's worth to the paper in its delicate state to risk antagonizing the Reagan people."

"Good point," said Allbritton.

"It may be," Yoder concluded, "that endorsing Ford is like lending half the capital of your bank to an unsound borrower."

Allbritton broke into a broad grin.

"Now you're talking my language," he said.

"Why doesn't Ed rework the editorial for publication on Friday?" I said. And that's how we resolved it.

But though Joe decided to bring his missiles home, my initial veto continued to rankle. After all, he was Joe Allbritton, and he did not like being overridden by one of the hired help.

So I stood up to Allbritton on the Ford editorial. Recently a journalist friend asked me, "Has your stubbornness always served you well?"

Washingtonian of the Year for 1976—Me

Most Washingtonians would agree that competition between newspapers is better for the community than monopoly, and editor Jim Bellows has worked miracles to keep the Washington Star *alive and growing. For years the* Star *was a pale imitation of the* Post, *perpetuating the illusion of competition and ending at the brink of collapse; under Jim Bellows it has developed a lively, distinctive style which often makes the* Post *seem dull and institutional by comparison. He has inspired and rebuilt the* Star's *staff, and the* Star *has become the best afternoon paper in the country. For bringing life, vitality, and a strong even hand to the* Star, *Jim Bellows is a Washingtonian of the Year.*

Announcement of award at Washingtonian annual banquet, 1976

Well, yes, I think it has. I think it's important to stand up for the things you believe in. ("That's the spin he puts on stubbornness," said my wife.) If you aren't stubborn, they think you aren't insistent on getting things done right. So I think stubbornness is a good thing, as long as you're not overbearing. And I don't overbear, I don't dominate people.

Of course, if you are pushing for something, and you are stubborn about it, there are times you have to back off. Sometimes you don't back off soon enough. And sometimes you aren't stubborn enough. And as the old bromide says, "God give me the wisdom to tell the difference."

On the heels of the Ford brouhaha, there was still another blow to Joe's ego. The new edition of the Washington *Social Register* appeared.

I had never seen the Washington *Social Register.* I had never even *heard* of the Washington *Social Register.* Then one dark day somebody came running into my office to tell me that I was in it. And *Joe Allbritton wasn't.*

In the newsroom of the *Star* we continued to produce a feisty, solid alternative to the *Washington Post*'s in-with-the-power-set approach. There were already many talented voices at the paper when I arrived—several Pulitzer Prize winners in the newsroom, solid local beat reporters, and some writers with great flair. I added some young blood to the staff and many new features . . . local news fresh with telling details . . . consumer coverage . . . pushing, insistent stories on government . . .

the Q&A on page one every day . . . focus stories explaining some aspect of the news. This was all an effort to give readers more *why* and *how.*

Two of the editors already at the *Star* were noteworthy. A few days before I arrived, I got a letter from Dave Burgin telling me he was already there. Dave was the only one who had been at the *Trib* when I was its editor. Dave was young and hot-blooded; his ideas were irreverent and he had a million of them. In later years (after the *Star*), Dave took his explosive personality to editor-in-chief jobs on papers in Dallas, Orlando, Houston, and San Francisco.

On my first day at the *Star,* Dave Burgin looked me up and took me to dinner. He invited along a young woman who did features at the paper whom he wanted me to meet. Her name was Mary Anne Dolan. I really got brought up to speed in a hurry by these two bright young people. Mary Anne was smart, tough, modern, and imaginative.

One evening a couple of weeks later, Keven and I were at a dinner party for 12 at Mary Anne's home in Old Town Alexandria. Mary Anne managed it beautifully with no serving or cooking help. As we emerged, I asked Keven, "Don't you think that someone who could pull that off without a ripple, with no serving or cooking help, could run a section at the *Star*?" I promptly put Mary Anne in charge of the paper's Style department.

It was Mary Anne who suggested that Diana McLellan and Louise Lague write The Ear, two very good picks. She also oversaw our new Writers-in-Residence column, which featured contributions by journalists such as Jimmy Breslin, Tom Wolfe, Dick Schaap, Willie Morris, Nora Ephron, Gay Talese, and Bob Greene, among others.

Mary Anne Dolan also rode herd on the seven *Star* staffers who created a daily piece of political satire called "Federal Triangle," a soap opera in print about Washington which ran for several months. Writers alternated doing daily pieces of the story, and the plot was developed daily at a joyous roundtable.

Mary Anne followed me to the *Los Angeles Herald-Examiner* in 1978, when my days at the *Star* ended, and when my peripatetic urges swept me off to *Entertainment Tonight,* she succeeded me to become the first female editor-in-chief of a major metropolitan daily.

Across town, the publisher of Washington's other major newspaper was having a little trouble. The pressmen at Katharine Graham's *Washington Post* were going on strike.

You've heard the cry in countless newsroom movies: "Stop the presses—tear up the front page!" Well, the pressmen at the *Post* got a little confused. They tore out the presses.

They were on their way out to form a picket line and they bloodied the foreman who tried to stop them.

Rather than stop publishing, the resourceful Katharine Graham had arranged to have the *Post* printed on the presses of six suburban dailies.

The *Post* continued to publish, but it was only a shadow of itself, a mere 24 pages long. *Post* executives started exercising the production skills they had learned at a school in Oklahoma City where Mrs. Graham had sent them against just such an eventuality as this.

For us at the *Washington Star,* it was a golden opportunity.

Readers turned to us. Advertisers turned to us. Our circulation ballooned and our advertising spurted. After five years in the red, we had our first profitable month.

There was an irony at work. When Joe Allbritton came to town from his Houston funeral parlors, he was hungry to join the journalistic establishment, eager to sip cocktails with Kay Graham at her private club. But he was not exactly embraced by his publishing peers.

"The little mortician," as some called him, was not a member of the newspaper aristocracy, was he? He wasn't a Hearst or a Sulzberger or a Meyer, was he?

But labor strife is a great leveler.

As Kay Graham saw us profiting by her adversity, she phoned Joe Allbritton. We publishers should stick together, shouldn't we? He couldn't endorse this kind of labor violence, could he? We publishers should form a united front against this hooliganism, shouldn't we?

Well, just how do we do that, Mrs. Graham?

Mrs. Graham demanded that the *Washington Star* print the *Washington Post* on its presses.

But wouldn't *our* pressmen go on strike? Wouldn't they tear up *our* presses as well? The *Star* pressmen were part of the same union.

To Catch a Falling Star

One of Bellows' most visible innovations has been what he calls the Star's *"writer in residence," in which a big-name author comes to town for a stint as a columnist. The* Star's *first star: Jimmy Breslin. He has been sitting in the city room belching forth morale-boosting obscenities, and writing lively front-page impressions of such local scenes as an unnamed bureaucrat's failed seduction of a coworker. Breslin will be followed next month by sportscaster Dick Schaap, writer Nora Ephron and New Journalism's Tom Wolfe. Most of these celebrities were attracted not so much by the money as by their long friendship with former* Trib *colleague Bellows and by the* Star's *fight for life. "The* Star *is the only place I would come to write in Washington," says Breslin. "It's no fun at the* Post. *Too big and successful."*

Newsweek, July 28, 1975

Well, yes, they probably would.

I don't think I could do that.

Well, if you're not willing to print the *Post* on your presses, you should just *cease publication.*

Yes, we could but—

It's the honorable thing to do. As members of the publishing fraternity.

Joe told me of his conversation with Mrs. Graham.

It is a testament to Joe's gentlemanly instincts—or his deference to the baroness of journalism—that his first inclination was to do as Mrs. Graham suggested.

The whole *Herald Tribune* horror story came flooding back to me. How Jock Whitney could not bring himself to keep publishing when the pressmen struck the *New York Times.* Jock had always said to me, "We want to be fair." Jock's devotion to fairness wouldn't permit him to keep publishing while a fellow publisher was being struck. And so, despite the pleading of the editorial staff, he shut down the *Trib.* We tried desperately to talk him into staying alive—we said it was our one shot—that the *Trib* could become a reading habit. But Jock was unbending. And though we resumed publishing when the strike ended, ultimately the paper perished.

Now history was repeating itself.

"Joe," I said, "the *Trib* began to die when Jock Whitney, out of the mistaken obligations of class, did not keep publishing."

I provided a little narrative. In New York, the typographical union had struck selectively—the *New York Times* and the *Daily News*. So all the other papers in town stopped publishing. It was a blood pact. The *Herald Tribune*, the *Journal-American*, the *World Telegram*, the *Mirror*. All except the *New York Post*. After a two-day pause, the *Post* resumed. All the papers were gravely wounded by the 114-day strike. And when a second strike hit two years later, the *Mirror* disappeared, and the *Trib*, *Journal*, and *Telegram* folded into a paper that soon expired. Only the *New York Post* remained in business. Of course, the *New York Times* continued its stately march through history. (So did the morning tabloid, the *Daily News*.)

"Joe," I said, "it will be the death of the paper if you shut down. When the strike ends, the *Washington Post* will resume. Its readers and advertisers will return. But if we stop publishing for even a few days, it will be a death blow."

Joe nodded solemnly.

"Joe, it is not your responsibility to bankrupt the newspaper as a show of solidarity. Your *first* responsibility is to your newspaper."

"True," he said.

That Friday Joe Allbritton attended a luncheon at Washington's tony F Street Club a few blocks from the White House. It was the sort of place where Joe would have enjoyed lunching with Mrs. Graham during the months he was being ignored.

On this particular Friday, Joe Allbritton was sitting down to lunch with Katharine Graham, me, and a surprise guest, Arthur "Punch" Sulzberger, the owner of the *New York Times*.

Punch was not there to persuade Joe to do anything. But he did rather feel that it was not quite right to profit by a fellow publisher's distress. Of course, the *New York Times* continued to ship hundreds of thousands of copies of the *Times* into Washington every morning during the strike. In fact, the *Times* had increased the number of copies coming in, to take advantage of the situation.

"I'm just here to tell you about our experience with the strike in New York," said Sulzberger helpfully. "The union whipsawed us against one another. We learned to stick together."

"I was in New York at that time," I said. "I was the editor of the *Herald Tribune*. And that's not the lesson I learned. The lesson I learned is that the papers who joined the strike went under. And the one paper that stayed out of it survived."

"If I printed the *Washington Post,* wouldn't they strike me?" asked Joe.

"Well, yes," conceded Punch. "They would undoubtedly strike you. That's the name of the game. But we should stick together."

Joe Allbritton did not choose to follow this fatherly advice. He said, in effect, that he'd rather not leap off the cliff. Even in such aristocratic company.

The day after the indigestible lunch, Scotty Reston wrote a column for the op-ed page of the *New York Times* under the headline "Burn, Baby, Burn."

Reston said the violence of the *Post* pressmen was more "vicious" than that of revolutionaries. "This is not a local or a trade union but a national issue," said Reston, "for if sabotage can be used as an instrument of collective bargaining . . . then the concept of collective bargaining and even the First Amendment principle of a free press are in serious trouble."

Reston jumped all over Joe. "The main burden has fallen to Joe Allbritton. . . . Should he come out against the sabotage of the *Post*'s pressmen and offer to print the *Post,* making a common front against this anarchy, or concentrate on his own immediate interests?" Reston acknowledged that "making a common front" might be fatal for the *Star,* but he asked Joe to take a chance. Reston chided Allbritton for choosing to "play the role of the fearful bystander," a virtual traitor to his trade.

Because the *Washington Star* was a subscriber to the New York Times News Service, I received the Reston column and the right to print it.

I phoned Jimmy Breslin in New York. Jimmy was the light of my days at the *Herald Tribune,* and was part of a writers-in-residence program we had instituted at the *Star*. I asked Jimmy to read the Reston column, which was in that morning's *New York Times*.

"So what do you think about that?"

He told me. In telling Jimmy how Joe had been roughed up by the establishment moguls of the *Times* and the *Post,* I could guess how he would react. He had little patience with the privileged classes.

"You want to type up your thoughts?" I said.

I ran the two columns—Reston for the prosecution, Breslin for the defense—side by side.

Breslin wrote of the luncheon meeting between Graham, Sulzberger, and Allbritton. He observed that the establishment press was trying to force Joe to shut down the *Star.* It was, Breslin wrote, "absolutely marvelous . . . threats to shut down the *Star.* Magnificent!"

Accustomed to writing about the felonious behavior of Marvin the Torch and Bad Eddy, Jimmy now reported on the extortionate demands of Mrs. Graham and Punch Sulzberger.

"These nice guys with their drawing room manners either go to too many Mafia movies or they've had it in them to be tough guys all

Joe Allbritton Conducts a "Sour Interview"

My earliest dream in this business was to work for the New York Herald Tribune. *The most interesting, most handsome, best written paper in America. But the paper was gone too soon. Still, maybe someday, maybe I could work for the* Trib's *Jim Bellows. His appetite for fixing the woebegone appealed to me. I was bopping along on my own career when Jim called me from the* Star. *"What about being general manager of this place? I think you'd be right for us." Of course I was interested. "You just need to see Joe Allbritton," he said. So I did. Most sour interview in my career. The guy clearly wasn't looking for anybody in that job who cared about journalism. It wasn't until later that I realized how much Jim was looking for—indeed, absolutely needed—an ally who cared about what he did. It turns out, of course, that Joe Allbritton wasn't looking to add any Jim Bellows allies.*

An E-mail from Dave Lawrence, Jr., former
managing editor of the *Miami Herald*

along. . . . I guess you've gotta come into the parlor to see a mugging like this."

Reporters asked Mrs. Graham to comment on the Breslin rebuttal.

"Utter nonsense!" she snapped.

At the start of the Watergate scandal, Attorney General John Mitchell had reportedly said of Kay Graham and the *Post* investigation: "Mrs. Graham is gonna get her tit caught in a wringer!"

Now it was Mrs. Graham's turn to issue a warning. Ed Yoder reported the threat in an article called "Star Wars" in *The Virginia Quarterly Review*: "According to reports that quickly got around Washington, Kay Graham grew very angry. Joe told me she said, 'Joe, I ran Richard Nixon out of town, and I can do the same to you.' Whether she had used those words I have no idea, but Joe persuaded himself that she had."

Mrs. Graham's warnings and her exclusionary manners were painful to Joe. He wanted to be a player. He formed a partnership with the *Star*'s old-school society columnist, Betty Beale, who had been covering capital society for years. Joe attached himself to Betty and worked at the task.

But if entering Kay Graham's circle meant killing the paper to get there, the price was too high. As it happened, Mrs. Graham didn't need Joe's self-immolation. She had won the strike from the word go. The pressmen had designed a public relations debacle when they opened their strike by storming through the *Post* printshop and sabotaging the presses. The *Post*'s reporters saw this as desecration, and the *Post*'s readers saw it as blasphemy. The reporters' union voted not to observe the strike, the paper was printed on presses belonging to nearby publishers, and its readers kept buying the paper. The strike began in October 1975; by February the printers were back.

The strike was over. Set and match to Mrs. Graham.

Fortunately for Kay Graham, Washington was not a very strong union town. But boy was it ever a strong social town!

Yet its social scene never attracted me very much. I was never too impressed by the White House or the capital establishment. So I went out of my way to avoid becoming a part of it. That wasn't what I wanted to do with my time. With so much work to do at the *Star,* I just didn't want to waste any time in the social whirl.

Keven was able to drag me to just one embassy bash, though we were invited to many. And I would seldom go to parties with congressmen or senators. I didn't get chummy with members of the party leadership. I didn't hobnob with the Georgetown set.

Fat Man in a Middle Seat: A Book by Jack Germond

The best years I ever had in the newspaper business were the three when James Bellows was editor of the Washington Star. *I did my best work, and I had more fun doing it. We didn't beat the* Washington Post, *and eventually they buried us. But we put out a newspaper that was a "must read" for the world of government and politics if not, unhappily, a "must buy" for advertisers. And we had a glorious time doing it . . .*

Bellows was never given the kind of budget that would allow him to go outside for many "name" hires. But he did manage to persuade Pat Oliphant to be our new cartoonist, and Edwin Yoder the editor of the editorial page. . . . He also created a writer-in-residence program under which outsiders with some reputation and talent joined us for a few weeks to write columns. We also had some significant assets, like Mary McGrory's column. . . . We also had a whole stable of excellent feature writers and a remarkable editor, Mary Anne Dolan. . . . Bellows also introduced a Q-and-A that started on the left side of the front page and jumped for several columns inside the paper. . . . We even had vastly overqualified dictationists, including Maureen Dowd . . .

One of Bellows's many strengths was his knack for firing up the troops to be even more zealous in competing with the Post, *which Diana McLellan always referred to in "The Ear" as "the O.P."—Other Paper.*

The relationship between Allbritton and Bellows deteriorated for several months until things reached a point at which Bellows left or was driven out, ending those three golden years. I remember getting off the third-floor elevator that morning and seeing Bellows at his desk, buttering a doughnut and wearing a mused expression. "I have been relieved of my command," he said.

1999

My feeling was that I was in Washington to cover these people, not to befriend them. It was a conscious decision on my part, but I noticed a somewhat different attitude at the *Post*. They had enough people to blanket the social scene. And their rationale seemed to be that in cultivating legislators, they were trading obeisance for access. But I think you lose more than you gain.

Keven had her own reasons for not adoring Washington. One evening, returning from a rare party, she said: "It's a men's club! Washington is the only town where a woman *longs* to be a sex object. Because it's better than being *invisible*."

I mumbled something sympathetic.

"We go to places," said Keven, "and people invariably say, 'This is Jim Bellows, the editor of the *Star* . . . and this is his wife.' I'm the nameless creature from the black lagoon. I'm an *appendage*."

My chief complaint with Washington was that "important journalists practiced important journalism." Washington parties overflowed with significant editors and correspondents. Sometimes these journalists, who were friends of both Ben Bradlee's and mine, would reproach me for needling him in The Ear. "Why are you doing this?" they would ask. "It isn't *worthy* of you!" They were working on my ego. They didn't realize I don't have one. I couldn't have cared less what those significant journalists thought of me. I was focused on my mission—pumping life into the *Star*. A lot of people would have killed for an invitation to a party that I wouldn't bother to attend. It used to drive Keven crazy because there were some great parties we never attended.

Well, there are no gains without pains.

But if Washington's social scene left me cold, it was a glittering target for Joe Allbritton. That's why his exclusion from Mrs. Graham's circle nettled him. Another thing that annoyed the hell out of Joe was the accolades I had been getting for transforming the *Star*. For years the paper was dignified and stately. Now it was developing a brisk style and a bold look that made the *Post* look institutional. But Joe wasn't sharing in the bouquets, and I guess it galled him to see me getting all the credit for the *Star*'s success.

Jack Germond, who led the paper's first-rate political crew and was one of our chief assets, described the Jim-Joe tension in his memoir, *Fat Man in a Middle Seat:* "Joe was already growing a little weary of all the encomiums being heaped on Bellows' head as the *Star* gained critical attention from other journalists. He was the one who put up the money, after all, but he was neither having any fun nor getting any credit. It was no surprise he was growing a little testy. . . . All the stories about how the *Star* had improved focused on Bellows and the innovations he had made. . . . But if a newspaper becomes a story itself, the editor, not the publisher, is going to be the hero of the story."

Joe was getting irascible. He told *Newsweek:* "I made him. People talk like I hired Michelangelo to paint a barn. Well, I took someone who was painting barns and gave him the Sistine Chapel." (Jock Whitney would have blanched to hear the *Herald Tribune* dismissed as a stable.) Of my changes at the *Star,* Joe said, "Yeah, Bellows has a lot of good ideas, but they all cost an awful lot of money."

The pecuniary theme would not go away. It never does.

When Joe hired a new general manager, James H. Smith of the Sacramento *Bee,* I didn't win any more arguments about money. Smith was

---

On Launching a Daily Q&A in the Washington Star

Everything with Jim Bellows was done daily, every day of the week. "Readers don't take weekends off," he'd say to his bleary staff.

Jim was never happier than when a bright new author or movie star or man on the street bumped some windy senator off the precious page one landscape. The Q&A allowed for quick turn-around. No need for long elaborate explanations, news pegs or nut graphs. We just did it. Do the interview. Transcribe it. Edit it. Put it in the paper. It enriched the page rather than trivialized it, as some of the pachyderms feared . . .

Jim's mission was that the front page should portray the colors of life and not be limited to the important but deadening "serious" gray matters of the instant.

Denis Horgan, who was responsible for the Q&As

a stiff, straight, follow-my-orders guy and his mind-set was to cut costs and put the *Star* in the black. He was trying to save us into prosperity.

I reflected on the situation:

I was being lionized in the media for my transformation of the *Star*.

Joe was feeling like Mr. Washington after his visit to the White House.

He was planning cuts in our already lean newsroom.

I was fighting to keep editorial control.

Joe and I were on a collision course . . .

Battle stations, everybody! The struggle was predictable. From the start, my relationship with Joe was civil but never warm. We were never bosom buddies setting out on a campaign to save the paper. As Dom Bonafede wrote in the *Washington Journalism Review:* "It was inevitable that Bellows, the roving old pro with gypsy in his blood, whose paramount concern was the quality of the product, would clash with a carpetbagger owner unacquainted with newspapering except in terms of the accounting ledger. . . . Involved were personality differences, a lack of communication, personal pride, private ambitions, and clash of egos."

By the second week in November 1978, *The Washingtonian* magazine reported on the widening war between me and James H. Smith,

---

■ Jules Witcover Discusses My Marriages of Convenience

Jim Bellows is guilty of perpetrating not one but two double-bylined political columns. After having inflicted the team of Evans and Novak on an unsuspecting world as editor of the New York Herald Tribune, *he repeated the foul deed at the* Washington Star, *when he created and obtained syndication for a similar venture by Jack Germond and me in 1977.*

Germond and I had spent countless years in countless saloons for countless late hours conjuring up the idea of a column of our own, but not until Jim offered to put it together for us did it get off the ground. He gave us no orders and no advice on what the column should say, launching it in the Star *on page one, eight columns across the top. Jim not only delivered the baby squawking in good health but also kept it in prominent view.* ■

Allbritton's financial gunslinger. They ventured the prediction that the money man would be the one left standing. Once more, "Mr. Smith Goes to Washington" and things get shaken up. Of course, this time around I saw *myself* as the Capra figure.

According to Ed Yoder's diary of these bloody days, Allbritton phoned him for the first time in weeks and said, "Ed, come up to my office but don't tell anyone where you're going." Very cloak and dagger. Allbritton's secretary was in the corridor beckoning him in.

"Prepare for a shock," said Allbritton. "Bellows is leaving. Probably by December 1st." It was November 12—my birthday, by coincidence.

"The new editor will have a lower profile than Bellows," said Joe, no doubt stewing over my good press.

Two days later, Yoder's diary read: "The walls still collapsing in slow motion. When I arrived today, Bellows had a handwritten notice for the bulletin board and asked me to read it. So the hour draws near. . . . Rumors sweep building by late afternoon. Little bands of people looking forlorn. Rumors of a cutback in personnel to accompany rumor of Jim's departure. . . . Allbritton was asked in newsroom Friday if Bellows is leaving. Allbritton nodded and walked off."

Washington, as I've already noted, is a gossipy town. So rumors were rampant. "Bellows is on the way out" . . . "Bellows has been fired" . . . "Bellows is going back to Los Angeles."

There had been so much talk in Washington when I came to town that it was a big story if I was leaving.

News cameras and news crews were staked out at our house. This was big news in the capital, where the media feeds on itself.

I had some other negotiations in the works, another suicide mission. . . . I went to see Allbritton and told him I would like to leave in a week or so; he said that would be fine. That was early in December 1978. I had been at the *Star* for three years. It wasn't a firing, or a resignation, just a mutual agreement. I cleaned out the personal effects from my office.

Someone reported they saw me standing on a Washington street corner with a couple of cartons. I looked like a war orphan. It was very dramatic.

A. J. Liebling, who loved newspapers, famously said that freedom of the press is confined to the people who own one. He also said that news of a dying paper always brought him up sharply. During the 30 years I worked in the newspaper business a lot of good papers went under. Most of our big cities have been reduced to just one paper, which means one voice, one opinion, one view of the world. In cities like Boston, Chicago, and Washington, daily papers are even buying up the pesky suburban publications.

The bottom line is that hot rivalries like the *Trib* and the *Times,* the *Post* and the *Star* dwindle. Noncompetitive cities become the norm.

In 1975 when I edited the *Washington Star* there were 174 multi-newspaper cities in America. Today there are 49.

I've always felt that newspaper work is a quasi-public service, no less today than it was in the crusading days of editor Lincoln Steffens. I've seen more than my share of newspapers expire. But does the disappearance of a newspaper matter to anybody except the people who own it and the people who write it? I think so. Newspapers have played a special part in American life—they've been the way we communicate what the country is about, the way we pass on the country's culture. As newspapers die, there are fewer, as Mencken said, to afflict the comfortable and comfort the afflicted.

Ben Bradlee once said, "Bellows hasn't been as lucky as some of the rest of us."

That's not quite right, Ben. I have been the luckiest guy in the newspaper business. I am never happier than when someone hands me a newspaper that is either not very good or in deep financial trouble. The *Washington Star* was both.

So I took risks, inspired writers, let talent blossom.

Despite Joe Allbritton's bewilderment at journalism and Washington, his heart was in the right place. He didn't quite get the access he wanted in Washington; he didn't make it into the stupid *Social Register.*

For a businessman, the *Star* had to look like a losing proposition. You could never catch up with the powerful *Washington Post.* But Joe stepped up to the plate and took a swing.

A few years before he came to Washington, Joe Allbritton was asked by a friend: "What do you want to be when you grow up?" Joe had made a fortune in banking, real estate, insurance, and mortuaries. He replied that it just so happened he wanted to own a newspaper. So he bought the *Star*. No matter that he had no publishing experience, or that the *Star* was in trouble. Skeptics said that rescuing the paper would be beyond him, but he was going to try.

He didn't try hard enough. After I left, Joe sold the paper to Time Inc. and kept the profitable TV stations he had bought along with the *Star*. Time Inc. ultimately drove the resurrected paper right into the ground.

Reports keep coming out these days that Joe Allbritton is now worth between one and two billion dollars, which ain't bad for a first-time publisher.

Willie Morris Talks About Quixote, Wallenda, and Houdini

Don't you understand? Bellows is the kind of editor any writer would follow into battle. . . . When I was at Harper's *everybody wanted to work for me because I promised them lots of space. But Bellows is like a combination of Quixote, Wallenda, and Houdini. He gets you out to lunch, starts talking to you about the thrill of the chase and how exciting being an underdog is, and being on the wire without a net, and the next thing you know I'm living on somebody's couch in Virginia writing three pieces a week!*

And you know what's funny? I was attracted to the Star *because it is after all in Washington, the most southern northern city, and it's the most powerful city in the world with the strangest social mores. But when Bellows made me the offer and I started writing the column, I realized how much I missed Washington and I think I did the best journalism of my life.*

That's why Bellows is a great editor—he got the best out of me. That's what everybody says. He gives you the assignment and then lets you have all the leeway that anybody can imagine!

As recorded by Ted Beitchman from a lunch with Willie Morris, January 1980

Joe was a man of extremes. He had very good moods and very bad moods. The good moods were better, of course. One of the most memorable examples of Joe Allbritton's mood swings occurred when I was cleaning out my desk preparing to go.

My phone rang. It was the publisher.

"Jim, Barbie and I want to give you a parting gift to show our appreciation for your work on the paper."

"Oh?" I said.

"I want you to go over to the Cadillac dealer and pick out a Seville. I've already alerted them."

"Thank you both," I said. "That's quite a nice surprise."

I grabbed my coat and left the office. I drove over to Capitol Cadillac. The showroom sparkled with emblems of greed and achievement. The 1977 Cadillac was a symphony in silver. A salesman descended on me.

"I think Mr. Allbritton has made arrangements for a Seville," I said. "I'd just as soon drive it away."

I signed some papers, climbed behind the wheel, and drove the car off the lot. With Joe's sudden mood swings, there was no sense in giving him a chance to change his mind.

When Jules Witcover, the reporter I had linked with Jack Germond to write a political column, heard that, despite all our acrimony, Joe Allbritton had given me a Cadillac, he smiled and said, "Being rich means never having to say you're sorry."

If Joe didn't exactly say he was sorry, a lot of good people said they were sorry to see me go.

A few of them threw a farewell party for me. Black tie. Candlelight and flowers. Dinner and dancing. Smart, funny, touching toasts.

Mary Anne Dolan said, "It was the kind of party that none of us could afford but the one party we couldn't afford not to give. It was a thanks-to-Jim-Bellows party."

Young columnist David Israel and sports editor Ted Beitchman joined Mary Anne in organizing the event, paying for most of it out of their own shallow pockets and accepting voluntary contributions. It took place at the elegant old Sheraton Carlton Hotel on 16th Street, not far from the White House, and it began with cocktails in the handsome first-floor Federal City Club, warmed by the streetlights outside. Jack Germond was a member of the club and got us in the door.

The back-of-the-newsroom guys looked amazingly at ease in tuxedos; there were ladies in gowns; and Eleni Epstein, the fashion editor and wife of Managing Editor Sid Epstein, teasingly watched out for bad behavior. There were about a hundred of us, including Jules Witcover,

David Israel Gets a Tip from Schaap and Breslin

It was probably the first and last coherent sentence I ever heard Jim Bellows utter.

This was on a winter's night in 1975. Bellows, the gaunt, ascetic newspaper legend who made Gandhi look like a picture of robust health even now, as he was a couple of martinis into the evening, sat on a couch across the coffee table. We were in a room I would later learn to call a parlor or a salon in his Georgetown crash pad.

Less than 24 hours earlier, I had been minding my own business writing a story about college basketball at my desk in the city room of the Chicago Daily News, *when the phone rang. Dick Schaap was calling. "Jim Bellows just became editor of the* Washington Star. *Breslin and I told him you should be his sports columnist," Schaap said.*

I was so flattered and eager for the job, I called Bellows without thinking how he might have asked Schaap and Breslin for the recommendation. All these years later, I have finally come to realize the question went something like this: "Where can I find a young sports columnist who'll work cheap?" . . .

That's when Bellows popped that uniquely coherent question.

"So what do you want to do with the rest of your life?"

"I want to write a newspaper column for you," I said, which wasn't a complete lie. Because in those days if you aspired to write a newspaper column that involved more than thumbsucking and intellectual pretense, you wanted to write it for Bellows. As an editor, he had brought Jimmy Breslin, Dick Schaap, and Tom Wolfe into this world, and made it a more comfortable place for Red Smith. You wanted to be sprinkled with that stardust.

■ David Israel wrote a fabulous sports column for the *Washington Star.*

Bradlee and I Duel over Bringing Mike Royko to Washington

James Bellows [was] one of the few rivals to Bradlee as the best editor in the country. . . . Bellows was also very interested in Royko and had also made his pitch, which Royko had apparently discussed with . . . David Israel, now working for the Star. *Israel then spoke with Bellows, prompting this Bellows letter to Royko:*

"Look, I'm ecstatic over the idea of Royko in Washington, writing in the Washington Star. *Monday, next week, next month, September, or even in 1976. The sooner, the better . . .*

"Yeh, I know, Washington ain't Chicago, but it is the seat of the world's power, etc., etc. And there are a hell of a lot of good crony bars in the South Capital area.

"Enough. I'm still counting on you sooner or later. We'll run you as you've never been run before."

F. Richard Ciccone, *Mike Royko: A Life in Print*, 2001

■ In April 1975 Mike Royko, stellar Chicago columnist, met with
Ben Bradlee, who was trying to get him to the *Washington Post.*

political cartoonist supreme Pat Oliphant, and the queen of columnists, Mary McGrory. Friends came from around Washington and New York, including Mark Shields, Jack Nelson, Bob Novak, Eunice Shriver and her son Bobby, Don Forst and Dave Laventhol from *Newsday*, Harry Rosenfeld and Richard Cohen from the *Washington Post,* and Doug Kiker from NBC. Ben Bradlee and Sally Quinn came by for cocktails, and so did Kay Graham. That showed a lot of class—and perhaps even a little affection—given the fact that the *Star* had needled them unmercifully in The Ear.

Joe Allbritton did not come to the dinner. Feelings were still quite raw at the time, despite the Cadillac Joe had given me as a parting gift. The *Washington Post* said, "[People] were talking about the remark by Bellows' wife Keven that he can always trade it in for three Volvos."

Reporters from the *Post* covered the party, and reading their story the next day, Mary Anne Dolan observed, "Understanding little of the love and sadness being felt that night, the *Post* portrayed the event as a gathering of old cronies from the *New York Herald Tribune* and some stumblebums from the *Star*."

There were some eloquent toasts, which Dolan summed up when she recalled, "What everyone tried to say and what we all felt was deep gratitude to Jim for reminding us what journalism was supposed to be about."

About a week after the party, Mary Anne received a note from Jack Germond with a substantial check. It read: "I gave my own check to Dave Israel. This one represents support for the party from an anonymous donor, whose money I agreed to launder. So don't ask." I suspect the check was from Joe Allbritton.

And a few weeks after that, when the IRS sent me a gift tax bill on the Cadillac for several thousand dollars, I sent it on to Joe with a note: "I thought the car was a gift." And he paid it. So there!

The Cadillac was the grace note that ended an acrimonious relationship. (Ed Yoder used to say, "The trouble is, Bellows can't talk and Allbritton can't listen.") But I think I could have handled the situation better than I did.

I paid a price for my stubbornness. For years I had wanted to be the editor of the *Star*. And I just couldn't make it work. Maybe I didn't have the finesse to work with Joe. Maybe if I'd had a little more polish, if I'd compromised a little more, if I had been more manipulative, I could have made it work. Instead, the paper went down. I was so damn clear about what had to happen that Joe and I were like two opposing fists.

There are people who blame me for the fact that the *Star* went under. They feel I could have made more of an effort, I could have played to Joe Allbritton's ego, I could have made him more a part of the editorial enterprise. But perhaps because I had this basic antipathy to publishers—it started when the *Ledger* publishers hung me out to dry—I just couldn't do it. I couldn't play the game well enough to stay.

When I was leaving the *Star*, I remembered that Ben Bradlee had felt it was a dubious proposition when I took over there.

"Bellows is holding a very poor hand," Ben said.

True, but I wouldn't have traded it for four aces.

■ The Pimpmobile Helps Me Lengthen My Legend

Bellows needed a car to get around Washington, so he had a dealer send one over. It was huge. On the trunk were phony plastic straps with gold buckles to give it a sporting air. It had chrome wire wheels. And it was pink. Any pimp might have sent it back. Four of us went to lunch in the new car. Bellows drove. Down at the waterfront on the river we swung in under the restaurant to the parking lot, and while we didn't know it, Bellows was about to add to his legend. We got out of the car and Bellows slammed the door and someone remarked that the engine was still running. The keys were still in the ignition and the doors had locked. We stood around wondering what to do and then turned to ask Bellows his opinion. He was in the distance, getting into the restaurant elevator. We saw what his priorities were, so we left the thing running and followed.

Pat Oliphant ■

CHAPTER 12

◆

Oh, Kay!

One of the first things I did when I took over the *Washington Star* was to establish a "Q&A" feature and print it every day on the left-hand side of the front page. The first subject I chose was the most powerful woman in Washington—and probably the most famous and admired—Katharine Graham. We were surprised and delighted when she agreed to sit down and be interviewed.

Further down the road, when we decided to profile her in a multi-part series, she was not so amenable. More on that later. First, let me tell you about the Q&A with which she was so cooperative.

When Mrs. Graham consented to the interview, Mary Anne Dolan, the editor of our style section, drove over to the *Washington Post* Building on 15th Street N.W. for the conversation. Dolan knew that the one area in which this most revered woman had been criticized was in using her position as publisher of the *Post* to meet and influence government leaders. So she took aim:

> **Q.** Mrs. Graham, do you see national policy being set over chocolate mousse and cognac in Georgetown?
>
> **A.** No, it really isn't. That's the most misleading sort of distorting view of it.
>
> **Q.** What about the clique of intellectuals and powerful people who gather socially and form government policy?

A. I think that to some small and on the whole negligible extent government people do see the press after hours. My own dining out is minimal. . . .

Q. If nothing of any significance ever happens at parties here, should newspapers care about covering them?

A. Yes, it's the one remaining town where social life is of interest.

Q. Do you feel a responsibility to other women because of your position?

A. I feel a dual obligation. . . . As a manager in a company these days, any executive feels a responsibility toward women, and if you are a woman in that role, you obviously feel it even more.

Q. Don't the majority of women still frown on their lives?

A. The old-fashioned way of living, in which women were brought up to please men instead of viewing themselves as equal, left their lives frustrated and boring when the children were grown. . . . People sometimes think that I put down housewives, and I don't at all. I just think that if somebody chooses to stay home, that they have their own interests and intellectual pursuits.

The interview ran as our first Q&A early in 1975, and got the kind of attention we had hoped it would.

If you read any of the articles that appeared about Katharine Graham in newspaper and magazine profiles at the time, you will not encounter much reproach. The Kay Graham America knew was a shy but courageous widow who had taken the reins of the *Washington Post* after her husband died, and dared to stare down Richard Nixon, which is more than Henry Kissinger ever did.

The *Washington Post* was the powerful paper in town. And Washington was a town that thrived on talk about its powerful people. And I knew that in order to succeed, the *Star* would have to get people talking, to stir things up.

So I called Lynn Rosellini into my office. This was in 1977, a couple years after we had bearded the lioness with our Q&A. Lynn had written a controversial five-part series for the *Star* on gays in professional sports, another good idea of our sports editor, Dave Burgin. I suggested to Lynn a full-blown profile on the baroness of journalism.

"That series on Mrs. Graham," Lynn recalled recently, "was a prime example of your willingness to take risks at the *Star*, taking on a taboo subject that was sure to prick the establishment." Well, when you are a second newspaper, you have to take risks to survive. We took some heat with the pieces on gays in sports, but we got a lot of attention in Washington and around the country.

Lynn had some reservations about the Kay Graham profile idea.

"It's a no-win proposition," she said. "If we do a critical piece on Mrs. Graham, we'll be accused of doing a hatchet job on the publisher of a rival paper. If we do a puff piece, people will think we're trying to suck up to her."

Looking back on our meeting, Lynn expanded on her reasons for wanting to get away from the assignment.

"I thought, what was the *Star* doing writing about the publisher of the *Post*, anyway? And I figured it was moot, since Mrs. Graham would doubtless refuse to do an interview, and that would be the end of it.

A brief Q&A piece was one thing, but a five-part profile? Never. But off I went and wrote a letter to Mrs. Graham requesting an interview, and then pulled the clips from the morgue."

Kay Graham was a controversial figure. She had just broken the pressmen's union. She had a reputation as a woman who changed her company executives as often as some people change hairstyles.

As Lynn anticipated, Mrs. Graham declined to do an interview. But we decided we would just do the series without her. Lynn put in a bunch of calls to Mrs. Graham's current and former employees, social friends, and others who had known her over the years.

That was when we started to get a sense of how feared she was in Washington.

I found this reticence to talk a little strange. If there was anything I had learned since I had arrived in the capital it was that everybody liked to talk about people—especially powerful people. Gossip was the coin of the realm.

"I'd never worked on a story quite like this," recalled Lynn. "I'd spend days putting out phone calls and not advancing the story one

Chicago Tribune Service Reports
on the Katharine Graham Series

Washingtonians learned, among other things, that the woman who carried on one of the toughest fights Washington had ever known with the Nixon Administration cried when her parents wrote that they would not attend her graduation from the University of Chicago.

Some of the other items included:

- *A dinner party in which the guests knew that her husband had left Graham for an "Australian popsy."*

- *A report by a former national editor that "she was like a schoolgirl" in the presence of Post editor Benjamin Bradlee. "She'd say, 'Benjy, did we have to run that story?' He could charm her. He could make her laugh."*

- *Statements by former employees that she was volatile and unpredictable, given to angry 2 A.M. phone calls, impatient summonses to her office, and sudden inexplicable demands.*

- *Criticizing her editors publicly, often in coarse, profane language. "Her mistake is not in picking bad people," one source said. "It's in emasculating them."*

- *Reports that Graham, who was often snubbed by her male fellow publishers at conventions, soon learned to use sexist attitudes to her advantage. A former Post executive said, "Don't make the mistake of thinking she's the ultimate liberated woman in the 'poor little widow' act—that's a number she uses all the time."*

Miami Herald, 1978

inch. Most people wouldn't even call back. And if they did, it was usually to say, curtly, 'I can't talk.'"

That master of investigative journalism, Bob Woodward, said, "If I'd known what you were calling about, I wouldn't have called you back." No, that wasn't Gordon Liddy talking, it was Bob Woodward. Woodward said to Lynn, "A profile of Mrs. Graham is a no-win situation—for you personally, for the *Washington Star,* and for me."

Lynn wasn't sold by this cautionary logic. She continued to forge ahead. "One day I got so frustrated I walked out of the newsroom and went to a movie," she recalled. "Other days, I had to force myself to go into the office every morning and make those dreadful calls."

Newsweek's Washington bureau chief, Mel Elfin, agreed to talk to Lynn but insisted on taking a cab clear across town to meet her at a restaurant on the riverfront, far from the downtown centers of power. Bob Woodward eventually met her—at a Georgetown hot dog stand. Maybe the mustard was good.

Another guy who knew Katharine Graham met our reporter in a dark bar and pleaded, "You've got my career in your hands!"

"Ben Bradlee, to his credit," recalled Lynn, "agreed to talk on the record, not just anonymously for background. But Ben's remarks were so careful and studied as to render them almost useless."

The only source that Rosellini found who knew no fear was that gabby social butterfly, Truman Capote. Truman was the one who, inspired by a scene in *My Fair Lady,* had held a masked Black and White Ball in the Grand Ballroom at the Plaza Hotel in New York with Kay Graham as the guest of honor. Truman Capote was not wearing a mask when he spoke to Rosellini candidly and in cold blood.

"With the Black and White Ball, Kay began to shed the dowdy, timid housewife image," said Capote. "It was the beginning of the new Kay Graham." She lost weight, had her hair redone by Kenneth, and began wearing Halston clothes.

Lynn was struck by the fear that was in the air. "I've thought a lot since then about what people were so scared of. This wasn't Watergate, after all. These sources weren't Deep Throat, and Graham wasn't Richard Nixon."

**William Safire Praises the Kay Graham Series—
Here's to Media Wars**

Although unreported by the embarrassed press sections of Time *or* Newsweek, *the media war broke out recently when the* Washington Star—*purchased this year by* Time—*published and heavily promoted a lively five-part series about Katharine Graham, the woman who heads the* Washington Post *and* Newsweek.

The series about Mrs. Graham was conceived over a year ago by the Star's *then editor, James Bellows, and written by the* Star *staff writer Lynn Rosellini. But publisher Joseph Allbritton suppressed it . . .*

Surely Mrs. Graham is a newsworthy subject. . . . Is this news-business rivalry of general news interest? Of course it is. . . . Media wars—out in the open, with no gentlemen's agreements to reduce the vividness of discourse— are not only of reader interest, they are important to the future of free speech.

To regulate political power, the Constitution sets up checks and balances. Similarly, to regulate the power of the media conglomerates, the best way to avoid abridgement of press freedom by government is to stimulate more economic and ideological competition: not only between television and the printed word, but among magazines, individual newspapers, and the huge conglomerates of news.

New York Times, *November 27, 1978*

No, but Mrs. Graham ran a powerful media empire, including at the time the *Washington Post, Newsweek,* and several TV stations and smaller papers. And she had social and professional connections that stretched throughout the media and into business and politics. No one who had any aspirations in Washington could afford to be on her personal hate list. She could, and would, blackball you.

Lynn observed a personal side to Mrs. Graham:

"Her caustic tongue was well known. She could greet someone warmly one minute and tear them to shreds behind their back the next. Some hated her because she would not just disagree with them, or in the case of her executives, fire them—she would humiliate them in front of their peers."

Mrs. Graham eventually decided to talk to Lynn Rosellini, after word got back to her that the *Star* was planning to do an article despite her silence. Lynn had two interviews and was surprised, given Kay's dragon-lady reputation, to find her quite likable, with an appealing air of vulnerability and a hesitant, diffident manner. Mrs. Graham was candid on some topics: the influence of her overbearing mother, her fears during the Pentagon Papers imbroglio and the pressmen's strike. But on other topics—like her marriage, her hirings and firings—she was less forthcoming.

But as Lynn listened to her talk, she was struck by a continuing thread of her narrative. "She seemed unable to reconcile fact with her own selective version of reality. Her marriage to the philandering Phil Graham was 'a barrel of laughs.' She couldn't comprehend why union officials hated her so much. If people criticized her for switching executives, it was because she was a woman."

Over the next few weeks, after the interview with Mrs. Graham, her willingness to cooperate opened doors for Lynn, to both family members and other sources. Over the course of the summer of '77, Lynn began to slowly pull together a fascinating story—enough not only for a profile but for what eventually became a seven-part series. She was trying to be scrupulously fair. "The series, I decided, would highlight the *contradictions* of Mrs. Graham's personality. The likable, kind, and vulnerable woman who could also be cutting, callous, and tough as nails."

Lynn interviewed more than 50 people. All the information was well documented. Every assertion and anecdote was well sourced. The piece was completed in September. It had taken Rosellini about four months. A fine piece of journalism.

And then Joe Allbritton decided not to run it.

Strangely enough, he asked me and the managing editor, Sid Epstein, to sign an agreement vowing not to run the piece without his personal approval. This reflects how seriously my relationship with Joe had eroded. Direct instructions would have been enough. Why the written statement? Epstein said of the written agreement, "It was a silly little document. Who in the hell would run a story that the publisher didn't want anyway?" Mary Anne Dolan felt that Allbritton's request for my signature on a pledge was "a terrible insult—but then Joe insulted Bellows every week."

But why had Joe spiked the story?

Word spread that Graham had such power that her competition was afraid to publish something she might not like. A *Star* official said it was because "Joe just doesn't have any guts." Mary Anne said, "Allbritton was totally insecure about what the effect of the series would be. He was frantic and paranoid, simply overwhelmed in a world he didn't know, where Mrs. Graham made all the rules." The *Washington Journalism Review* reported that an Allbritton pal had said, "Joe was

---

■ **A Bid for Washington Attention**

Newspaper rivalries of the old-fashioned, gut-cutting kind are about dead in this country, partly because the press had lost much of its old fire, but mostly because few communities have truly competitive papers.

That is why what the Washington Star *did last week had the news business buzzing. The* Star, *with unprecedented fanfare and dead aim at the jugular, published a five-part profile of Katharine Graham . . .*

The subject of the series was a valid one. Katharine Graham is a power in Washington and the country—"the most powerful woman in the world," some call her. Also the Post *is true to a tradition that grants a newspaper's own publisher immunity from this sort of coverage [in its own pages]. So if Washington newspaper readers were to read a personality piece about Kay Graham, it had to be in the pages of the* Star.

But the result was less than great journalism. Rosellini's articles were not totally unfriendly. A glimmer of admiration sometimes showed through. For the most part, though, they read like five long gossip columns about one person. They relied heavily, as gossip columns do, on unnamed sources, and the stress was on inside dope, titillating to the reader and embarrassing to the subject.

Charles Seib, ombudsman of
the *Washington Post,* 1978 ■

scared to death of Graham. And he was convinced that she was about to kill the *Star* and run him out of town."

I have always felt that rivalry in the news business makes interesting journalism. A media power struggle deserves attention. But the people involved in the struggle, like Kay Graham and Joe Allbritton in Washington, Jock Whitney in New York, Otis Chandler in Los Angeles, shouldn't shrink when the bull's-eye is painted on their forehead. Tradition is served in the thundering of press lords at one another. Bill Safire has said, "Such healthy combat is good for editors and publishing pundits." Amen.

Eventually, the Kay Graham profile *did* run in the *Washington Star*, after I was long gone to the *Los Angeles Herald-Examiner* and Joe was gone, too, having sold the paper to Time Inc. in February 1978. Time lost no time in exhuming the piece. They had no concern about Mrs. Graham's sensibilities or her power. They knew, as I did, that the article would cause a stir and bring the *Star* new readers.

So they ran the series and promoted it like hell. They billboarded the story on the side of every *Washington Star* delivery truck, on newspaper coin boxes, in radio ads. For three days running it got a page one banner above the *Star*'s masthead: "The Katharine Graham Story." The series was the talk of the town. In restaurants, at parties, and particularly in newsrooms and bureaus all over the city, people relished the details. And nowhere was it read more avidly, I'm sure—albeit surreptitiously—than at the *Washington Post* itself.

The series passed along family anecdotes that told of her "joyless" childhood with her brilliant but indifferent parents; it talked of a troubled adulthood prior to her becoming president of the *Post* after the suicide of her husband, Phil Graham.

Mrs. Graham told friends that she was so humiliated she couldn't leave the house. Mind you, she never claimed there were errors in it. She just hated to see her personal life, complete with warts, spread all over the front page of a newspaper—and who wouldn't?

But it always struck me as a little odd that Mrs. Graham was so outraged at the notion of seeing her personal life appearing in the pages of a newspaper. After all, it was the *Washington Post* that helped pioneer the

Mary McGrory Lauds the Courage of Katharine Graham

*I am subdued by the knowledge of other recipients who are known to me and
are plainly more deserving of this honor. . . . [One of these was] Katharine
Graham, chairman of the board of the* Washington Post, *the paper where
I work. When she was publisher of the* Post, *Mrs. Graham had the crushing
responsibility of deciding whether or not to print the Pentagon Papers and,
soon after, whether on not to go forward with what turned out to be the
story of the century, Watergate. . . . Mrs. Graham is no bomb thrower, but
she stood up to it all, the taunts, the threats, the fears, and she presided over
the publication of stories that led to the first resignation of an American president. She put her newspaper's fate, and her own, in the hands of two reporters who were under 30 years of age. I don't think many could match her
courage. I know I couldn't.*

Accepting the Elijah Lovejoy Award
from Colby College, November 1985

modern no-holds-barred personality profile. Sally Quinn, the *Post*'s style
reporter, was even less sympathetic to some of her subjects in her profiles.

There is a bizarre epilogue.

Lynn Rosellini ended up marrying Graham Wisner, whose mother,
Polly Fritchey, was Kay Graham's best friend. Not surprisingly, Kay refused to come to Lynn's wedding, and for several years Polly Fritchey
judiciously avoided inviting Lynn Rosellini and Kay Graham to the
same functions.

Then one Saturday morning about three years after the series ran,
Lynn's phone rang. It was Kay Graham.

"This can't go on," she said, and asked Lynn and her husband to
lunch. Here's how Rosellini remembers that unusual meal:

"While the three of us sat huddled at the end of her banquet-length
dining room table, she began to rant. Her words echoed in the huge,
empty room. She talked about how incredibly unfair it had been for
the *Star* to run the series, how humiliated she had felt, how Joe Allbritton had been out to get her.

"Her tirade went on for about an hour, while a servant crept in and out bearing salad, entrée, and dessert. My husband and I were speechless.

"Afterward, she abruptly stood, bid us good-bye, kissed me on both cheeks, and said, 'All is forgiven.' But of course it wasn't. Over the years, various of Kay's pointed barbs found their way back to me, and I noted with interest that she devoted a page or two of her autobiography to rehashing the series."

Now for Kay's turn.

In Katharine Graham's best-selling memoir, *Personal History,* which Alfred Knopf published in 1997, she presents her side of the story.

She says that the series was originally suggested by Joe Allbritton, but that "in the end, he had ordered it killed, because it was so negative."

"I'm not exactly objective about the series," writes Mrs. Graham, "but my memory is vivid that I was portrayed as a sort of Jekyll-Hyde. Not that some of what Rosellini said wasn't true, but I was pictured so negatively that I feared that no one would ever work for us again."

Mrs. Graham feared in vain. I have never met a newsman or news executive who did not welcome the chance to go to work for the *Washington Post.* Present company excepted, of course.

Mrs. Graham's memoir quoted from a sympathetic letter that the *Star* received from Barry Goldwater. His empathy must have trumped his politics. Said Barry:

"Now I don't happen to be one the *Washington Post* has been kind to during my political life. In fact, I

Mrs. Graham Recalls Time Dusting Off the Series

One of the first things the new editor of the Star *did under the Time Inc. regime was to exhume a five-part profile of me by Lynn Rosellini that initially had been suggested by Joe Allbritton himself as a kind of hands-off look at me. In the end, he had ordered it killed because he thought it was so negative. Time Inc.'s people at the* Star *resurrected it, promoting it to the skies and even running the first two parts of the series on the front page. . . .*

From *Personal History* by Katharine Graham. Copyright © 1997 by Katharine Graham. Used by permission of Alfred A. Knopf, a division of Random House Inc.

Oliphant Cartoon Takes Mrs. Graham's Breath Away

I felt like we were being lambasted in the press for being Goliath to the brave little David, partly through what I thought were stories planted by our competition. I certainly believed that the Star was doing everything it could to hurt us. Nevertheless, because we have to live together in the same town—and, in fact, had helped each other in many ways over the last forty-plus years of my family's ownership—I also believed in maintaining civil relations. Consequently . . . I rushed back from New York, where I'd been for an ANPA meeting, to attend a reception at the Mayflower in honor of Joe Allbritton. I made the effort to go through the receiving line and tried to say something nice to Joe. However, on my way out, my breath was literally taken away when someone showed me a cartoon being circulated around the party. It was drawn by Oliphant, the Star's cartoonist at the time, and used the famous (John) Mitchell quote to depict me brutally with my breast drawn out at length in a wringer, this one from a press. I found it terribly wounding, said nothing and left.

From *Personal History* by Katharine Graham.
Copyright © 1997 by Katharine Graham. Used by permission
of Alfred A. Knopf, a division of Random House Inc.

imagine I have suffered as much from its editorial and reportorial whims as any person in politics, but that's beside the point. There comes a time, in my opinion, when decency in reporting must have some consideration, and neither your reporter nor your publication showed any inclination toward that. You can be critical in a decent way of the manner in which Mrs. Graham conducts her business, but I don't believe you have any right to be critical of the way she has conducted her life, nor have you the right to be dishonest about it."

Or to paraphrase Barry Goldwater: "Extremism in the defense of publishers is no vice. Moderation in the pursuit of journalists is no virtue."

On the strength of the Graham series, Lynn Rosellini got a job as a reporter in the Washington bureau of the *New York Times*. After several years at the *Times,* she moved on, wrote some fiction, and wrote pro-files for *U.S. News & World Report.*

"The Graham series was a turning point in my career," she now says, "and I still believe it is one of the best things I ever wrote. At the same time, when I look back I am reminded of what a snakepit that whole episode was. And what power does to people in this town and what fear does, too."

Kay Graham was a strong woman and a great competitor. We spent some time at an adversarial luncheon when she tried to convince Joe Allbritton either to shut down his paper or print hers. But even then, her strength and devotion to the *Post* were impressive.

Kay Graham and I had a lot in common. At her funeral, Ben Bradlee remembered a letter she had sent him one Christmas about the plea-sures of journalism: "My God, the fun. It's unfair. Who else has this kind of fun?" Kay Graham loved the news, loved the search for the facts. Ben told of her describing the morning when she rushed drip-ping from the shower to take a phone call from President Ronald Reagan, and scribbled notes on soaked paper: "Brenda Starr, girl reporter . . ."

Kay Graham was a widow, in the shadow of her husband's brilliance and her father's cultural myopia—the business has to go to the son or

Ben Bradlee Leads the Eulogies for Katharine Graham

Mourned as a friend of the powerful but a foe of the imperial presidency, Katharine Graham was buried today after an eloquent farewell from lead-ers of the ruling establishment where she flourished as publisher of the Washington Post.

"Maybe all of you do not understand what it takes to make a great news-paper," Ben Bradlee, Mrs. Graham's former executive editor, told an over-flow crowd of more than 3,000 gathered to honor her at Washington National Cathedral.

"It takes a great owner, period."

New York Times, *July 24, 2001*

son-in-law, right?—and suddenly, she was handed the reins of the *Post*. She turned it into a remarkable newspaper. She opposed the "imperial presidency" of Richard Nixon, she pursued the Watergate investigation, she published the Pentagon Papers. She had a wry sense of humor: "If this is such a great story," she asked Ben during Watergate, "where the hell are all the other papers?" And she was undaunted by John Mitchell's warning that if she didn't abandon Watergate, she would get some part of her anatomy "caught in a wringer."

The grande dame of the *Post* was, in Arthur Schlesinger's words, "a very gallant lady." It was a delight and a challenge competing with her and Ben and the *Post*.

She put it very well: "It's unfair. Who else has this kind of fun?"

Art Buchwald was the *Trib*'s satirical columnist in Paris for years. We moved him to Washington where he splashed about, and his widely syndicated column grew and grew. Buchwald and Breslin exchanged bristling, hilarious interoffice memos. Photo by Wally McNamee.

Jock Whitney bought the *Trib* in 1958 at Ike's urging. Here he is, five years later, with his lineup of editorial managers—from left, me, editorial page editor **Ray Price,** managing editor **Buddy Weiss,** New York editor **Clay Felker,** and national editor **Dick Wald.** Here we are after a big newspaper strike, during which we created a new Sunday *Trib* that received a lot of attention. W. Sauro/*The New York Times.*

Jimmy Breslin has arguably been the best city columnist in the country for the last 35 years. He worked the streets for his column about the people he knew so well. Jimmy's success had the effect of jump-starting the *New York Times*'s local coverage. He and Tom Wolfe were also the stars of our *New York* magazine supplement. Cover courtesy Jimmy Breslin.

JIMMY BRESLIN THE WORLD OF JIMMY BRESLIN

by James G. Bellows and Richard C. Wald

Evans and **Novak,** who I linked on the *New York Herald Tribune*, became the most successful team of syndicated political columnists in newspaper history. Roland "Rowly" Evans was sophisticated; Bob Novak was, well . . . Someone said: "A day without Novak is like a day without darkness." By permission, Robert Novak, photo by Rich Bloom.

Joe Allbritton was the banker-mortician from Texas who bought the *Washington Star* and brought me in to edit it. Kay Graham threatened to do to him what she did to Nixon. Here he and his editor stride from the *Star* building with **Gov. Jerry Brown.** By permission, Martin Luther King Library.

Tom Wolfe outraged the literary establishment with his wicked send-up of *The New Yorker*. Bill Shawn, J. D. Salinger, and E. B. White screamed, and Tom responded by becoming famous. I like David Levine's sketch of him. Drawing by David Levine, reprinted with permission from *The New York Review of Books* © 2002, NYREV, Inc.

Jack Germond and **Jules Witcover.** I united them as a political tandem in 1977, after which they became widely syndicated columnists and wrote best-selling election-year books. Germond was a busy fellow—he was also a regular on Sunday morning TV panels; and he and Bob Novak were my political experts on the Prodigy Internet service in 1988. By permission, *Baltimore Sun.*

Ben Bradlee and **Kay Graham.** It looks like Ben and Kay are happy about actually finding something nice about themselves in our "The Ear" column. No, it's not that, it's just that the *Washington Post* has won another prize. Courtesy of *Washington Post,* photo by Associated Press.

The "Federal Triangle" was a daily feature in the *Star*, a fictionalized soap opera about life in the Capital. It was written on rotation by **John McKelway, David Richards, Louise Lague, Diana McLellan, Richard Slusser, Michael Satchell,** and **Gloria Borger,** except for when they forgot to do it, and then it was written by night editor **John Walter.** Amazing things happened in Federal Triangle—wide-eyed young women lost their innocence, back-room deals were cut on the Hill, and a features reporter on the *Morning Moon* cooked breakfast for her boss. (The two "Ear" writers are in the group, uncharacteristically at rest, Louise atop the bus, Diana standing at center left.) By permission, Martin Luther King Library.

The last editions of the *Washington Star* and the *Herald Examiner,* as they bowed to the might of the local monsters, the *Washington Post* and the *Los Angeles Times.* The *Trib* bowed to the *New York Times* by turning into a hybrid called the *World-Journal-Tribune* before disappearing. From the collection of Jim Bellows.

Bellows and family. This photo was taken at our home in L.A. soon after our youngest daughter was born in 1973. Shown are **Billy Savoy, Laurie Savoy, Keven Bellows, Scott Savoy, Felicia Bellows, Justine Bellows, Jim Bellows, Mike Sohigian, Amelia Bellows, Priscilla Bellows.** From the collection of Jim Bellows.

My four wonderful daughters, Justine, Amelia, Priscilla, and Felicia. They turned out to be remarkable achievers that would make any father proud. Justine must be held responsible for this volume, by lobbying me to write it. From the collection of Jim Bellows.

The war years. The Navy taught me to fly high and land an F6F Hellcat on a tiny carrier deck, which proved good training for trying to find success with an underdog newspaper. From the collection of Jim Bellows.

Cub reporter Bellows (25) and friends. After being roughed up by members of the Ku Klux Klan, we examine our wounds. Klansmen forced whiskey and drugs into us, and set us up for arrest in 1948, launching my 77 page FBI file. My colleagues are **Carlton Johnson (22)** and photographer **Joe Talbot (36)**. Photo by Associated Press.

Jim Fain and Bruce Wilder. My first mentors—Jim Fain, left, overcame his initial misgivings about me at the *Columbus (Georgia) Ledger,* and gave me some big stories to cover. Later he helped me to escape to the *Atlanta Journal.* Bruce Wilder, in wheelchair, was a courageous newsman who helped me find my legs. From the collection of Jim Fain.

Nick Williams and Otis Chandler. Editor Williams and publisher Chandler ran a metropolitan paper better than any team I had ever seen. They shook up the paper and improved it mightily, despite chafing some conservative members of the Chandler clan. From the collection of Otis Chandler.

Anyone
who enters here
must celebrate

MAGGIE

Maggie's book. When Maggie died, I took the sign from outside my front door and put it on the cover of a book dedicated to her memory. My friends joined in making the book the best thing I ever did. From the collection of Jim Bellows.

Dave Burgin and the author. Dave played better golf than me. He helped a lot at the *Trib* and the *Star* before moving on to become editor of numerous papers across the country including the *San Francisco Examiner*—twice! He also helped edit this manuscript. From the collection of Jim Bellows.

Paul Conrad was the *Los Angeles Times*'s multiple Pulitzer Prize–winning political cartoonist. He suggested Pat Oliphant to me when I took over the *Washington Star*. And Pat was another Pulitzer Prize winner. By permission, Paul Conrad.

"Doonesbury" is a comic strip that I have enlivened with my presence through the years. How did I ever become a punching bag for Garry Trudeau? And I've never even met him! By permission, Garry Trudeau and Universal Press Syndicate (an Andrews McMeel Universal company).

Don Forst and me. Don was my executive editor on the *Los Angeles Herald*. He helped to turn around the paper, before moving on to become editor of the *Boston Herald*. He is now editor of the *Village Voice*. From the collection of Jim Bellows.

Mary Anne Dolan and her predecessor. Mary Anne headed my feature section on both the *Star* and the *Herald Examiner*. She succeeded me as editor-in-chief of the latter, becoming the first woman editor of a big-city American newspaper. Here, in the *Her-Ex* newsroom, she gives me a feisty, rebellious look. From the collection of Jim Bellows.

Bill Schorr was my editorial cartoonist at the *Los Angeles Herald*. He drew this on my departure. He now wields his pen at the *New York Daily News*. By permission, Bill Schorr.

Mary Hart and friends at *E.T.* After 30 years in newspapers, I was invited by Barry Diller to enter the mysterious world of TV. One of the things I did to brighten the show was to bring in Mary Hart as a co-anchor. Also on hand in this 1982 publicity shot are **Ron Hendren** and **Vin DiBona**. Courtesy of *Entertainment Tonight*.

Prodigy was an on-line computer service years before the Internet was ubiquitous. I brought a bunch of experts for Prodigy users to query one-on-one—Jane Fonda, Howard Cosell, Gene Siskel, and others. This was my Q&A for computers. Shown at my going-away party are **Mary Langer, Mark Benerofe, Jennifer Carney,** and me. From the collection of Jim Bellows.

Excite editorial managers and some of our young bosses gathered at my home to discuss the future—when we were still on a roll. Left to right, back row, **Adam Turteltaub, Ben Cosgrove, Tim Robinson, Larry Dietz, Vinod Khosla, Tony Cook,** and **Digby Diehl;** middle row, **Alex Auerbach, Joe Kraus, Mary Pitzer, Marnie Davis;** bottom row, **Ron Gross, Rob Wood, Brett Bullington,** and me. From the collection of Jim Bellows.

CHAPTER 13

◆

Mary Not Contrary

Are you on a safe phone, Mary?"

That was Ed Yoder, my editorial-page editor, talking to our premier columnist, Mary McGrory. They were conspiring in a secret campaign to soothe our volatile publisher, Joe Allbritton.

"Yes," recalled Yoder. "That was when Mary and I were in a conspiratorial mode, attempting to jolly Joe along when he was pouting."

"Ed's code name was Lighthorse," remembered Mary.

"I think it was my southern nature," said Yoder.

"We were all trying to keep the place going," said Mary.

"We did what we could."

Mary and Ed were watching nervously the growing enmity between Joe Allbritton and me. I don't think Mary felt I was giving enough tender loving care to the little guy up on the top floor. Hence, she supplied some of the nurturing that I didn't provide.

"Well, you had other things to do," she acknowledged. "You were trying to run a newspaper, not humor a temperamental man, which could take quite a bit of time. You had to be tough."

But for Mary McGrory, there was reason to show compassion. She wanted the paper to keep going. "We had to have Joe. And I was very willing to put up with him if he was going to save the paper."

Mary McGrory liked her role of mediator. "It was very enjoyable being in the middle of something like that," she admitted. "That's as good as it gets."

As the journalistic queen of the Potomac, Mary was secure enough to humor Joe.

"I didn't feel any loss of pride or dignity to go out of my way to be nice to him," said McGrory. "You were naturally nervous about these assaults on what was totally your turf. You couldn't have him writing a page one editorial endorsing Gerald Ford. That was out of the question.

"But I liked him for buying the paper and taking a chance on us. Because otherwise it was extinction."

Mary had an interesting take on Joe Allbritton, the Texas titan of banks and mortuaries: "I would watch him come into the newsroom and see all these losers in their unpressed suits, and they were all having such a good time! And they were talking to each other and laughing, and there was a great deal of affection and kindness.

"And I thought, this was a man who hadn't had many loves. When you take banking and mortuaries, that is not the place where people have a very good time. But here he was at a place where all these people were working for a declining paper, not getting much money, and *reveling* in it. I always felt that was what Joe was looking for—to be accepted in this absolutely weird world, where people didn't wear good suits and plainly weren't going anywhere. . . .

"And he could see they had something that he didn't have."

Then one day Mary was confronted by what Ed Yoder in his diaries headlines "The Feb.-March Crisis."

Ed's home phone rang at 7:30 one Friday morning. It was Joe Allbritton and his tone was ominous. He told Ed that he hadn't slept at all.

"Ed," said the publisher, "I have decided to take my name off the masthead."

He ran through a list of grievances. He never knew what was going on at the paper. He had to be told by strangers about important things that were happening. The list of complaints included the news about the Germond-Witcover collaboration. I had combined them in a tandem political column for the paper. Allbritton protested that he had learned about the column from Kay Graham!

"Bellows never tells me anything!" said Joe.

Yoder begged Allbritton to discuss the move with someone before taking his name off the paper. "You can't just tip-toe out," warned Yoder. "This will be noticed and written about in all the papers, especially the *Washington Post.*"

Next thing I knew, Joe had disappeared. Vanished. No one knew where he had gone. So I went to that font of newsroom wisdom, Mary McGrory.

"Have you heard from Joe?" I asked.

"No, have you?"

"Nope."

Mary was the soul of propriety. "You know," she said, "the relationship between a publisher and an editor is kind of sacred. I don't think anybody should meddle in that without knowing that it's wanted."

I nodded.

"Would you like me to try and get in touch with him?"

"Yeah, why don't you?"

Mary tracked Joe down in Houston.

"He was sulking big-time," recalls Mary. "Felt very left out. Felt not wanted. Very bad humor."

Ed Yoder Recalls the Great Masthead Crisis

When Joe returned from the West Coast, I gingerly suggested—with Jim Bellows' approval—that he make a joke of the masthead matter [Allbritton had removed his name from the masthead]. I even drafted a jocular news release. Joe did not act, but he sent word that if his name went back on the masthead it would be as . . . chief operating officer, a familiar title in banking and business but entirely strange in journalism. I suggested a memorandum. It had to do with the traditional relationships of publishers to their newspapers. . . . A publisher, I suggested, works a bit like a constitutional monarch, with the right to be notified and to warn. It was an elaborate project. I sent it to Joe, but there was no answer, written or otherwise. Months later, I asked him one day whether it had been helpful. "Not very," he said.

"Star Wars," *The Virginia Quarterly Review,* autumn 1993

So the publisher and the columnist talked. And talked some more.

"I told him," said Mary, "that if he came back, I would make him something he'd like very much for lunch, and we could talk things over. He loved veal, and I make a good veal dish. Lots of butter in it."

And so Joe agreed to come back to Washington. The *Washington Star* would be saved by veal.

"We had a very nice talk, and he told me he didn't feel appreciated. He didn't feel included. He wasn't happy. And I told him I thought this was all remediable."

All this reminded Mary of the time in 1974, before Joe took over the paper, when Joe had suddenly called off his deal, and Mary and the rest of the newsroom didn't know what to do about it.

"We were all sitting around and wringing our hands," recalled Mary, "and I thought—I have an idea. I'm going to write him a note, one line. 'Dear Joe—Say it ain't so, Joe. Yours truly.' So in reply, he sent me a note saying, 'It ain't so. Joe.' And with it came fifty yellow roses. They covered my whole desk. And everybody on the paper came to see them. So he seemed to be saying to me, 'You know, I really want to do this.' That was a very nice introduction, to send the roses. I thought that showed imagination and a little humor."

Mary did what she could to persuade Joe Allbritton that he should buy the *Star* and enjoy the pleasures that Washington had to offer: "My first acquaintance with Joe was when Newbold Noyes, former editor of the *Star*, told me that the deal that they were negotiating with Joe to buy the paper had fallen through. Newby and I were going to the Gridiron Club. We were going to meet Joe there. And I said, 'Well, I think I'll be nice to him anyway.' So we really knocked ourselves out. We told him everything about the Gridiron, we tried to make him laugh, we sang "Wouldn't It Be Loverly." And Newby was the soloist in one of those patter songs, based on Noel Coward. Joe had a pretty good time, I think. And I thought that's what he was looking for."

Sometimes Joe bristled when he wasn't a part of an important social event. Like the unsinkable Molly Brown, he wanted to be "up where the people are, up where the action is."

■ McGrory Writes of the Passing of Kay Graham—
the Evolution of a Newspaperwoman

Katharine Graham died as she lived, doing only what she would have seen as her duty, attending a business conference in Idaho. The preeminent personage in American journalism spared herself nothing. The English poet Gerard Manly Hopkins described her well: "Strung by duty . . . Strained to beauty."

I first met Katharine Graham when she was the doting wife of Philip Graham, a brilliant, volatile Florida lawyer, whom her father chose to be the publisher of the Post. *. . . . After Phil died, Kay, with her usual conscientiousness, set about training herself to run the paper, even though the men in charge advised her to just sign the documents they brought her. That was not her way. As part of her self-education, she came out on the campaign trail with Barry Goldwater. We sat together, and she was an endearing companion. She was humble about "the professional writers" around her—she was later to write them into the ground with the stunning autobiography . . .*

From across town, I watched the evolution of the "doormat wife"—her phrase—into the daring, resolute newspaperwoman. At the Star, *we heard tales of her unsuspected business acumen; we knew the hiring of Ben Bradlee, a Wasp with pizzazz, meant trouble for us—we had no idea how much. . . . In 1981, the* Star *died, and finally I came to the* Post. *Kay told me she thought Phil, "wherever he is, is pleased." For me, it was a different world. At the* Star, *we did no end of laughing—perhaps more than consonant with survival. At the* Post *people took themselves seriously.*

Washington Post, July 19, 2001 ■

Mary recalled one such occasion: "I was invited to the National Press Club when Walter Mondale and Morris Udall and the British ambassador were there. And we sang Scottish songs. (I suggested we do that because I didn't want to make a speech.) And for some reason or other, NPR put it on the radio. And Joe Allbritton heard it. And, of course, this was absolutely up his alley. This was big names—the National Press Club—the British ambassador—Fritz Mondale. And Joe heard it on the radio! So we had a chat, and I told him all about it. . . . But that was a real crisis. Joe really wanted to be there."

Like most everybody in Washington, Joe Allbritton had a lot of affection for Mary McGrory. She was the paper's premier personality and Joe deferred to her. When she received the 1975 Pulitzer Prize for commentary for her coverage of the Watergate scandal, she had a party at her home. Joe Allbritton came, and so did many of the capital's movers and shakers. One of these was Clark Clifford, adviser to numerous presidents. At Mary's parties there was always a lot of singing.

"Clark had a swell time," recalled Mary. "I can't remember what was going on, or what was said, because everybody sang. But I remember Clark Clifford came up to me and said, 'Now, we don't have to wait till after dinner to start singing, do we?' And I said, 'Absolutely not.'"

Mary has always had a special niche in Washington. She'd been there so long and been revered so long. Mary earned a national reputation in 1954 for her coverage of the McCarthy hearings for the *Star*. She became a national columnist in 1960. Her commentary on the Kennedy assassination in 1963 made her one of the best-known print journalists in the country. Mary's column has always been a little oasis of very good writing.

Notwithstanding her conciliatory approach to Joe Allbritton—because he had saved the *Star*—Mary did have her contrary moments. One day, Richard Nixon came for lunch and was walking through the *Star* newsroom, shaking hands with reporters and editors. Work had stopped in deference to the president of the United States. Well, not *all* work. In the respectful silence, from Mary's small cubicle in the corner of the newsroom, a single typewriter could be heard defiantly clacking away—a clear signal that at least one journalist refused to be a party to any fake affability to a president she despised.

Mary was grateful to Joe for saving the *Star* because she had a strong attachment to the paper. The *Star* was more than a job to her—it was a daily love affair with life. Of her first day on the job, she has said: "When I stepped over the threshold of the *Washington Star*, I knew I was home. I also acquired a family, a wonderful company of titans and eccentrics. We were part of a large, untidy, noisy operation that resulted every day in the production of five editions, ending with a splendid Night Final!"

Mary recalled the *Star*'s former owners, their closeness to the people who worked at the paper, and the closeness of the staffers to one another:

> The *Evening Star* was owned by two families, the Kauff-manns and the Noyeses, who sent their employees to college, helped them buy homes and sent city kids to summer camp. It was the most successful evening paper in the country. . . .
>
> When John Kennedy died, we gathered together and, with broken hearts, put out papers that showed we had no equals in reporting breaking news. In the newsroom, people spoke quietly and kindly to each other and worked around the clock. We were professional, we were civil. We were the *Star.*

Mary Talks About the Absence of Passion

I accept with great gratitude the Elijah Parish Lovejoy Award. I will not be-labor my unworthiness. If I were to go into detail about my misprecisions . . . the wrong judgments, the off-the-mark predictions—you might want to take it back, and I don't want that to happen.

I have decided to talk to you about something I know something about. I was prompted to do so by Jim Bellows, who, for three heady years, was editor of the Washington Star. *When I asked him what in the world I should say to you, he suggested that the absence of passion, from newspapers and their readers, could be a theme. He didn't suggest whether it begins with us or with them, whether we've stopped writing it right, or whether readers simply don't care anymore. I think the fault may be on both sides . . .*

Elijah Lovejoy did what editors and reporters are supposed to do. He told people things they did not want to know. In the face of their wrathful and violent rejection, he persisted and paid with his life for the principle that in a democracy, the press has an obligation to report what is happening, and to explain to its citizens what is expected of them in the face of these facts.

Accepting the Elijah Lovejoy Award
from Colby College, November 1985

It was no wonder that the matriarch of Washington journalism remained at the *Washington Star,* and during the life of the *Star* was never lured away to the prosperous *Washington Post.*

But Mary wasn't alone in her feeling for the *Star.* She told of a reporter named Betty James, who was on the city staff. Betty talked about coming to the *Star* and being overwhelmed with the fun and the foolishness, the craziness and the odd people.

Betty James spoke for a lot of us when she said, "As I was riding on the bus in the morning, I used to look around me and feel sorry for everyone who wasn't going to work at the *Star.*"

There was another extraordinary woman who greeted me when I arrived at the *Washington Star* and her name was Mary Lou "Ludy" Forbes. What made Ludy extraordinary?

She won a Pulitzer Prize in 1959 for her articles about the desegregation of southern schools.

She gave a dictationist named Maureen Dowd her first story assignments.

She gave a copy boy named Carl Bernstein one of *his* first story assignments.

Star management was sure that a woman wouldn't want to walk around a newsroom showing her pregnancy, so the rules prohibited her being there after her sixth month. Ludy worked till her due date.

Ludy enjoyed my arrival at the paper, but she had no illusions that I would be able to save the falling *Star:*

"Jim was fun, exciting, a savvy newsman. He put great emphasis on graceful writing and he came up with new ideas at a time when the *Star,* like most afternoon papers after the advent of television, had started a downward trend. Jim tried to give the paper momentum, but the spiral was well in place."

Ludy Forbes believes that the newspaper business was unique in giving opportunity to women. "It offered you the chance to demonstrate what you were capable of doing, because you, as the creator, were so close to the end product. That is seldom true in a business environment. But in the news business, by golly, you could show 'em!"

Ludy always thought our young dictationist, Maureen Dowd, was terrific. "She was always sharp, good at anything you gave her to do." One Sunday they were having a Bay Bridge Walk across the Chesapeake Bay Bridge, from the western shore to Maryland's eastern shore. We would occasionally use the dictationists to cover stories. You didn't have to go to journalism school. The *Star* was your journalism school.

Ludy told Maureen Dowd to do a feature on the walk, to see what it was like walking across the Bay Bridge. "She did an outstanding story about the families and the people. It was a graceful, entertaining, informative piece of writing." There have been a couple of U.S. presidents who wish she hadn't done so well.

Ludy ran into Maureen Dowd at a recent *Washington Star* reunion and said, "I brag to people now that I gave you your first assignment," and Maureen said, "I still have that clipping." And I still have some Ludy Forbes clippings. She crossed a few bridges herself.

Martha Angle was another spectacular woman journalist at the *Star* when I arrived. She had joined the paper over a decade before, in 1963. She was steered through the door and to an interview by Mary McGrory. Mary took the time to invite Martha Angle to her home for coffee and a chat, looked at her collection of clips from the Elyria, Ohio, *Chronicle-Telegram,* made a phone call or two, and got her in the door at the *Star.*

Martha was shunted to a copy girl job in the dreaded women's department, where "my assignment included frequent runs to the next-door liquor store to pick up a bottle for the women's editor."

Martha loathed the women's department but did her best there, using her spare time to get acquainted with reporters and editors in the real newsroom. She spent two years taking dictation from reporters on the phone, watching in anger while a succession of male Ivy Leaguers put in their three to six months on dictation and then were promoted to reporter.

Of course, life on the dictation bank had its moments. "I helped many a frazzled, tongue-tied reporter find the lead when he called to dictate his jumbled raw notes," recalls Martha. "I cleaned up the syntax and unscrambled the grammar."

Sid Epstein, the city editor, had announced that he didn't want any more women on his reporter staff. "Women get married, have babies, and quit," he said. This was demonstrably untrue. All the women dictationists were single and childless. Ironically, the bright young men the *Star* so eagerly promoted in those days were the very reporters who stayed a year of two and then jumped ship to *Time, Newsweek,* or the *New York Times.*

Ludy Forbes, who was a state editor at the time, became Martha's champion, sending her on increasingly important stories. After Martha finished her eight-hour shift on the dictation bank, she began an eight-hour shift as a reporter. Finally she screwed up her nerve and presented herself and her growing pile of bylined stories to the managing editor, Bill Hill.

"Of course I know your work," said Hill. "You're excellent! I thought you were a reporter."

Martha told him that the city editor didn't want any more women on his staff. Hill laughed and said, "That's ridiculous. Women make

Katharine Graham on the Star's Fall

Despite the good things that were happening, the Star *was in a real decline, which of course had started long before Allbritton entered the picture. There is no question [but] that its long-time dominance and success had bred self-satisfaction and lack of drive.*

It never seemed to occur to the ownership that the world could change.

Even so, the extended Star *family wasn't the main reason we started to gain and the* Star *started to decline. A societal change in the country strengthened morning newspapers, while at the time bringing hard times to the traditionally strong afternoon and evening papers. Principally, the growth of television network news, the flight to the suburbs from the inner cities, and urban problems affecting late-day home deliveries all weakened afternoon dailies. . . . Once the momentum got going, there was not much that could be done.*

From *Personal History* by Katharine Graham.

better reporters than men lots of times. They know how to get information out of male sources who wouldn't talk to a guy." Said Hill: "The next opening is yours." And it was.

Martha Angle went on Ludy Forbes's staff as a full-fledged reporter. She was promoted rapidly. She covered the governor's office, the legislature. Then to the metro desk. Then she covered the U.S. Senate. Then to the national desk and lead reporter on the Senate Watergate hearings!

Early in my newspaper days I noticed that the few women in the newsrooms were much more eager to accept unusual assignments and work hours than the men. Of course, in retrospect, I realize they had nothing to lose, because they were going nowhere to begin with. I also probably identified with their second-class citizenship in the newspaper fraternity. I knew a lot about coming from behind.

So the women were willing to try new things. I used to urge my people to "spread your wings and do a thousand things," and most of the women jumped at the opportunity.

For example, in Miami I sent Rollene Saal to cover a heavyweight championship prizefight, and I promoted Agnes Ash to business editor. At the *Star,* Lynn Rosellini was assigned to do a series on gay athletes. And at the *Los Angeles Herald-Examiner,* I not only made Mary Anne Dolan managing editor, but also hired one of the first female sports columnists in the country, Diane Shah.

As far as I'm concerned, feminism was a great movement, and it did wonders for newspaperwomen. Maybe I was unduly influenced by the fascinating time I spent with Germaine Greer and Maya Angelou, among others. Certainly, Maggie helped my education. But I also think of my appreciation for my mother and respect for her strength under pressure. And it has been nurtured by watching my wife, Keven, reinvent her professional life time and time again to accommodate the zigzags in my career path.

Having four daughters also opened my eyes and sharpened my attitude about equality of opportunity in my own profession. I have consistently supported women reporters and editors, and I'm proud of that. Despite the fact that most of the media projects I've been associated with are no longer here, the people I hired and trained have gone

A Star Falls, a Star Moves to the <u>Post</u>

On August 7, 1981, the 128-year-old Star ceased publication. There was no gloating. . . . The city and the country had lost a great American newspaper . . .

I knew the Star's folding would present problems as well as opportunities for us, including resentment of our dominance and the loss of the other much-beloved voice . . .

Almost a month later, when it was clear that no one would come forward to revive the fallen Star, we bought its land, building, and presses. We hired a number of its writers, most notably, Mary McGrory.

From *Personal History* by Katharine Graham.
Copyright © 1997 by Katharine Graham. Used by permission of Alfred A. Knopf, a division of Random House Inc.

on to pretty impressive successes. Many of those are women, and many of them have contributed to this book. I think that's a nice legacy for my grandchildren—girls, of course—all four of them, with a fifth one on the way.

The barriers against women in newsrooms have continued to come down, thanks to the talent and resourcefulness of women like Martha Angle, Ludy Forbes, Mary McGrory, Mary Anne Dolan, Diana McLellan, and Lynn Rosellini, whose exploits are recounted on these pages.

But it wasn't always without a struggle. One part of Martha Angle's pivotal interview with the managing editor was jarring. Recalls Martha: "Then Bill Hill said something that almost made me lose both my cool and my shot at a promotion. He said: 'Take off your glasses, sweetie.' I froze, paralyzed, trying desperately to decide whether to stand on my pride or go for the job. But I swallowed my pride and took off my glasses. He looked at me and said, 'You really ought to get contacts. You look so much better without your glasses.'"

In the years before I came to the *Star* in 1975, women journalists had a tough road. The Gridiron Club, a prestigious club for Washington newsmen, practiced severe discrimination against newswomen. Women were not invited, not as guests or as members. Of course, the issue of women guests didn't arise much, since there were no women among the important members of Congress nor in the national administration. The National Press Club had no women members either. If a woman reporter was assigned to cover a speech there, she was not allowed to sit downstairs and eat lunch; she had to sit in the balcony to take notes.

Women accepted a lot of what would today be considered overt sexism. Barbara Cohen Cochran, who was national editor at the *Star,* recalls: "We wanted to get along, be one of 'the boys.'" Barbara wanted to advance off the copy desk and needed to learn page makeup. But her boss told her he couldn't let her go to the composing room "because my skirts were too short and one glance at my dimpled knees would bring everything to a halt." Barbara lengthened her skirts and did get to go to the composing room.

In the early seventies, the women on Washington's three newspapers—the *Post,* the *Star,* and the Hearst paper, which was bought up by the *Post* before I arrived—formed a caucus and formulated demands for their papers to abolish sexist language in news stories such as "leggy blonde." One night, while the caucus was meeting in someone's apartment on Capitol Hill, three armed men entered the place and robbed the thirty of them of money and jewelry. When Barbara came to work

Dear Jim,

Re the Ford editorial flap . . . I seem to recall that Joe Allbritton gave you a heads-up of some sort a few days earlier at a party at the house . . . something like "reserve a space on the front page, but I'm not going to tell you what for because you'd veto it."

By the way, re your account of Ben Bradlee's left one, at Ben's retirement party at the Washington Post, *Kay Graham told the famous story, and then quipped: "I accepted his offer."*

Letter from Ed Yoder, 2001

the next day, the copy desk at the *Star* was handling the story for the front page—and the story treated the robbery as a joke!

By the time I arrived, in 1975, there were a lot more women sharpening their skills as reporters on the *Star*. When change finally came for women in Washington, it all happened in just about five years. Barbara witnessed the transformation: "The *Star* went from a newsroom where women were few in number to a newsroom where women started at every position and had no limit on what they could aspire to. Everyone worked on equal terms, everyone's idea was worth hearing. Gender didn't matter; talent was what was respected and nurtured. You were never told what you couldn't do, only what you could."

Which is a pretty fair description of the kind of newsroom we all ought to be running.

CHAPTER 14

◆

Citizen Bellows

When I arrived at the *Herald-Examiner* at the beginning of 1978, Los Angeles was a city of gleaming skyscrapers of glass and silver. That was the *northern* end of downtown where the *Los Angeles Times* was. The southern end where the *Herald* sat was a place of seedy theaters and boarded-up windows, stores selling bargain wedding gowns, drunks curled in corners, pawnshops, and garment factories.

Amid this glorious clutter stood the famous Julia Morgan–designed Herald-Examiner Building, like an ancient Hollywood star waiting endlessly for her close-up. Some mornings when I stepped through the security entrance, I could imagine photographers with flash cameras and reporters with press cards tucked in their wide-brimmed hats. The Moorish-style lobby offered more aging ostentation, high sculpted ceilings, and a carved marble staircase leading to the city room.

It was the most suicidal of my suicide missions. The paper was pretty thin. There was a huge number of editions every day, in order to deliver track results.

Mayor Tom Bradley said to a *Herald* editor, "People are pulling out the sports section, reading the race results, and throwing the rest of the paper in the street. You're clogging our drains!"

We covered the track in more ways than one.

Mel Durslag, the *Herald-Examiner* sports columnist, remembers:

Long Strike at the <u>Herald-Examiner</u>

The Her-Ex *unions spent six years on strike and doled out $6 million in strike pay to their unemployed members. Then they gave up. George Hearst Jr. [the publisher] had won.*

But for all the good this did the Herald-Examiner, *he might as well have run up a red flag over the building and moved to Moscow. Once the unions realized that George Jr. wasn't just maneuvering for financial advantage, but meant to be rid of them permanently, they went for his groin: his advertisers. . . . Local union officials went around urging local advertisers to stop advertising in the* Herald-Examiner. *. . . Striking* Her-Ex *employees or their sympathizers broke hundreds of windows in advertisers' stores and lobbed stink bombs into theaters that persisted in advertising in the* Her-Ex. *. . . After an advertiser's windows were trashed three or four times, he was unlikely to continue his* Her-Ex *advertising.*

Peter Benjaminson, *Death in the Afternoon,* Andrews McMeel, 1984

At the *Herald-Examiner* the sports department considered itself a leader. We had, for example, three bookmakers available on the grounds. No other sports section could claim such volume.

One bookmaker operated in the circulation alley. To engage his services, you placed your money and your written selection in a bucket and lowered it by rope from the second floor to the alley below. Our second bookmaker served as copy cutter in the print shop. Copy from editorial went to him by pneumatic tube. Our bets did too.

And then there was Cocky Lou, so named because one of his eyes was cocked. A veritable member of the editorial family, Cocky Lou spent the day in our department, fielding bets. You could pay him in cash or run a tab. It was unthinkable for staff weddings, parties, bar mitzvahs and the like to exclude Cocky Lou from the guest list.

Once the pride of the Hearst chain, the *Herald* was now rated one of America's ten worst big-city papers. Thanks to a ten-year strike, a lockout, and a labor boycott, the *Herald-Examiner* had lost 65 percent of its advertising lineage. The editors and reporters were reeling. The best of them had left and their replacements were often picked up off the street.

In 1967, the prestrike *Herald* had a daily circulation of 729,000, the largest of any afternoon daily in the country. Even before the strike, circulation was dropping, but the strike hastened the decline, and by the time I arrived in 1978, circulation had fallen to about 322,000, less than a third of the *Los Angeles Time*'s 1,018,000. The paper was an editorial disaster, the editing sloppy, the stories truncated, and the headlines sensational. The underpaid reporters punched a time clock.

Bellows to the rescue. I had a mandate from the Hearst people to change the paper, make it successful, and do it quick.

There was a lot to be done.

In the first year I did a rapid staff turnover. I replaced about 80 of the 150 people on the news and editorial staff and virtually the whole

---

■ **Rick Du Brow Remembers Riffs and Solos at the Herald**

I am leafing through my copies of the Herald-Examiner *and having a very good time. Well, why not? They were heady times, and happy, and productive.*

I have a lasting vision of the Herald*: It was like sitting in on a jam session every day, riffing on your stories on the keyboard, taking exhilarating solo flights that Jim encouraged, and then having him pull everything together at the editorial meeting late in the day. Am I romanticizing? Probably a little, but if something still feels so good more than 20 years later, it must have been special.*

There was a swagger in the city room, and flair in the air, and lots of laughter. And Jim presided from his spartan office in the far corner, visible to all and easily accessible.

His informality was infectious. I received exactly two memos from him during his reign there, each two words long: "Nice job" and "See me."

Du Brow was hired as TV critic in 1978. ■

entertainment division. I brought on Don Forst to ride herd on hard news, Mary Anne Dolan for soft news, and Will Hearst III for design. New critics, new columnists.

I redefined news. Not just the regular big three of national, foreign, and local. Now entertainment was news, gossip was news, finance was news, sports was news, anything that was *new* and would interest people was news. Whatever was *unusual* was news! I started up a writers-in-residence program for Los Angeles, just as we had at the *Star.* Big-name writers from my past—Jimmy Breslin, Jane O'Reilly, Willie Morris, Dick Schaap—would sit right down in the newsroom for a one-month or six-week stretch, write three columns each week about Los Angeles, drink with us in our bars, and dazzle and inspire our staff.

I featured a Q&A on the front page each day, another carry-over from the *Star.* Our first interviewee: Bob Dylan.

When the *Los Angeles Times,* on advice of counsel, decided not to run Garry Trudeau's syndicated "Doonesbury" comic strips that needled Frank Sinatra about his Mob connections, we picked them up and ran them. We developed a "Your Money's Worth" feature that was a watchdog of your tax dollars at work. Once we sent a reporter and photographer to tail a crew of city tree trimmers and found they were only working three hours out of their eight-hour days. Once we found a cop

---

The Bar Stool Test

Jim told me one time, "The way to write a story is, you imagine a big news event, and you've just heard about it, and you run down to the bar to get the reporters to come back to the newsroom. And there's two guys sitting on bar stools, and you go in between them and you're trying to explain to them this big story that just broke, and they should come back to the newsroom. Now ask yourself—What are the first three or four questions they're going to ask you? And make sure those are answered in the lead." So we used to call that "The Bar Stool Test."

William Randolph Hearst III, when he was
graphics designer at the *Los Angeles Herald-Examiner*

who was on permanent disability with a bad back and photographed him riding a bull in a rodeo.

I instituted a column that ran at the bottom of page one every day called "In Focus," where reporters tried to make sense of a confusing local story that other media had not treated fully enough.

We launched Page 2, a saucy gossip column that dealt mostly with entertainers and members of the local media. It was peppered with swipes at the *Times,* which we referred to as The Whale, a tribute to the advertising heft of their Sunday pulp extravaganza and daily ad pages.

Much of the newsroom spirit during my years at the *Herald-Examiner* could be traced to John Lindsay. The Big Guy, in his Beach Boys Hawaiian shirt, was there when I arrived and watched over the newspaper as news editor, assistant manager, and later managing editor. He was a brooding volcano of creativity and wit, and he provided the paper with something of an institutional memory—he knew the town, its communities, its cops, its teams, and its geography.

John really stoked the fire for me. During that era he rallied the troops toward spectacular coverage of the Hillside Strangler case, with maps and graphics showing the locations of the killings and touching stories of the victims.

Lindsay recalls the ferment of that time: "People would sit around and talk and someone would say, 'Hey, I saw this thing in my local paper,' and we'd say, 'Bring it in,' and 'Let's do a series on that.' We tapped into everything and tried to turn it into something. The *Herald* was a real creative soup." It sure wasn't consommé.

People knew that I was going to completely remake the paper. John Lindsay noted, "There was suddenly energy and fun in the place because there were so many young energetic people that were brought in. And it just became a great place to be. We felt—we're going to do something—we're going to change this newspaper—we're going to put this paper on the map—we're going to make the town notice it and buy it and advertise in it. There was no doubt that was the mission."

It was never business as usual in our city room. Every day was different. Every day I said, "Okay, if there's news, how are we going to cover it differently—more compellingly?" And when there is no traditional

A Reporter Remembers an Assignment from the Top

I took one look at the city room of the Her-Ex *in 1978 and retracted my landing gear. Everything was essentially unimproved since the '40s, when William Randolph Hearst still berthed in an apartment upstairs—cracked checkerboard linoleum, paralyzed Venetian blinds, grimy metal desks, mechanical Olympic typewriters . . .*

"You start Monday," said Bellows. And I did.

The most remarkable episode of my career came from a Bellows assignment.

The job was a news story that played off the entertainment phenomenon of the day, the TV show Dallas *and the big "Who Shot J.R.?" episode. Bellows had an angle in mind. The assignment gave voice to widespread public sentiment.*

"He wants you to find somebody who's been shot—for real," the city editor said. "The angle is 'I don't care who shot J.R.—I want to know who the hell shot me!'"

Rip Rense, cityside reporter

news, if Congress hasn't acted and no peace treaties have been signed, what are we going to tell people? "Well, *this* happened. It may not *look* like news on the surface, but we're going to figure out how to report it, write it, package it so you know it's *news*."

We didn't have a lot of people, and our people didn't make a lot of money. But we were on a higher mission. We were going to save the *Herald*! We were going to raise the *Titanic*! And we were going to save L.A. from becoming a one-newspaper town.

Despite the old building, the low salaries, and the propensity of newsmen to gripe, it was definitely more interesting coming to work every day if you didn't know what was going to happen. It was practicing journalism without a net. It was more like *The Front Page* than *All the President's Men*.

I liked being editor of the *Her-Ex* because it put me smack up against an entrenched power. During my years at the *Los Angeles Times,* I called it "the velvet coffin." The columnist Jim Bacon commented, "Leaving the *Times* for the *Herald* is like trading a stateroom on the *Queen Mary* for a deck chair on the *Lusitania*." Maybe. But I liked assaulting the mammoth power of the *Times*.

The *Her-Ex* was lean and mean, local and lively. We let the *Times* enjoy their "establishment" role. They were the sober, responsible paper in town. Their sheer weight proclaimed their dullness. They carried many, many more stories. Yes, the *Times* had weight. They were a ton of feathers.

Youth, energy, and positive spirit got us lots of good stories. I had assigned a six-part series on Nancy Reagan to two young reporters, Wanda McDaniel and Caroline Cushing Graham.

Herald Hires First Woman Sports Columnist

I was working at Newsweek *when I was sent to Los Angeles on assignment. David Israel, then a sports columnist for the* Chicago Tribune, *asked if I'd like to go with him to a party at Jim Bellows's house. Yes, I said, of course.*

Bellows was a journalism legend—a brilliant renegade who seemed to mint one talented writer after another, though how he did this was not clear.

He greeted me at the door, handed me a glass of wine, and sat me down on a sofa. "So," he began, "what do you want to do with the rest of your life?"

"I want to write magazine articles and mystery novels," I replied.

"Nope." Bellows was adamant. "That's not what you're going to do."

"I will," I replied. "Soon."

"I don't think so," he said.

I grew indignant. The man didn't even know me and he was already dismissing me. More firmly than before I said, "Yes, that's what I'm going to do."

"No you're not," Bellows cheerfully replied.

And so it went till finally, exasperated, I said, "Okay then, what do you think I should do?"

"You're going to be my new sports columnist," he said. Bellows had been tracking me for a year and the offer was a legitimate one.

Diane K. Shah recalls her hiring in 1979

The series appeared in the *Her-Ex* the week before the election of 1980, which took Reagan to the White House, and through syndication it hit every news desk in the country. It was the first major piece on Nancy Reagan and it went worldwide. Its hard-hitting headline: "The Woman Who Would Be Queen."

Nancy Reagan would remember Wanda's series. In her memoir *My Turn,* written after the White House years, she recalled Wanda as one of the "radical feminist militant journalists" of the time. Germaine Greer Wanda definitely was not!

A quote found its way into the series that rattled the Reagans in those prepresidential days. Caroline Graham interviewed the Hollywood publicist and Reagan courtier Rupert Allen and scribbled a quote in her notebook. Rupert had said that once the Reagans reached Washington, "The White House will be full of Hollywood comings and goings, and all of their non-Jewish friends will be among their closest buddies."

■ Bellows Retreats in Disarray

Jim is a guy who likes girls, but he's very proper.

His daily conference was a 4 P.M. meeting. I used to describe it as High Mass for Jim. That's when he would decide what was going to go on page one and lay out the page. That was where the paper's personality would come across to the reader the next day, so he didn't like to play around at those meetings. It was a serious thing for him.

And one time, on his birthday, Don Forst and I passed the hat. And somebody misguidedly suggested that we send a Playboy bunny in costume into the news conference to sing "Happy Birthday."

So she walks in, and she is a knockout. And a lot of things were hanging out. And Jim takes one look at her, and he picks up his cigarette holder and his cigarette and he stalks out of the conference room and he goes to the far end of the building. And he wouldn't return until she had left.

Tom Plate, editorial page editor who won awards for best page from the L.A. Press Club in 1979, 1980, and 1981 ■

That quote did more than drum Rupert Allen out of the Reagan circle. It flashed around the country and the world. Caroline remembers the uproar:

> It's a sort of delicate subject. Rupert Allen was a friend of mine. So when Wanda and I were doing the Reagan series, I spoke to Rupert. And he told me that about the Reagans' anti-Semitism. It was an off-the-record description of them. It was never supposed to go in quotes. But what the *Herald* did to me, they ran it in quotes! So when it came out, everybody was off the wall.
>
> Rupert Allen never spoke to me again before he died.
>
> I remember taking the quote down. I was on my phone in the kitchen at my house on Woodrow Wilson Drive. When Rupert told me that, I put the quote in my notebook, I did the piece, and handed it to Mary Anne Dolan. And the paper ran Rupert's words in quotes.
>
> Jim had to take responsibility for running something on the record that was told me off the record. That was a pretty fiendish thing to do, on dynamite like that. It was a pretty sensitive issue at the time.
>
> The paper was sued by the B'nai Brith and Wanda and I were named in the suit.

When Wanda set out on her reportorial odyssey to track down the Nancy Reagan story, I told her, "The key to this series is interviewing Loyal Davis." He was Nancy's stepfather, the famous neurosurgeon whose conservatism had turned Reagan from a Roosevelt Democrat into a Reagan Republican.

It is arguable that it was Nancy Reagan who really created the blueprint for Reaganomics when she introduced Ronnie to her stepfather.

Loyal Davis had retired to Scottsdale, Arizona. And the problem in making him the key to Wanda's series was that he absolutely refused to be interviewed. He didn't trust journalists. On the phone he sounded to Wanda like a gruff Marine general. Wanda told me of Loyal Davis's thumbs-down on an interview.

"So what?" I told her. "The best interview I ever got was when my editor told me to interview General Omar Bradley. I was a cub reporter on the *Columbus (Georgia) Ledger* in 1947 when Bradley was staying with relatives on the outskirts of town. Bradley told me he would do no interviews. My editor, Jim Fain, said, 'Just go and knock on the door. If he looks you in the eye and still says no, then you have your answer. But that's what a journalist does.'"

Wanda McDaniel set off for Arizona and had quite an adventure in the desert:

> I was 24 years old, driving in a taxi around some country club in Scottsdale. It's the middle of the summer. I'm sweating bullets over the fact that I have to walk up to this man's door and confront him. I hid the taxi in the bushes down the street. I walked up and a nurse answers the door. She says Nancy Reagan's mother is quite ill. And I can see she's in a wheelchair in the living room. And I say, "I'm here to see Dr. Loyal Davis. I'm Wanda McDaniel from the *Los Angeles Herald-Examiner*." And she says, "Is he expecting you?" And I say, "No, probably not." Boy, is he ever not expecting me. So she closes the door and I'm standing outside in the Arizona heat. And three or four minutes pass, and the door suddenly flies open and bangs against the wall. Loyal Davis is standing there in a Marlon Brando T-shirt. And he scowls at me and says, "Oh, what the hell! Come on in."
>
> But he won't let me tape. And I have a tape recorder and pad. And he says, "Turn that off." So I put it down next to my side on the sofa. . . . So I'm listening to what he's saying and I'm watching the way he presents himself, because this is the man who presented himself to Ronald Reagan and changed his life. So he's railing on for ten minutes about journalists and how you can't trust them. So finally I walk out of there. I am stunned by this experience. And at the door he says, "How the hell did

you get here?" The taxi is stashed in the bushes like a get-away car. So I point to it, and he calls it over and he puts me in the cab. And I'm five minutes away from the house—and I suddenly realize I've left the tape recorder in his house! So I said to the driver, "We've got to turn around." We go back to Loyal Davis's house, I knock on the door. He flings it open again, it smashes against the house. He says, "See, I told you, all you journalists are alike. You won't leave me alone! . . . Here's your tape recorder." And that was my lesson—if you're a journalist, you never stop.

At the *Herald-Examiner* we embraced the occasional frivolity.

One of our more controversial innovations involved the movie reviews written by our critic, Michael Sragow. He and his editor, Mary Anne Dolan, used to have long debates about whether or not to rate the movies. And they finally came up with a delightful scheme for rating films.

Decades earlier, William Randolph Hearst had decreed a ban on mentioning the movie *Citizen Kane* in Hearst newspapers. We had taken

---

Don Forst in Praise of Imagination and Unconventionality

We were always the underdog at the Herald. *Which allowed you to do anything—there were no restrictions on you. You didn't want to be stupid, but you could be as imaginative as possible. You could divert from the conventional way things would be covered—if you wanted to send a boxing writer to cover a city hall political fight, it would be fine. There was nothing you couldn't do that was intelligent, witty, and smart, and that the other guy would never do, because the other guy's stock in trade was conventional journalism, which can be boring as hell.*

■ Don Forst went on to become editor of the *Boston Herald* and the *Village Voice*.

the risky step of lifting that ban when Michael arrived. He wrote a piece declaring *Citizen Kane* his standard for the finest film ever made.

Now, Mary Anne took it further. She decided that the ideal way to symbolize the paper's rating of films was to award them rosebuds in honor of the famous wooden sled in *Citizen Kane*. A movie got one, two, three, or four rosebuds. Marvelous.

The Hearsts went bonkers.

CHAPTER 15

◆

Big Stories

I was turning the pages of that morning's *Los Angeles Times*—The Whale, as we affectionately called it—on April 16, 1979.

On page two they print a roundup of local news, in which they devote 50 to 100 words to things that are happening around town. Suddenly I noted a brief, one-paragraph story about a thirty-nine-year-old black woman named Eulia Love who had been gunned down in her front yard. The killers were two Los Angeles police officers. They had emptied their revolvers into her body at point-blank range. She had failed to pay a gas bill.

The story shook me. It outraged and appalled me. It was one too many stories of police brutality. And the *Los Angeles Times* had shrugged it off with the same indifference as the L.A. Police Department.

On any given story, the *Times* could bury us in resources, sending ten reporters to our one. But I knew that on any one story, we could pour it on, challenging the *Times* with passion and detail.

Local coverage was the only way we could compete with the *Times*. But we had to choose our stories with care. And the story of Eulia Love, a woman who died of eight bullet wounds in her chest, was such a story.

Today, if you are brutalized in a precinct house lavatory, or shot down in your doorway, or stopped on a highway because of your skin color, it is more likely that the media will pay attention.

It wasn't so on that crisp January morning when a man from the local gas company went to Eulia Love's Orchard Avenue home to collect a

$22.09 gas bill. When she chased him off, he went for the police. He returned at four that afternoon with a pair of Los Angeles's finest—Officer Edward Hopson, who was black, and his partner, Lloyd O'Callagan, who was white. "Eulia Love was in the back yard with two of her three teenage daughters. She was holding a kitchen knife and," testified the officers in extenuation, "she was sort of waving it around." As she backed toward her house, the police cornered her, knocked the knife from her hand with a weighted baton, and emptied their .38s into her. She died.

My Magic Scissors Strike Again

Flipping through the Times, *Bellows had spotted a one paragraph item about an LAPD patrolman shooting and killing a woman when she tried to stop a utility company workman from shutting off her electricity. The item struck Bellows as anything but a routine cop story, so, as was his habit, he cut it out of the paper with his ever-present pair of scissors. (A friend once joked: "If you stole Bellows's scissors, he'd never have a story idea.")*

Tim Harrell, our police reporter, quickly got the official version: Eulia Love, who was the size of a football lineman, had provoked the shooting by threatening police with a knife. The police fired in self-defense. End of story.

But the official version established a new fact and raised all sorts of questions. The fact was that the LAPD routinely assigned armed patrolmen to accompany private utility workers when they were about to shut off electricity in certain neighborhoods, namely low-income minority areas.

The story stewed in that pot for several day with the Her-Ex *in pursuit and the* Times *on the sidelines. Then we got a breakthrough. The coroner's report established that Eulia Love was nowhere near the police when the patrolmen opened fire.*

The story exploded from our pages onto local radio, leaving editors of the Times *no choice. They assigned a team of reporters—in memory, more reporters than the entire* Her-Ex *city room staff—and joined us in producing penetrating articles that dented the LAPD's false facade of infallibility and hastened much needed reforms in police training that surely saved lives.*

Frank Lalli, who was city editor of the *Herald*

The *Times* had decided it was worth a paragraph. At the *Herald* we ran a 22-paragraph story on the front page. A few days later we ran another story on page one. And a few days after that we ran another front-page story, this one illustrated by a smiling photo of a young Eulia Love. Our headline: "The $22.09 Gas Bill Tragedy."

L.A. Police Chief Daryl Gates was not enjoying our front-page and editorial-page visits to his department's excesses. Our editorial-page editor, Tom Plate, felt his sting:

> Jim had a certain sense of what journalism ought to be. So he put the Eulia Love story repeatedly on page one. And we wrote many editorials about it. And it got to the point where Chief Gates invited me to lunch, and basically tried to intimidate me. I didn't know what I was getting into. I thought I was going out for a pleasant lunch. And he is sitting with his goons around him. And he says to me, "Maybe you can get away with this kind of journalism in New York, but you can't in Los Angeles."
>
> So I went back to the *Herald* and I told Jim about this lunch, because Jim didn't even want to have lunch with Gates. He was smarter than me. And when I told him what had happened, Jim said: "Well, there's only one thing to do." And I said, "Write." And he nodded.

Thirteen years later, Chief Gates wrote a book called *Chief: My Life in the LAPD* (which he wrote with the former *Herald-Examiner* sports columnist Diane K. Shah). In it he recalled the Eulia Love inferno. It had started for him when he received a phone call from Lieutenant Charles Higbie of Robbery Homicide:

> "Chief, late this afternoon two patrol officers in South Central shot a black female. They both emptied their weapons. She's dead."
>
> "They fired *twelve* shots?"
>
> "Yes, sir. Eight of the bullets struck her."
>
> The terrible shooting of Eulia Love on January 3, 1979,

would turn into a powder keg. For the next ten months the city of Los Angeles and the police department would be in utter turmoil, fomented by relentless newspaper stories that played up the facts selectively and turned a mentally unstable woman's death into a nightmare that continues to haunt the black community and the LAPD today.

Here are some of the facts, not very selectively chosen, that are presented in Chief Gates's memoir:

Eulia Love was a widow who lived with three daughters, aged twelve to fifteen, in a three-bedroom house on a quiet street.

Her husband had died of sickle-cell anemia six months before, and she was paying her bills with a monthly $660 Social Security check.

Eulia Love's gas bill was six months and $69 overdue, and when the gas man, John Ramirez, visited her that morning, he told her that she must pay at least $22 or he would shut off her service.

When Ramirez went to the gas meter, Mrs. Love came up behind him brandishing a long-handled shovel and he fled.

Mrs. Love promptly took her Social Security check to a local supermarket and used it to buy a money order for $22.09.

The gas company dispatched another vehicle at 4 P.M., driven by Robert Aubrey. Love offered Aubrey the money order, but he said, "I don't know anything about your gas bill, I'm just here taking a break."

At 4:15 a police car drove up and stopped beside the gas van. Officers Hopson and O'Callaghan, threatened by Eulia Love and a serrated boning knife, emptied their service revolvers into her.

When Lieutenant Higbie of Robbery Homicide reported the killing to Chief Gates he said, "It was not a medal of valor shooting."

Richard Reeves wrote a white-hot piece for *Esquire* magazine in which he deplored the *Los Angeles Times*'s scanty coverage of the affair; he called the article "Mr. Otis Regrets." And in his history of the LAPD, Joe Domanick wrote of the affair. Joe's book was called *To Protect and to Serve,* the motto of the LAPD, which Mrs. Love's survivors would find arguable. Said Domanick: "The *Herald* had a large black readership, and the stories created an uproar in the city's African-American commu-

---

■ "Mr. Otis Regrets" by Richard Reeves

The Times *probably didn't give a damn one way or the other about Eulia Love and assumed its readers didn't either. . . . The longest* Times *story came on March 2 under a two-column headline leading the second section: "Gates Assails News Media in Death Case."*

Gates is police chief Daryl F. Gates. Most people seem to agree with Gates— in Los Angeles, the cops can do no wrong . . .

In New York City, which has more than double the population of the City of Los Angeles, sixty-seven civilians were shot and killed by policemen in 1977 and 1978, compared with fifty-three in Los Angeles. . . . New York police officials refuse to go on the record about their California brothers' procedures, but one assistant police chief in New York said he had recently been told by his Los Angeles counterpart: "Your problem in New York is that you don't have a high enough kill ratio."

Esquire, April 1979 ■

---

nity, setting off a chain reaction of follow-up stories by the *Times* and the *Herald* on the LAPD shootings, choke-hold deaths, and spying. What everybody in L.A. with an ounce of street sense had known for years was finally being investigated by the establishment press."

In the years since the Eulia Love killing, things at the LAPD have only gotten worse, and the *Los Angeles Times,* in my view, has consistently failed to vigorously pursue the growing signs of abuse of citizens' rights by Los Angeles police.

Domanick commented on the deficiencies of the *Times's* coverage of the local police: "The *LA Times* was the agenda-setting newspaper of record. And although it had already made its historic transformation from right-wing rag to one of the nation's best papers, hard-hitting investigative reporting—particularly of local institutions—was simply not its forte. As a major investor in the city's financial life and in the redevelopment of downtown L.A., it seemed disinclined to make waves."

Since the *Herald-Examiner* closed its doors, without a second newspaper in town, the LAPD's militaristic attitude and tactics have led to the infamous beating of Rodney King, captured on videotape for all the world to see.

Now, I don't mean to lay blame for all of this at the *Los Angeles Times*'s door. But, as a major institution in the city of Los Angeles—one that enjoys the constitutional protections accorded the Fourth Estate—it has to share the responsibility for the depth and duration of a largely rogue police force. It's a perfect example of why newspaper competition is of such vital importance to the public. It's also why I have been irresistibly drawn to second newspapers, because the big guy in town inevitably gets fat and satisfied, which makes him vulnerable to energetic competition. If the second newspaper does its job, it awakens the sleeping giant and goads it into more aggressive coverage of the city. Everyone benefits.

There was another "big" story during my second year at the *Herald-Examiner*. It had more fun than gravity, at least at the beginning. And it was my rotten luck to be on a two-week vacation in Europe when it broke. But Executive Editor Don Forst spotted it and threw all our slim resources at it.

In February 1979, a hippo named Bubbles had escaped from the Lion Country Safari in Orange County. I guess it had gotten tired of

Bubbles, the Runaway Hippo

Here was a story for the new Her-Ex. *It had three elements Bellows loved. It dripped with human interest; it was inherently amusing; and therefore, Bellows correctly assumed, it would be largely ignored by the always sober Los Angeles Times.*

After several days of fun, the story came to an abrupt end. The authorities decided to subdue Bubbles with tranquilizer darts and truck the hippo back to the park. But once tranquilized, Bubbles literally dropped dead.

Executive Editor Don Forst was at dinner at my house when he got the call. As he hung up, Forst announced gravely, "Bubbles is dead." My wife, Carole, shook her head and said, "You mean, Bubbles is burst!" Forst said: "I'll steal from anyone." The next day, Her-Ex *readers learned of Bubbles's untimely death under Carole's banner headline: "Bubbles Is Burst."*

Frank Lalli, *Her-Ex* city editor

cement and bars. Here was another chance to show those potted palms across town how to cover a real human interest story. Don saw in the Bubbles story a little of the cry for freedom that is universal. And in time, it also became a tale of government inefficiency.

They hunted for Bubbles, they surrounded Bubbles, they tried to bring her back to the bars and cement, and, given the natural ineptitude of government, they killed Bubbles.

We covered the Bubbles story—the saga of a 4,000-pound hippo heading for freedom and managing to escape the bureaucratic oafs who trailed her. She had dug through mud at the zoo, squeezed under a chain-link fence, and headed for freedom. Once on the loose, she rambled over miles of bushy hills and grassy meadows, before finding a home in a rain-filled pond.

We covered the escape, and when Bubbles reached her pond, we began a daily page one feature, "Hippo Watch." The hippo editor (whoever was available at the time) was in charge of the letters and phone calls that started pouring in after we asked our readers for suggestions on the morality of hippo hunting and other issues. Our "Hippo Watch" produced more than 11,000 letters. It crowded some of the other news off our front page. Most of the people in our newsroom found the story fun and exciting, though there were a few who winced at our pouring our resources into the story of an escaped hippo.

Bubbles was capturing a lot of hearts. She was drawing national attention to what had once been a bad second paper. The story captured the imagination of kids. When we asked for suggestions as to how to capture Bubbles, one nine-year-old boy sent in a sketch of the pond surrounded by elephants with their trunks in the water. "Have them suck out the water," he suggested.

Zookeepers wanted Bubbles to come home. But Bubbles had her own agenda. She was going to have a baby. (Maybe a "baby hippo" sounds like an oxymoron, but not if you're a hippo.) Now the story had everything—freedom, bureaucracy, motherhood. The hippo hunt was costing Orange County $1,500 a day, and there is nothing as damaging to morality in municipal government as a $1,500-a-day expense.

We sent an eager and impassioned young reporter, Ann Salisbury, to the scene. Night and day she covered the story.

"Because Bubbles emerged from the pond at night, I didn't sleep much for days. I'd bundle up in a parka and wrap myself in a sleeping bag, waiting at the edge of the lake for Bubbles to come out—along with a growing army of 24 reporters who were arriving late to the scene of this big, breaking story. This was joyous. They all jumped into the story, all the networks and even the lofty *Los Angeles Times*. These reporters, with all their intellects, all their national exposure, all their arrogance, were clearly miffed about having been assigned to cover something like this. They were above it. And they blamed the lowly *Herald* for starting the whole thing."

Tension, Fatigue, and Muttering Among the Bubbles Media

Every night this week, more than two dozen reporters and photographers have gathered in a meadow near Clucker Lake, in Orange County, awaiting the capture of Bubbles, the errant hippopotamus.

They're on Hippo Watch, 30 newsmen and women standing behind banks of strobe lights and movie and still cameras mounted with telephoto lenses. . . . The reporters are staring out into the darkness, smoking, sipping coffee, swigging beer from cans, and muttering silent oaths.

Some have been here a week, without a bath. Some arrived only days ago. Most are cranky. They are not getting much sleep while they wait for Bubbles.

Last Tuesday, Lion Country officials passed out guidelines for covering the capture.

"Notice to All Media at Clucker Lake," it read. "Now that the capture of Bubbles is imminent, we at Lion Country Safari would like to make a request of you, the media assigned to the capture attempt. Please do not use lighting of any kind during the capture attempt, until the animal is completely unconscious in the net!"

With newspapers and TV stations investing thousands of dollars on the venture, the big question is, "How do you take pictures in the dark?"

Ann Salisbury, *Herald-Examiner*, March 3, 1978

Bubbles came out of the lake for the last time on the evening of March 10. Workers from Lion Country Safari shot Bubbles with tranquilizer darts. She fell by the side of the pond. Her lungs were crushed by the weight of her intestines as she lay in the pond with her head lower than the rest of her. They hadn't planned on that. It took her about an hour to die. She was two months away from delivering her baby.

One of the escapades in which we found news in unconventional places surrounded one of the highest-rated shows in television history, the "Who Shot J.R.?" episode of *Dallas*. When Lee Rich, chief of Lorimar, the company that produced the show, announced with great bravado that there was such security surrounding the script that no one who wasn't supposed to would ever see it before the episode aired, we pounced. Our gossip column, Page 2, declared in a cheeky bluff that we had had our own copy of the script for weeks, but were keeping the identity of the shooter secret.

The Page 2 editor, Jeff Silverman, arrived at the newsroom the next day to find an offer on his answering machine from a recently fired *Dallas* crew member who had a copy of the script to sell. He wanted $500. Knowing our improvidence, Jeff talked him down to $50.

Over the next few days the *Herald-Examiner* crowed about its prized possession and dropped bits of scenes into the paper to prove it.

Lee Rich went ballistic. He threatened to have Jeff arrested by L.A. Police Chief Daryl Gates himself for holding stolen property. Jeff walked into my office and explained his predicament. He could shortly be in jail over a hot script. I promptly arranged a news conference in my office for four o'clock that afternoon at which I would personally hand the script over to Chief Gates for safe delivery back to Lorimar. Lindsay Gardner, the reporter who wrote the story, remembers the press circus:

"As the press conference began, *Herald-Examiner* publisher Frank Dale announced to the assembled TV cameras that being aware of its ethical responsibilities, the *Herald* was returning the script to Lorimar via Police Chief Gates, and pledged not to reveal the name of the script's fictional assassin. While I was writing the story and scanning the wire stories that were being flashed across the country, I was fielding calls from newspaper and radio correspondents who had missed the press conference and wanted the facts. Both the *Times* and the *Mirror* called from London."

Across town, the *Los Angeles Times* would often embrace the *Herald-Examiner*'s audacities. In his book on expiring newspapers, *Death in the Afternoon,* Peter Benjaminson wrote: "The editors of the *LA Times* used their cash, and their own savvy, to imitate many *Herald-Examiner* innovations. *Times* writing became more human and more colorful. The paper jumped on local stories faster and played them better, and its entertainment coverage improved; the *Herald-Examiner* had wakened the *Times* to its shortcomings. All of this was a great service for the newspaper-reading public."

While our reporters and editors were busy as hell, chasing down stories on escaped hippos, Dallas millionaires, and dinosaur cops, behind the scenes at the *Herald-Examiner* some stories were playing themselves out . . .

The *Dallas* story not only made the TV news shows that night, it made so much noise that even The Whale was awakened by it. It had to respond that evening to the media "event." The paper that muffed Watergate and dismissed Eulia Love moved quickly enough to slap an entertainment story into its next morning's edition. So readers of the *Times* were able to read about the purloined script at the same time they watched our satirical coup unfold on the *Today* show and *Good Morning America.*

Frank Dale, the publisher of the *Herald-Examiner,* had come aboard shortly before I did. He had an interesting background. Frank had been the publisher of the *Cincinnati Enquirer*, and Richard Nixon had made him chairman of the Committee to Reelect the President, affectionately known as CREEP during the Watergate years, and widely publicized by the team of Woodward and Bernstein. Frank had escaped the Nixon administration with clean hands and nary a blemish, which couldn't have been easy.

Before my arrival at the paper, he had replaced the forbidding security guard at the front door with a pretty receptionist, he had repaired

John Lindsay Recalls a Phone Call from the Editor

I got a call. I was living in this kind of depressing apartment on the west side in 1981, and the phone rang, nine or ten in the morning, and I had gotten to bed as usual at three in the morning. I said hello, and he said, "Hello, this is Jim." And I thought I'd done something wrong. And he said, "I just wanted to let you know before you found out that I'm leaving the paper." I was stunned. At that point I was the news editor and one of his confidants. And I felt I'd learned a lot from him, not just about the newspaper business, but how to think, and how to treat people, and how to look at the world differently. And there was a huge number of things that he did for me and to me. And I couldn't really articulate at that point. But I said, "I appreciate your calling me so I didn't hear about it from somebody else. And I'll see you when I get there on my regular shift." And I hung up and I sobbed.

the digital clock outside the building, and had removed the dreaded time clock that reporters and ad salesmen were obliged to punch. All good moves. Frank Dale's Republican credentials pleased the Hearst family, and he had had the good judgment to agree with the Hearsts and to hire me. So it would be somewhat graceless to reproach him in any way.

But I must.

It's true that publisher Dale did make an effort to stay clear of the threepenny opera taking place in the newsroom, but there was one area where he and I constantly locked horns.

On a second paper there must be a clear separation of advertising and editorial—the two departments should be completely distinct. There must be a *wall* between them. You've got to write stories that are worthwhile as news, not intended to promote some particular advertiser. News should be what's unusual, not prostitution in print.

Unfortunately, on the *Her-Ex* I was being pressed into the oldest profession, and the pressure was coming from the publisher's office. A series of letters descended on me from Frank Dale urging me to do more to promote our advertisers in our editorial columns. Memos like this one:

JB:

I'm curious that we do very little promotion for any advertisers. Our automobile advertising classification needs it!!

FD

And that was one of the tame ones. There were many more with specific advertiser names, claiming that we were hurting business by criticizing the advertisers and never helping them.

The relationship between advertising and news has always been a source of concern to me. Frank Dale would have liked to see closer ties and more interaction between the business and news sides of the paper.

I have always fought that kind of publisher interference with the newsroom. Particularly on a second paper, where integrity is everything, content has to be controlled by editorial people. Why would reporters stick around if they don't have any respect for the place? Why would they work as hard as they do on a second paper, for lower pay and longer hours, if their editors are not really backing them up?

Of course, I have always had trouble genuflecting to publishers. (I have this trick knee.) William Randolph Hearst, Jr., son of the founder

Finding Stories in the Rosetta Stone

Jim had this Teletype machine in his office that had a big roll of yellow paper, and it was kind of like the headlines from the news services. And this thing would be spewing yellow paper on the floor all day long, and Bellows would be picking up these folds of paper, and he studied this thing like the Rosetta Stone. And he'd make these marks on them with a red pen. And he'd tear off these little things and he'd say, "Go find this story!" or "Don't you think this is kind of oddball?"

Will Hearst recalling his time at the
paper his grandfather founded

and chairman of the board, wrote a Sunday column. It was widely syndicated in all eight Hearst newspapers, where it appeared without fail on the front page. Well, we needed the space. So one day I moved Mr. Hearst's column inside. This wasn't very well received on the executive floor.

One battleground where advertisers engaged editorial folks was the movie front. Our film critic, Michael Sragow, had been called "the John Simon of the West" by the *Village Voice*. "He is a merciless reviewer and Hollywood has never seen the like from its daily newspapers, whose critics tend to stroke the industry." But when Sragow panned Universal's *Sgt. Pepper's Lonely Hearts Club Band,* the studio promptly canceled all advertising in the *Herald-Examiner*. On that one Frank backed me all the way. He said, "Bellows is backing Sragow and I'm backing Bellows. I don't think any advertiser can tell you what a critic can do."

The *Los Angeles Times* recently put some nicks in The Wall, raised a storm among its editors, and embarrassed itself when it made a deal with Staples Center, a new sports arena in L.A., where the Lakers and Clippers play and Madonna and Cher sing. The *Times* and Staples agreed to share the profits from a special edition of the paper dealing with the arena. A newspaper sharing profits with the place it is covering? Hmm.

I had to fight another fierce battle about integrity at the *Herald* over the tradition of "news for sale." Too many of our reporters would allow ball clubs and movie studios to pay for their air fares, hotel rooms, and meals when they covered games and movie openings. Not surprisingly, this spawned uncritical approval from the reporters and columnists. Said Don Forst: "There was so much puffery when we arrived here that we could have opened a bakery and sold Napoleons."

I let the staff know the ground rules on my watch by posting the following bulletin: "There should be no freeloading, junketing or freebies. If any of you have any question about past practices, or possible conflicting work or associations, please see me. It's best to put the issue on the record now. If later events turn up activities in conflict with good professional standards, I would consider dismissal a reasonable recourse."

In 1978 I had come back to Los Angeles to run a dying paper, to take it against the toughest media giant around, in a town where people didn't read all that much. Well, my wife said I was a man who equated comfort with death, and came out of the womb like a wind-up toy that can't wind down.

Small wonder that my attention began to wane after three years. I had done as much as the Hearst Corporation was going to let me do. I had pressed them for as much money as they were going to spend on the news department. It was at this point that I received a phone call from Barry Diller, who was then president of Paramount Pictures. Barry invited me to run a new TV entertainment news show called *Entertainment Tonight.*

In my typically untraditional way, I had not set up a system by which someone would replace me at the *Herald.* At the time, Mary Anne Dolan was acting as my managing editor and had a lot of hands-on experience running the paper. She had followed me from the *Star* to the *Herald-Examiner* and had worked with me for six years. When my peripatetic urges threatened to sweep me off, it was Mary Anne who deserved to become my successor, and I supported her in that quest.

The question was: Would Frank Dale agree to appoint a woman? Just how Mary Anne arranged it is a reflection of her brains and resourcefulness. Her contract was just about up as I prepared to step off the cliff into television.

At the time we were meeting with various people about how the *Herald-Examiner* was going to cover the 1984 Summer Olympics in Los Angeles. Mary Anne represented the paper at these meetings.

Paul Ziffren was in charge of this enormous enterprise. This was his shining hour in politics and power. He was an elder statesman of business and finance. He was negotiating everything important in Hollywood. He represented the top actors and directors. He was the power behind every deal. He was the Howard Hughes–Clark Clifford–Lew Wasserman of the hour. And Mary Anne impressed the hell out of him.

When she learned that I would soon be gone, Mary Anne seized the moment and had a chat with Frank Dale about what she would do at the paper once I left. "I went to Dale," she recalls, and said, 'I hope you

■ Escapades with The Who, the What, and the Why

I never bought into the theory that Jim Bellows was impossible to understand because he garbles his words and emphasizes with his hands for effect. I was always able to decipher what he was trying to say because I have the attention span of a flea and his first sentence was almost always his last. I guess that means we were a good match. I've been listening to those fractured Bellows sentences, and taking direction from him, ever since I joined the Los Angeles Herald-Examiner *in 1978, a few months after he got there. I was hired to cover rock and roll.*

Once my beat took me to San Diego where The Who was performing in concert. I went with Ken Tucker, the paper's rock critic, and Chris Gulker, a photographer. We traveled down the San Diego Freeway in Gulker's car.

After my post-performance interview with the band's leader, Peter Townshend, we piled back into Gulker's car and headed north. It was a little after 3 A.M. We didn't get far because the engine in Gulker's car blew up and stopped dead. As we waited to rent a car, Gulker told us how the photographers at the Los Angeles Times *were routinely provided with company cars when their assignments took them out of the L.A. area.*

By the time we got back to the paper, I was hungry and tired and frustrated enough to repeat what happened to Bellows, who was finishing the morning papers at his desk.

I couldn't help being upset that the Herald *didn't have a company car program similar to the one at the* Los Angeles Times.

"But you're here," Bellows said with a laugh, "because you like adventure. The Times *would never offer you this kind of adventure."*

Mitchell Fink, who later became *New York Daily News* gossip columnist ■

don't mind but I'd like to bring somebody in to help me negotiate my new contract, because I'm not that comfortable doing it myself.'"

Notice the studied humility. Next day she went up to Dale's office for her meeting. He had the old William Randolph Hearst office with its mosaic tile, its arches, its huge desk that was so intimidating to young editors.

"I said to Dale," she continues, "'You know my representative is going to be here in a minute and I'm thinking we need to be frank about what will happen if Jim were to leave. It's important that I know the intention of the organization.' Frank coughed and said, 'Well, we really don't do that. . . .' And I said, 'I'd prefer that you talk to my representative.' And right on cue, in walks my representative, Paul Ziffren.

"Frank Dale slides down very low in William Randolph Hearst's chair. He is in his shirtsleeves, so he jumps up and races to the coat rack to put on his jacket. Then we all sit down and I never opened my mouth. And Paul Ziffren starts talking. And he concludes, 'Therefore if you don't mind, my office will fax you a contract for Mary Anne this afternoon which says that should Jim Bellows leave, she will be the editor.' Bang. Sign here."

And that's how Mary Anne Dolan became the first woman editor-in-chief of a major metropolitan newspaper in these United States.

CHAPTER 16

◆

E.T. and ABC

I suppose Barry Diller can be cordial on the phone when he wants to be. But when Diller, who was then president of Paramount Pictures, called John Goldhammer, senior vice president of programming at Paramount and producer of *Entertainment Tonight,* on this occasion he found it necessary to be less than cordial. He snapped:

"I hate the writing. Fix it."

"What's wrong with the writing?" said Goldhammer.

"Just fix it." And he hung up.

Sometimes charm doesn't get it done. Barry could be a tough task-master, but it should be noted that *Entertainment Tonight* is still a giant hit 20 years after he launched it.

When I was editor of the *Washington Star,* Barry Diller sent me a nice note about how I was making the paper lively and exciting. Now, out of the blue, his phone call to me at the *Herald-Examiner* in October 1981 was genial and gracious.

"I just wonder," said Barry, "whether you ever thought about running a TV show about entertainment news."

"No, I never have."

"Well, would you consider it?"

"I don't know. But I'd be happy to talk about it."

I was the editor of the *Los Angeles Herald-Examiner,* and the Hearst people had made it clear that they weren't going to spend enough to make it any better. So why not a leap into the unfamiliar world of TV?

"The fact that at his age he would even consider putting himself in the middle of this kind of fray was insane," said John Goldhammer.

Barry sent me several tapes of the three-month-old show. And he set up a meeting for me at Michael Eisner's house in Beverly Hills. Michael was then Barry Diller's right-hand man at Paramount. He had not yet left for Disney to rescue the Mouse Factory. Also at the meeting were John Goldhammer, Rich Frank, the head of Paramount's TV division, and other TV executives.

Bellows Under Stress in World of TV

When things appeared more bleak than usual, Jim would begin a marathon walk around the rectangle of inner offices at a brisk pace, head down, arms pumping, deep in thought, round and around.

In the office next to mine, a writer kept a caged hamster which enjoyed running on a wheel. I was always aware when Bellows was under way in the halls because, without looking, I could hear the hamster pick up the pace, inspired by Jim going by the door, and the resulting racket from the hamster could be heard through all adjacent rooms.

If race-walking didn't set things right for Jim, he would on occasion disappear out the Vine Street door to an early-opening bistro for a touch of vodka on the rocks.

Jim's conversational code resembled Sgt. Preston of the Yukon grilling King, his trusty Malamute canine sidekick:

"ARF ARF ARF."

"WHAT IS IT BOY? TROUBLE?"

"ARF ARF ARF ARF!!!"

"LITTLE LIL HAS FALLEN DOWN THE WELL?"

The real magic of Jim Bellows may well have been wooing the angry media which was constantly pasting E.T. with slings, arrows, and predictions of doom. One headline after Jim arrived read:

"Why Is This Respected Editor Directing an Airhead Show?" But over time, Jim brought the reviewers around.

Bob Flick, head writer on *E.T.*

"Look," I told them, "I know what I don't know. I don't know anything about television. But I'm a pretty fast learner."

I told them I thought of *E.T.* as a sort of back-of-the-book *Time/Newsweek* type of show, with newsy, bright, talk-of-the-town entertainment, a fun show.

The year was 1981 and *E.T.* was off to a rickety start. It had arrived in an uncharted land when it premiered. Never before had a syndicator tried to produce a daily news program about entertainment or transmit it by satellite to stations around the country. Paramount had even given big satellite "dishes" as gifts to stations in Tier B markets like Boise, Little Rock, and Albuquerque if they would commit to carry the show for a guaranteed 26 or 52 weeks. So they had the markets; but the concept was muddy.

The atmosphere on the show was what Goldhammer called "extremely formative craziness." In their offices near the fabled corner of Hollywood and Vine, the staff was enthused but perplexed. There were a lot of eager people there who had never done this kind of show before. Nobody had. *E.T.* was breaking new ground.

Critics were lashing *E.T.* for its lack of credibility. "It won't give you gallstones or yellow fever," said Howard Rosenberg of the *Los Angeles Times,* "but it won't give you much information either. It is so soft that it squishes."

The show was being dismissed as puffery and a press agent's dream. "All they need to get automatic acceptance when they call in with a story is a celebrity's warm body," one critic smirked. "Any press agent who can't get a client on *E.T.* should be fired."

I got Ed Hookstratten, an agent in town who handled Bryant Gumbel and other TV notables, to work out a deal for me with Paramount. I signed up to start in two weeks. I wanted to give the *Herald* a chance to decide what they wanted to do about replacing me. (They named Mary Anne Dolan the new editor.)

When I reported to work as managing editor of the show in November 1981, John Goldhammer became my mentor. The show had launched in September and was fighting for its life in the middle of its first major sweeps rating book, which occurs in late November. The staff was broken into two camps. The veterans, who had come from a hard TV news background, were uptight with a "newspaper guy" running the shop. The others, who wanted the show to be fluff and puff, were already sending their résumés out.

So began my transition from newspapers to TV. It was another country. There seemed to be a lot of screaming and yelling going on in a TV operation. It isn't that way in a newspaper newsroom. Unless something very out of the ordinary happens, things are more sedate. People are in the business of writing, which is a little more of a private occupation than getting all the colors right, and the film right, and editing the videotape, and using the on-camera people in the right way.

New to me was the frantic activity, the editing bays, the video feeds and taping schedules, the egotistical and overworked staff. The overall appearance of quasi-ordered chaos took me by surprise. The only time I saw such frenzied behavior in a newsroom was in movies like *The Front Page* and *Citizen Kane*.

"The first few days, Jim looked like a deer in the headlights," remembers John Goldhammer. Ten days after I reported to *E.T.*, Natalie Wood died at 43 on a boating trip off Catalina Island. The events of her drowning were a mystery. We worked hard to illuminate the story, but it eluded us. (It has remained a lingering puzzle for 20 years.) Natalie Wood drowned after inexplicably paddling away in her nightclothes in a dinghy from her 60-foot yacht, on which she was staying with her husband, Robert Wagner, and actor Christopher Walken. Covering the cloudy circumstances of the actress's death in dark waters was my baptism by fire in TV.

My subsequent attempts to deal with the staff—to explain my philosophy—were usually greeted by blank stares. I left John with the task of translating what was fast becoming known as "Bellows-speak."

But whether you are a TV show or a newspaper, you are still dealing with the same ingredient—*news*. I knew news.

Barry Diller deserves a lot of credit for recognizing that the show needed an objective newspaperman. Barry was running a major movie studio, and *E.T.* had a movie critic. Barry wanted someone in charge who would make sure the playing field stayed level for all the studios.

■ Marian Christy Reports My Pulling the Switch
from Journalism to <u>E.T.</u>

Jim Bellows is tense and intense, a wiry man who likes to gamble on the odds and win. Shortly after his 60th birthday, when retirement should have been his mindset, Bellows pulled a switch. The veteran newspaper wizard took on a television dare dangled to him by Paramount's Barry Diller. Could he, a famous newspaperman who knew nothing about the inner workings of tele-vision, bring respectability and an audience to the floundering syndicated television show Entertainment Tonight? *That was Diller's question and Bellows answered yes, he'd try.*

And at a luncheon at the Beverly Wilshire Hotel, Bellows tells you how his newspaper associates snickered that he'd be a loser. Today Entertainment Tonight *is seen on 133 stations by 11 million people nightly, a bigger audi-ence than the* Today *show and* Good Morning America *combined. Bellows, managing editor of* Entertainment Tonight, *is suddenly a hot television property, reportedly being wooed by ABC-TV. . . . This remarkably imagina-tive man says success is simply "overcoming something." He's tough, too, a man who warns: "Fawn not upon the great." Bellows never has.*

Boston Globe, April 28, 1983 ■

Otherwise the others would gang up on Paramount for using the show to push its own product and there would be hell to pay.

Considering the fact that I was an alien from another culture, the staff treated me with a mixture of respect and befuddlement.

John Goldhammer, said, "Jim can be the most enigmatic of human beings. He is not somebody you would send to negotiate with the Russians. Because they would walk away from the table saying, 'What did he say?' And the next thing you know we would be at war."

I would express myself with some perfectly comprehensible gestures and this spawned confusion. Goldhammer: "Sometimes when he ges-tured, his hands would be high in the air, sometimes lower. They used to say, 'What is it today? Is it a High Roadie Day?' If he got really upset his hands would go high. On a normal day his hands would move in the middle of his body. That was a Middle Roadie Day. If he was depressed, his hands were low. That was a Low Roadie Day."

Bob Flick, the head writer for *E.T.*, was the only member of the staff who actually had a news background. A former NBC news producer, Flick was no friend of authority or dress codes. One of his favorite stories is about the time he was told the New York contingent of bosses would be visiting the NBC newsroom the next day and Flick should be sure to dress well. So Flick came to work in a tuxedo. He was promptly fired.

Before I arrived, Bob Flick used to quit weekly. He recalled: "Goldhammer came into my office to bum a Marlboro and deliver what he termed terrific news. 'We've hired the editor of the *LA Herald-Examiner* to be our managing editor. You're going to love this guy.' I immediately typed up a scathing letter of resignation, which he read, ripped into small pieces, and tossed on the floor.

Bob Flick Finds Priceless Notes

Came across a copy of verbatim notices I typed up moments after a 1981 conversation with you about Diana Ross.

Flick: *"So we're set on the Diana Ross story?"*

Bellows: *"I'm sort of worried that there are so many trees in this story that we'll wind up forgetting how this thing was supposed to go out and so forth and we'll find ourselves too close to the, um, trees."*

"Over many years in TV, the 'wonderful new guy coming to save the day' spelled disaster. Without fail, these guys were cordial at first, and without fail, a few weeks later they would turn on me like a jackal. Bellows was different. Instead of becoming loud and pushy, he hardly ever uttered a sentence."

I was trying to bring some star power to *Entertainment Tonight*.

I called Barbara Howar, whom I had met when I was at the *Washington Star*. She had what today we call "edge" or "attitude" and in those days we called "point of view." The show needed it. Barbara was as charming as ever.

"Why in God's name would I go chasing after a bunch of movie stars with a microphone?" said Barbara Howar.

"For the money," I said. "And the fun."

Barbara had written a best-seller called *Laughing All the Way,* about the Kennedy-Johnson era. But this was the Reagan era, and what had she done for me lately?

"Why me, Jim?" she asked.

"You've been around and you can help give the show some special recognition," I told her.

I was betting where the mainstream media was heading. I sensed that the country was teetering on an obsession with celebrity and would soon be demanding ever more information about the lives of movie, TV, and rock stars. With Barbara I knew it would be sharp and sassy. Barbara knew New York and she could be our correspondent in the Big Apple.

But she was disinclined to come aboard and start "chasing movie stars with a microphone." She was in Los Angeles on a visit, and after our meeting she drove to the Chateau Marmont to meet her friend John Belushi. He didn't show up. Several days later he was dead of a drug overdose and the event brought a flood of media coverage.

"The era of celebrity journalism has begun," reflected Barbara, and called me.

"I think I'd like to give that job a try," she said.

Barbara became our star reporter in the New York bureau and she added a lot of glitz to the show. As we moved along, we added heft by doing some stories that poked into the entertainment industry's shadowy corners—stories exploring Hollywood's taste for drugs, the proliferation of sexual sleaze on cable TV, the career problems of black actors in a white-dominated business.

But what should *Entertainment Tonight be*? As I joined the show, it was still an open question. There were two clear groups, diametrically opposed. Taft Broadcasting owned a third of the show, Cox Communications owned a third, and Paramount a third. Like most partnerships, as far back as Gilbert & Sullivan, this one was full of disagreement. Cox and Taft wanted the show to be the *National Enquirer.* Paramount, in the perspective of Diller and Eisner, wanted it to be *60 Minutes.* John and I agreed that both sides were wrong. If the show became *60 Minutes* it would bore the audience to death. And if it became the *Enquirer,* the stars we needed wouldn't cooperate.

I felt the show should be a mixture of the *MacNeil/Lehrer Report* and *People* magazine. I told Harry Waters of *Newsweek,* "We've got to have a mix of the heavy and the light. We have to please the viewers as well as the critics."

There was another reason the *Enquirer* route was bad. The show needed credibility. The *National Enquirer* was not credible, and if we were not credible we would have nothing.

Nothing illustrates the issue of credibility and integrity better than a big story that we covered—the death of John Belushi.

Right after lunch that day, John Goldhammer took a call from Rich Frank, his boss at Paramount. Frank said, "Listen. This call never took place. John Belushi was supposed to have lunch today with Michael Eisner. He's not going to because he's dead. He died from a drug overdose at the Chateau Marmont. But it can't come from me!"

"What?"

"Good-bye."

Goldhammer came in and told me of his non–phone call. We quickly assembled the troops on the studio floor.

"John Belushi has just died. We can't give you a source for the news. You guys have gotta go out and find a source."

"But you *have* a source."

"You're not listening. We can't *use* that source. Go out and find two good sources."

We found an ambulance driver and a hotel manager.

That was the kind of thing I brought to the table. Get two credible sources. When we put out a story, people could believe it.

It was important to define the difference between gossip and news. *E.T.* was a great idea, a daily TV show about the world of entertainment. But the crucial thing was to stick to the *news* and make news. And cover the waterfront with criticism of the popular arts.

After all, *E.T.* was using a satellite for same-day program delivery. The only reason to do that is to deliver up-to-date news. First and fore-

The Los Angeles Times Leaves No Turn Unstoned

You can get virtually 99 percent of your clients on if you can think of even the flimsiest of reasons. It's a puff show that you can fill with more has-beens than you ever dreamed of. They will put pretty boys of the '50s on in a moment's notice, and you don't even have to go there. They send remotes everywhere . . .

This is a video fan magazine that doesn't miss a party, moving breathlessly from one "star-studded Saturday night" to another.

If you're opening a disco in Cedar Rapids, Iowa—anywhere—E.T. will be there faster than you can say Brooke Shields, and the show's anchors will give it an awestruck intro.

Even the occasional worthwhile segments and guests are only trivialized by the show's apparent determination to ruffle no feathers and keep celebrities happy enough so they remain willing to come on the show and fill time.

Howard Rosenberg, *Los Angeles Times* TV critic, March 10, 1982

most, this was a news program. Otherwise we didn't need the satellite; we could have sent out the tapes by UPS.

I was determined to make the show newsy. I was determined to really cover the events we attended, not merely chat up the celebrities.

"When we go to a media party," I said, "we're not there to taste the shrimp."

When our media producers on assignment attended a glittering Hollywood benefit, a dinner dance studded with stars, they were to work the party for *news,* not just report who showed up and what gown they wore. They were to ask the tough questions—like drugs, the Natalie Wood case, Belushi, the latest studio conflict, et cetera. Not, "What's your favorite color?"

I wrote a staff memo at the close of our first year: "It's very important to stick to the news, the stories at the top of the news, and the features about people who have something happen in their lives."

Newsy and credible—but what about an audience?

Barbara Howar phoned to carp, "I have to beg for an interview because nobody in New York is watching us in the middle of the damn night."

"Hang in there," I told her. "We'll find an audience. It'll go through the roof one of these days."

I was right. We started finding an audience. In part, we were doing a better show. In part, John Goldhammer's business troops had done their job: they managed to switch the station airing the show in New York City. We went from 1 A.M. to 7 P.M. The media capital of the world was watching! Our ratings were heading for the roof.

In its July 4, 1983, issue, *Time* sang our praises. Under the headline "Turning Show Biz into News," *Time* called us "a glitzy hit that celebrates celebrities." We were "a TV hybrid" that was "news in form, entertainment [and] content" and "the hottest, and certainly the fastest-paced, syndicated show on television." We were being delivered to a growing audience of 21 million.

We were getting into the studio around 5 A.M. and often not leaving until 7 at night, which contributed to the frantic atmosphere. It extended to everyone. One morning we arrived to find a videocassette

My TV Mentor Disclaims Mentorship

Bellows added his very special touch to every corner of Entertainment Tonight. *In addition to focusing the editorial point of view, Jim brought in talents like Barbara Howar, Ben Stein, Carl Reiner, and Mary Hart, to name a few. He created an investigative team, establishing for the first time a truly unprecedented (and many times unwelcomed by "the biz") dissection of the problems inside the halls of the entertainment business. It is doubtful the series would have survived without the credibility his name, reputation, and skill brought to this new venture. Jim often called me his "mentor" in regard to his transition from print to video. The reality was once Jim figured out that both mediums used words to describe ideas, he needed little help from me!*

John Goldhammer, Paramount's senior
vice president of programming

shot around midnight by the news crew of the station that carried us in San Francisco. A taxi had crashed down the block from the station, and the cameraman turned on his camera as he ran toward the scene. *Bump-bump-bump*—and suddenly we're looking at a bloody Mary Martin in the taxi.

Well, we edited a solid 60 seconds out of the footage that was too horrific to air, and put it on that day's show. Around seven that night John Goldhammer came into the office and wondered what our follow-up was going to be. Assignment editor Larry Dietz remembers that enchanted evening: "Since the hospital where they took Mary Martin was not allowing anyone into intensive care, I thought we'd just have one of our anchors report on her condition. John started bouncing off the walls. Why couldn't someone sneak a camera into her hospital room? Sneak a large, professional, three-quarter-inch camera into a hospital room? I'm sure I didn't convince him it couldn't be done. I think he finally just figured that this wimp from print couldn't hack it."

It wasn't all about adding a hard edge to the fluff. In bringing Hollywood to the heartland, I wasn't entirely happy with some of the on-camera talent. One of the changes was Leonard Maltin, who brought his astute movie reviews to the show. Leonard was a writer of movie encyclopedias in New York when we found him, with his name appearing in small print on the paperback covers. Leonard recalls the interview before the onslaught of fame:

> When I arrived in Hollywood, Jim Bellows greeted me cordially and said, "You understand, we're interested in having you do movie reviews. Can you tape a couple tomorrow morning?" My mind instantly flashed to stories I'd read about the early days of silent film, when an assistant director would come to the studio gates to hire extras. If he spotted someone who had the right look and asked, "You! Can you ride a horse?" the only acceptable answer was "Yes." So I said yes, wrote my first television scripts, taped an audition, and got the job. To my astonishment, I'm still there.

Leonard Maltin's name is a bit more prominent these days on his best-selling annual movie books. The cover now has his picture, and his name is above the title, as it is with every star's.

Television was a journalism frontier for me. And I plowed right in. And the show proved wildly successful. Perhaps I helped create a monster. For better or worse, much of what we see on TV news shows today started with the flashy electronic features of *Entertainment Tonight,* and that made the show successful beyond anyone's dreams. It changed things.

When Peter Jennings's *Nightly News* began, they adopted *E.T.*'s flashing graphics. Funny, *E.T.* had been dead meat in the water, gasping like an asthmatic on Olympus. "Nevertheless," recalls Barbara Howar, "in a year's time, ABC's *World News Tonight* was doing flips, paint boxes, twirling cubes. *E.T.* made a huge difference in the TV industry because it showed that people really could relate better to that kind of graphics, that fast music, the ups and downs and ins and outs."

We had another instrument of integrity and credibility. I wanted to do some serious investigative pieces—some serious journalism. So I turned to Joe Saltzman, who had produced several groundbreaking documentaries for CBS, and was now a professor of journalism at the University of Southern California. I needed a seasoned documentary producer who knew TV but also had a print background.

"Mutual friends brought Bellows and me together," Joe recalled, "and for me, it was love at first sight. Here was the legend of the newspaper world who wanted to do serious journalism in the most frivolous of media."

One afternoon I called Saltzman in.

"What do you know about the tabloids," I asked, "especially the *National Enquirer?*"

I wanted him to do an investigative report on the *Enquirer* and celebrities. Somebody needed to do an accurate job examining this controversial tabloid. Saltzman told me it couldn't be done. That really got my attention. Anyone telling me something can't be done makes me very alert. Joe explained that the *Enquirer* would never cooperate and the celebrities would be afraid to talk about the *Enquirer*.

■ **A Memo of Rambling Thoughts from**
  Bellows to Goldhammer

It's my opinion that we will get the ratings and the stars if we do much better with the quality of the show's news and comments. We will win greater respect and we will be a show the stars want to be on.

Right now I think there is a sameness to the show that could hurt.

We need to convince field producers and directors to bring back a story. We want more than tape—we want the tape to tell a story.

We need to set up one of our talents as the Home Interviewer. Somehow all our interviews seem to be in offices and we ought to do the Ed Murrow walk around the home and garden routines.

I'm trying to find the right "face" for a gossip person. Then we would have several people provide anonymous info she could cull and rewrite for use on the program.

Fall 1982 ■

"Bellows never really told you anything," recalled Joe. "But when you left his office you knew what you had to do. And when I left his office, I knew he wanted this series and it was my job to deliver it."

The publisher of the *National Enquirer* had vowed never to let a camera crew into the inner sanctum of his Lantana, Florida, offices. They had been burned by *60 Minutes* and said never again! But we had a secret—many respectable journalists were moonlighting for the *Enquirer* because it paid well. We knew these people and they were able to vouch for us, persuading the *Enquirer* to let us do the definitive piece on the publication.

An *E.T.* camera crew was allowed complete access to the editorial offices, the personnel, the *Enquirer* morgue, and its presses. We interviewed the publisher, the editors, reporters, and researchers. We also found a bar frequented by former *Enquirer* editors and writers who had been fired by the paper. That was a bonanza.

Then one day Joe made an off-hand remark.

"You know, Jim, the *Enquirer* has moles all over Hollywood."

"Great. Find one."

"That's impossible," he laughed.

I gave Joe Saltzman the Bellows look that said, "Nothing is impossible." There is no greater power than a challenged journalist. Go and do it. So Joe found an *Enquirer* informer and we found a dozen or so celebrities who would talk about their experiences with the *Enquirer*.

Joe Saltzman screened the four-part series for me. It was great. "The *Enquirer* and the Stars" got wonderful press and did everything I wanted it to do—it gave *E.T.* enormous credibility as a serious player in the world of journalism.

"That year with Bellows was one of the best of my life," wrote Saltzman years later. "It was a chance to see how it was possible for one person to do so much with a shrug, a pause, a quiet word of encouragement. I learned from Jim that the key to success is to hire the best people you can find, and let them do their work in a creative, exciting atmosphere."

In 1983, after two years in the soft-news latitudes of entertainment, I was getting a little fed up. I was hungry to bite into hard news again. So I proposed a prime-time newsmagazine show to Roone Arledge, president of ABC's news division, and signed on to develop the show.

I called the show *Seven Days* and I wanted it to emulate the approach of *Life* magazine. Just as *Life* gave you a broader perspective than the daily newspaper, with a greater concentration of pictures, I wanted *Seven Days* to bring coverage and graphic excitement to the week's events and maybe break a few stories too.

ABC was familiar with my extensive newsroom résumé, and I had proved, with *Entertainment Tonight,* that my skills were transferable to television. It should have been a pathway to triumph, right? Wrong. ABC News and I were not a perfect fit. They hungered for prestige and respect, while I was an old-fashioned newsman who wanted to tweak the prestigious and the respected.

To ABC News's solemn corridors I brought my childlike glee about journalism. I wanted to play in the sandbox of news, orchestrating a medley of stories you just had to see and talk about.

But there was one little problem. I was adrift there. It was the first time in my life that I didn't have a daily deadline. Nor did I have my "troops"—no staff to organize, motivate, shepherd, and cheer on. I didn't have a task or a challenge either—nothing to "fix," nothing to turn around and breathe life into. There was no clear-cut chain of command.

Probably my chief deficiency was my lack of political skill in a corporate environment. Though I had worked for corporations before, a newspaper newsroom was like an island of safety for me. I was totally sure of myself in a newsroom—I knew just what to do and when to do it.

At ABC News I was lost. I didn't know how to maneuver in the power game that everyone played. It was an intensely competitive environment. People didn't work together. They had their own little fiefdoms and power bases, and I didn't have the faintest idea how to build one or the faintest desire to do so.

ABC News wanted me to replicate the success of *Entertainment Tonight. Seven Days* was hatched in the same audacious spirit as *E.T.,* but it was an hour-long weekly review, not a daily report confined to show business. ABC asked me to produce a pilot. A staff was assembled. The ABC people assigned to the show were devoted to the self-important network style; they were not long on the rollicking spirit. The outsiders I brought in—free-wheeling types from the newspaper field—were smothered by the alien culture.

The network approach when reviewing a script is to remove the producer's spleen, liver, and lungs. My method, by contrast, was to blurt out a few half sentences, wave my hands, and charge out of the room. The show's chief writer, Steve Zousmer, recalls, "For the staff, adjusting to the lack of personal abuse was difficult enough. And it was a challenge to cope with this renowned editor espousing the go-for-the-gusto news values [the staff] had been taught to regard with abject horror."

We taped the pilot in May 1984 with Kathleen Sullivan and Tom Jarrel as cohosts and such correspondents as Jeff Greenfield, Pierre

Steve Zousmer Remembers <u>Seven Days</u> at ABC as a Holiday from Stalinism

Everyone was hopelessly bewildered. It turned out that I was only mildly in the dark. It was my strange gift to be able to get the general drift of what Jim was saying. I was on the staff as the show's writer, but now I became Jim's interpreter.

It was fun and liberating, despite the common agreement that the guillotine was being sharpened down the street. Office hijinks surpassed anything I'd ever seen in network news. In the hallways there was constant hilarity and good cheer, and it found its way into the product, doomed as it was.

An early question about Bellows—why was this wild-eyed lunatic regarded with such legendary affection and admiration?—was gradually answered. Meeting him later, my wife said he reminded her of James Stewart in a Frank Capra movie. He was good-hearted and good-humored, undaunted, modest but somehow heroic. His ego never got in the way. He got an enormous kick out of good work. He was the boss you always wanted.

Working on Seven Days was like a holiday from Stalinism, going down to the Black Sea and drinking and laughing at all the nasty little schemers back at the Kremlin. It was too short, but holidays are like that.

Salinger, Dick Schaap, and Sander Vanocur on hand. The set was a huge calendar with the highlighted week lit up. The pace was brisk. One critic of our rat-tat-tat rhythm referred to the pilot as "McNews." Another said there would be no reason to tune in unless you "had been out of the country the previous week." But you know how people love to criticize.

Seven Days never made the ABC schedule. I worked out my contract trying to help out on *World News Tonight*.

But was I disappointed about *Seven Days*? Listen, I am a professional, a stoic, I can handle failure. Of course, if anybody would like to see the pilot for a great magazine show, I can be there in thirty minutes.

CHAPTER 17

◆

On to the Internet

I had never touched a computer before. It was another country. When I hooked up with Prodigy, they sent me a computer, and I got to work. It was amazing—the feeling that you were part of an electronic community that was to become a global community. A network of connections to people and ideas.

There was a sense of immediacy that I felt with the readership in an on-line environment that I hadn't felt anywhere else. In any other medium, you create your piece and you let it go, and the audience sees it and may react. On-line it was a much more connected sensation— you create it and instantly *it's read*. And the feedback comes in, and there is the loop. Unlike with TV or broadcasting, people are able to communicate with one another. Unlike a newspaper, where a letter to the editor may bring a response in days, you get an instant reply.

I got it! I instantly understood that there was now a connection to the universe of readers/users/members that can be exciting and highly rewarding.

With the on-line service I tried to offer all the same departments as a newspaper, but the system of reporting was different. I insisted that Prodigy react immediately to news events. I loved beating TV or radio on a story—the print guys were not even in the same league.

This was the first attempt to sell a computer network to a national audience. But it was more than just an electronic newspaper. Much more. Bruce Thurlby was head of Editorial Business Operations when I came aboard. Here's what he saw as my contribution:

"Jim had the vision of an on-line service as a daily companion to its users. He saw a technology that could become part of the 'fabric of America,' as he expressed it. He understood at a basic level how to connect this machine to real people and create a relationship between them that was much more intimate than newspapers or TV could ever be. And he did all this while being the most technically illiterate human being on earth."

It never fails to please me each time I discover that the same basics apply in almost every form of journalism. I have worked on many newspapers, a variety of TV shows, and a few magazines. At first glance, giving information to people connected by computers seems like a different job. But they want exactly what Aristotle said the ancient Greek audiences wanted—to be informed and entertained.

Don't Get Bogged Down by the Technology

One of my favorite quotes from Jim is "I may not be right, but I'm never in doubt."

The other Bellows quote that I love and that I use to this day is "No one ever said of a failed enterprise that they stayed within budget."

And it's so true. Of course, you pay attention to budget when you run your business and you're responsible, but when push comes to shove, you do what you've got to do to make it work.

The technology of computers was foreign to Jim. I'm not technically competent either, but Jim used to turn to me for advice! That will show you how desperate he was.

Not knowing much about computers gave him a certain edge in terms of making it easy for the user, making it clearly understood.

And Jim would never get bogged down by the effort required technologically to have the end goal something that he wanted.

Bruce Thurlby, Prodigy's manager
of editorial business operations

■ Lost in the Corporate Latitudes

You have to understand the environment Jim walked into at Prodigy. The officers were men (no women) who had spent most of their careers navigating the ladders of IBM and Sears and other corporate giants. Only one officer had ever worked, briefly, in journalism. They were generally politically conservative, suburban dwelling, fairly affable guys, but Jim's résumé must have looked checkered at best and unlikely to fit into their world.

These men envisioned a computer service that was interactive to a point, limited to subscribers requiring information from the cultural neutral zones of news, weather, sports, and managing stock portfolios. . . . "Content" had second-class status in a world of computer scientists, not media types.

Mary Langer Butler, Prodigy's director of marketing services ■

I had a three-year contract at ABC that ended in 1986, and I was out of work in high-cost New York. An inquiry came to me from Peter Knudsen, Prodigy's search consultant. They were looking for a content editor and had turned to David Burgin, my great idea man at the *Washington Star.* Dave wasn't interested, but he suggested they call me. So Knudsen called and told me about something then called Trintex— by startup time the name was changed to Prodigy—and it was to be the first on-line newspaper. I agreed to visit their offices in White Plains, New York, and met with Henry Heilbrunn, the Prodigy creative vice president, who was a former Associated Press executive. He offered me the job of vice president of media, and I took it. Two months after the end of my ABC stint, I started a daily reverse commute from Manhattan to White Plains.

Once again, as I had done when I left newspapering for television, I was jumping to another news field. I didn't know anything about computers. So I told them, in a paraphrase of what I had told Barry Diller when he beckoned me to *Entertainment Tonight,* "I know what I don't know, and I don't know computers. But I can figure out how to put the right content on a computer screen just as I learned about content and a TV screen."

Prodigy had begun as a joint venture of IBM, Sears, and CBS, so it had the benefit of being well funded. The promise of an interactive on-line service was exciting to me because for the first time in media history, the "reader" had a chance to talk back—to have exchanges with the reporters.

A Hardcore Newsman Comes to Technoland

Jim Bellows doesn't interview well—when he is on the other side of the table.

The year was 1986. Jim had been identified by an executive recruiter as the ideal experienced candidate for editorial director of the unknown Prodigy on-line service. He brought a rare résumé that demonstrated he could work across different types of media, was willing to risk his reputation on starting new ventures or reviving failing newspapers, and had the requisite gray hair. He was being asked to parent dozens of 20- and 30-year-olds who had been hard at work for two years creating a new way for people with recently invented personal computers to get information, electronically communicate with each other, and to shop from home.

CBS, IBM, and Sears reportedly would eventually spend $1 billion on Prodigy over 10 years to reach—at its peak in the early 1990s—some 1 million house-holds. Still unprofitable, the service would be sold to a company that would take it public during the Internet IPO frenzy.

Jim was being considered to spend some of the billion during Prodigy's pre-launch years. He was on an all-day round of interviews among the top exec-utives of Prodigy when I met him, the lowest-ranked and least interested in his arrival—and about half his age. I was taking on new responsibility and reluctantly giving up my passion for editorial. The company wanted brand name. Jim more than filled this, with his recent credentials from ABC News, Washington Star, Los Angeles Herald-Examiner, *and* Entertainment Tonight.

The problem, as Jim readily admitted during his halting job interview with me, was that he had little understanding of personal computers or technology, was a hardcore newsman with a few trips into entertainment, and had minor interest in the shopping or advertising that the owners were depending on as the profit lifeblood of Prodigy.

Henry Heilbrunn, Prodigy executive vice president

I did a lot of new hires—some of them from my newspaper years—to write news briefs, punchy factoids from all over. Then we worked out contracts with AP and UPI, and then with the *Wall Street Journal*.

There was a problem. CBS was the *news* partner at Prodigy; IBM was the *technical* partner, and Sears was the *marketing* partner. But when Larry Tisch bought CBS he opted out of Prodigy. With CBS gone, the most knowledgeable communications people were gone too. IBM and Sears had no media experience and their executives had little respect for news. They thought of it as fillers between the ads. They saw the home computer as a dandy new selling tool. A favorite graphic was a computer, chock full of recipes, sitting on a kitchen counter. The tagline of Prodigy's first TV ad campaign was: "You Gotta Get This Thing." Apparently J. Walter Thompson had no idea what the hell they were advertising. So against these corporate walls, breaking news fought an uphill battle.

Then I developed what seemed to me a promising idea. I felt that there not only had to be a personality to this whole thing, but there had to be *personalities* involved in it.

If you wanted to lose ten ugly pounds, what could beat asking Jane Fonda? If you were wondering about the meaning of the last scene in *Casablanca,* who better to query than Gene Siskel? If you wanted to ask about presidential policy, how about asking Bob Novak or Jack Germond? Asking them *directly,* on your *computer*. And getting a personal answer.

I thought: Let's get all the areas we want to keep people informed about, whether it's food or finances or relationships, and let's get the best people not only to write a short tip on the subject matter once a week, but also to answer questions from our subscribers. What could be more exciting than that in luring people to our service?

Basically, I was trying to create for Prodigy a group of star columnists, very much as I had done in the world of newspapers. The subscriber could e-mail a question to a celebrity; the expert would respond privately via e-mail, one-on-one. These notables were going to have an intimate interaction with users of the service.

Of course, it wasn't easy to get these luminaries involved. When you read this today, the Internet is ubiquitous, it's where the action is. But

I Fall Back on My "Quiet Magic" and Serendipity

What would you do to make [Prodigy] appealing to early adopters of personal computer owners, I asked of Jim. He was silent, clearly thinking. Then he waved his arms and uttered an incomplete sentence about having similar challenges through his career. It would come to him, he promised, and to the people he would enlist to help. Not very satisfying to me, fully acceptable to him.

That was Jim's quiet magic. It did come to him and to the rich mix of people he drew in to Prodigy from his past associations. He spent his part of the billion—in spite of management's lack of comprehending his arm-waving vision and their continual resistance—bringing Howard Cosell, Dick Schaap, Jane Fonda, and Bob Novak, among other notables, to the tiniest screen that they would appear on, the personal computer. He persuaded them to respond in a unique two-way forum to questions posed by the general public. It was a moment of genius that gave the editorial a sense of purpose and innovation and the marketing message instant substance and promise of interactivity.

Only someone with the depth of experience and Jim's Rolodex could be confident in pulling it off. Jim visited Prodigy for two years, by which time you could see his restlessness for his next adventure. As always in his career, Jim moved on, carrying with him what he had learned and whom he met to continue writing his legend in a different city, at a new desk, mixing new and old acquaintances to evolve his current favorite medium—with his same style of staccato, incomplete sentences accompanied by a wave of the arms that launched so many media innovations.

Henry Heilbrunn, in letter, September 2, 2001

in 1986 it was an unknown. So when you told Gene Siskel about this on-line thing and asked, "Do you know what a PC is?" "Have you ever seen a modem?" "Have you ever logged on?" his answers were (a) no, (b) no, (c) no.

But I tried to be persuasive with these busy people. I said, "This is going to be fun—this is going to be interesting—we will make it worth your while—give it a shot." In short, I tried to convince people that it was going to be an adventure. And it was.

I had been talking to Jane Fonda's company about her doing a column on physical fitness. Jane and I had met in L.A. She had been a prep school classmate of my wife's at Emma Willard. In 1987 her books and videos were selling platinum. It got to the point where I was going to meet with Jane Fonda herself and show her what the service was going to be like. This was before it actually existed, of course, but I was undaunted. I would demonstrate a prototype model of the service and explain how Jane would communicate with the network's members.

So Bruce Thurlby and I took off for sunny California. The machine we used for our demonstrations was an IBM XT; at the time it was state of the art—today it's a doorstop. It was just a big old boxy machine with a huge monitor. It traveled in two huge metal crates, which we would check in at the airport. Not quite a laptop. So off we go to magical Hollywood. We check into a swank hotel, and because we want this to be the best presentation ever, we set everything up in our hotel room the night before and rehearse. This was a canned demonstration that was on the hard drive. So we turn on the computer . . . nothing! It's not there. The machine won't boot. It's dead.

We sit there depressed and befuddled. We are trying to figure this thing out. Here we are, we've come all the way to California to get the gem of our celebrity list. This was to be our big moment. But it's going to be a disaster.

But we decide to go for it. The meeting is scheduled for first thing the next morning. We have with us Polaroid snapshots of the screens in the presentation. So we decide to show up smiling and confident at Jane Fonda's office. We will set up the computer and make the usual verbal pitch. Then at the fateful moment, we will hit the "start" button. It will fail to start. We will register chagrin. We will whip out our little Polaroid pictures. Listen, Jane Fonda knows that things go wrong. Didn't she star in *The China Syndrome*?

So we taxi over to her office on Robertson Boulevard, we meet Jane Fonda, we set the thing up, and we start our little pitch. I look glowingly at Jane, Bruce, and the machine. I turn it on. The demonstration pops on the screen! *It works!* We go through the entire presentation. Jane is

---

A Portion of the Experts List

Julian Block . . . . . Taxes	*Digby Diehl . . . . . . Books*
Heloise . . . . Household tips	*Robert Novak . . . . . Politics*
Jane Fonda . . . . . Fitness	*Jack Germond . . . . Politics*
Howard Cosell . . Sports	*Mary Anne Dolan . . "Dear Jane"*
Dick Schaap . . . . Sports	*Larry Beard . . . . . . Pets*
Gene Siskel . . . . . Movies	*Lisa Robinson . . . . . Rock and roll*
Leonard Maltin . . Movies	*John Mariani . . . . . Restaurants*
Sylvia Porter . . . . Personal finance	*Brendan Boyd . . . . Stocks*
Encyclopaedia	*This Old House . . . . Home repair*
Britannica . . . . General topics	

As reconstructed by Bruce Thurlby, manager, editorial business operations

---

impressed. We shake hands on the deal. Me Bellows, you Jane. We emerge into the California sunshine. Slow fade out, music up.

A Hollywood happy ending? Not quite. We go on to our next meeting, we plug in the machine—not only does it not work, but *smoke* comes out of the back. Stories of our demonstrations in this primitive age of the Internet are legion. Full of daring and challenge. Like landing on a carrier at night.

We wanted Heloise as our expert on household tips. I sent Bruce on to San Antonio. For years Heloise, like many other newspaper journalists, had been writing her column on yellow pads with a ballpoint pen. She would send her scribbles to the syndicate, someone would type it up, and it would show up in a hundred or so newspapers. Bruce reported that when he walked in her door and said, "Now you're going to use Prodigy, the on-line computer service," she said, "What's that?" Her household tips did not embrace the Web. We managed to get her on the service. A lovely person, Heloise, but the classic pen-and-pad columnist.

We told her what kind of computer to get. Heloise obediently bought one. We hooked it up, hooked up her phone line, taught her how to use on-line word processing and how to send her column in to Prodigy. Wonderful lady, Heloise.

Jack Germond was great too. Jack had written politics for me at the *Washington Star.* I had linked him with Jules Witcover to create a successful syndicated column. He is a journalist whose honest, no-nonsense reporting and wit are hallmarks of punditry and he became a TV star too. Jack was interested in joining up with us. Germond said of our meeting, "You know, Bellows told me all of this on the phone, and I didn't understand a word of it. But when he was down here and we got together for a drink, I could see his *hands,* and I got it immediately!"

One trip I visited Abigail Van Buren, the famous advice columnist whose Dear Abby column has brought coherence into so many lives. Abby had no idea what I was talking about, but because I had known her for years, she listened. I showed up with my two huge white boxes of computer equipment at her beautiful home in Beverly Hills.

"Where shall we set it up?" said Abby. "Maybe on the bar."

She ran into the bedroom, grabbed a comforter, and spread it over the bar. Then we set up the equipment and did our stuff.

Robert Gehorsam, our editorial tech expert, recalls the meeting: "It was a wonderful afternoon. I found Abby to be lovely, a nice woman with tremendous dignity, cordiality, and poise. Setting up a computer in her house in 1987—I mean, what did she know about computers? She was very gracious, but she's very serious about what she does. She reads every letter, answers every one, even if she doesn't print it. It was a revelation to her. 'This is going to revolutionize communicating with people!' she said."

But Abby feared the volume would be overwhelming and I couldn't persuade her to join up.

In fact, whenever I mentioned to people like Abby that people would send them questions to answer, there was always a fair amount of resistance. Their concern was immediate: What if I can't handle it? What if I start annoying people with my answers instead of helping them? The basic problem was that these people were busy, they were always in demand, so the big impediment was: How do I fit it into my day? I was pleased by how often we got people to step into the batter's box.

One of our experts was not a celebrity but a celebrity institution—the *Encyclopaedia Britannica*. I remember flying to Chicago to meet with the stolid executives of the Britannica company around a football-field-sized conference table. It was a cold November day and I got a chilly reception. Their business was built around what their salesmen could sell, so the idea of an electronic encyclopedia did not thrill them. They could not dream what was happening to the encyclopedia business. The door-to-door salesman could not outrun the Internet. I tried to make it unthreatening. I talked about how amazing it would be for a kid to ask a question of the *Encyclopaedia Britannica*.

I was struck by a basic irony: This was the cutting edge, but all these companies were so damn conservative.

But, to their credit, Britannica took the plunge. Prodigy members would e-mail questions to the *Encyclopaedia Britannica*'s editors. The idea with Fonda and Siskel was a quick question, a quick answer. "Dear Jane, how do I get a flat stomach?" But the Britannica folks had no experience with brief answers. They are a group of erudite, scholarly professionals who were offended at the very thought of giving anything less than the most complete answer. So when people sent in a question, they would get a twenty-page essay. The scholars would take weeks to prepare it. Unfortunately, Britannica was losing a bloody fortune on the deal. We were tying up their entire research bureau. That contract never got renewed.

Our book expert was Digby Diehl, former *Los Angeles Times* book critic and a good friend. There were fewer people coming on-line to talk about books than about movies or health, so Digby had the time to engage in yearlong "tutorials" with subscribers who kept returning to talk to him about books.

Digby was more than our book expert. He was able to bring on various "guest experts"—authors like Stephen King, Tom Clancy, and Anne Rice. He would solicit a group of questions for a particular author, then pose them to his guest. The answers were posted on the screen for the questioners and the rest of our viewers, the birth of on-line "chats."

Tom Clancy was fascinated at getting on what was then a brand-new medium. He observed that people who were writing in questions to him "had to take the time to sit down and think of what they were asking, so their questions were more thoughtful than somebody standing up in the *Oprah* audience, or calling in to a radio talk show."

Digby found there was a more intimate interaction with his audience than he had ever experienced in any of the media in which he had written about—books, newspapers, magazines, radio, TV. "I've never had the feeling of connection that I did on Prodigy. And there was an immediacy of response. With a newspaper, someone might write a letter a week later. On Prodigy, people came right back at you. It seems like a cold medium, banging away at a keyboard, but the intimacy is marvelous."

It was hard to get Prodigy to commit much in the way of resources to my "experts" project. They did not view editorial matter as the priority. They focused on the financial data, and then the shopping material. So they assigned their weaker technical staff to me.

There was a lot of reorganization in the company. That's part of the corporate culture, I guess. Every few months, desks and credenzas would be moved up and down the elevators, and new organization charts showing who was now reporting to whom would be issued.

A Hard Day at the Encyclopaedia Britannica

We were in Chicago, in a classic boardroom. We had a demonstration of what Prodigy was going to be, which ran on two computers. And the demos were protected by a password. And I was the guy who was going to run the demos. And Jim is explaining the whole thing. And how great it will be for children to ask questions to the Britannica. *And I'm trying to get the demo going. And I can't get the password to work. And Jim is talking. And I'm thinking, "I think they changed the password." And I run out and I'm desperately trying to find someone in White Plains who has the new password. And it's getting late in New York, and they have a 9 to 5 operation. And I reach someone, get the new password, and run the demo. And the* Britannica *went along!*

Robert Gehorsam, our editorial tech expert

There was a lot of secrecy too. Why a company that occupied a building in the boondocks of White Plains needed locked doors on every floor was a mystery. White Plains is one of New York's bedroom communities. The Prodigy building was on the outer edge of town, a rigorous 15-minute walk up from the train station. Each morning I would lead the New York contingent up the hill just before nine, and down again in time to catch the 5:02.

The walk was invigorating. But the corporate culture was not. I could have done without all the meetings—complete with blue suits, white shirts, and photo-sensitive name tags. IBM had brought with them a management system built on a relentless schedule of meetings morning, noon, and night. They made it hard to get any real work done. I had lived in a world of daily deadlines for decades, and I would often murmur, "I don't think I'm going to this meeting."

Mary Langer Butler, Prodigy's director of marketing services, was a colleague of mine who was seated in the peanut gallery at those meetings, awaiting her own turn to stand in front of the Rosewood Table. She recalls my first presentation:

> The required method of presentation was by carefully crafted outlines and diagrams displayed by the overhead projector. Jim put up his first and only transparency. It contained a column of single words including "movies, TV, romance, books, teens, politics, travel, rock, fashion, Hollywood, advice." Jim began a tortured explanation, never completing a sentence, and gesturing as he spoke. "You see . . . we're going to have these experts. . . . We'll have these columns . . . and so, in other words . . . people will write in . . . and so forth . . ." When he was finished, the men around the Rosewood Table were dumbstruck. This new guy was actually proposing that subscribers determine content, in a truly interactive way.

I remember the first time we got the "usage" figures back. We had started out testing in two markets, and had since spread to twenty. And we had our first record of who was using what on the Prodigy service. This was the big blessing of on-line: You could measure it exactly. When the first usage figures came back, lo and behold, 72 percent of the usage was "editorial," and 9 percent was what we called service areas, meaning directories and indexes. Another 10 percent was e-commerce and shopping, like stock brokerage, grocery buying, bookstores, and record shops.

Mark Benerofe, general news manager, recalls the meeting when management learned of the appeal of editorial:

"Jim and I were really excited. These usage figures showed that people were using and enjoying the stuff we were creating—the experts' columns, the one-on-one questions, the special reports. Yet there were only 40 people out of the 900 at Prodigy assigned to our team. The Sears CEO, Charles Brennan, was at the meeting. He was not happy with the usage numbers. They showed that not enough people were *shopping*. The CEO of IBM, John Akers, was there too, and he wasn't pleased either. Said Brennan: 'This is not good.' And Akers said: 'Don't worry, the novelty of editorial will wear off.'"

But Prodigy was educating its audience. We spent a fortune educating people on how to use the system, how to navigate, how many great things were available. We taught the public how wonderful the Internet was. Now, teaching computer navigation to complete novices was an expensive and time-consuming process, but it paid off—for AOL. As soon as Prodigy had created a base of computer-literate users, AOL stole Prodigy's thunder by making its own service younger, sexier, and cheaper.

I was outraged by the censorship required by the Sears-trained management. Prodigy was getting bad press for censoring words of the four-letter variety and preventing members from exercising free speech. By letting it all hang out and ignoring its "publishing responsibilities," AOL attracted a lot of eyeballs, avoided the expense of monitoring the boards, and got credit for sticking up for the First Amendment.

The experts program lasted eighteen months. Finally the volume became too great. It became a victim of its own popularity.

As time went by, the Sears notion of creating a sales medium was a clear failure. Running an Internet service had become, as my young friends at Excite would say a few years later, "an eyeballs game." Prodigy simply wasn't getting eyeballs as fast as AOL and was destined to fade into its present half-life.

Perhaps if management had agreed with my way of thinking, they might have succeeded. But they didn't, and so I took my personal brand of journalism elsewhere.

Prodigy and AOL Talking Dirty

Prodigy's chat room had proctors. There were people who were checking on what was being written all the time. One of my responsibilities was to yank messages off the boards if people were using improper language, or inciting to riot. AOL had one advantage that Prodigy did not—AOL was a free-for-all. For kids that was nirvana. They weren't going to be censored, no Big Brother was looking over their shoulder, and AOL got to be the place where kids could talk dirty to each other. That was a big thrill for them and a big attraction of the site. It's grown up since then . . .

Jim was thinking about ways that the Internet could be used for people to exchange information. Almost as soon as the Prodigy news page was up, he started using Prodigy members who lived near news events. His news desk encouraged members to write in with their eye-witness reports.

Jim found young, energetic people who had the technical skills, if not the journalistic skills, and imbued them with his own brand of enthusiasm. He would call in to the newsroom at all hours to suggest an idea for them to try or a news source they might have missed. For a time, the Prodigy newsroom became a model of what the Internet was trying to achieve: people connecting with other people electronically and sharing information that was important in their lives.

Digby Diehl, former *Los Angeles Times* book editor

CHAPTER 18

$\blacklozenge$

USA Today and *TV Guide*

Before it was launched on September 12, 1988, *USA Today: The Television Show* was the most successful show ever created for syndication. It was one of those "could not miss" sure things. It had the *USA Today* brand name, which was unassailable. It had Grant Tinker, the TV genius who had turned the third-ranking NBC into the No. 1 network. It had Steve Friedman, the live TV producer of the *Today* show who had made Gumbel and Pauley household words. It had Gannett's money.

It was the most successful show in history.

That is, until it actually went on the air.

Then—"It was greeted with Bronx cheers from the critics and 'We're not interested' from the viewers," said Jeremy Gerard of the *New York Times*. "A stillborn series," said Lee Winfrey of Knight-Ridder. "It doesn't fill a void, it *is* a void," said Howard Rosenberg in the *Los Angeles Times*. "As insubstantial as cotton candy and more frenzied than a three-ring circus," said Alvin Sanoff in *U.S. News & World Report*. If they didn't like the show, why didn't they come right out and say so?

But what promise! The show had been presold into every major market and scores of minor ones—156 stations in all. And those stations reached 95 percent of the viewing public. Quite an achievement for a show without a pilot. It had been sold to station owners on the strength of its pedigree, no taped sample was needed.

The New York Times Magazine Reports on "The Big Turnoff"

The pitch was simple. When salesmen from a new company called GTG Entertainment visited television stations across the country early last year, they would hand the station manager a copy of USA Today. *Next, they would talk about the newspaper's appeal, its colorful graphics, its crisp, upbeat stories. Then came the clincher: "This paper was founded by Al Neuharth, right? Let's say Al Neuharth came up to you and said, 'I just made a deal with Grant Tinker, the guy who bought NBC back from the basement to No. 1, and I told him, "Use my name, here's my newspaper, do whatever you want with it, here's a check for $40 million."' And then Grant got Steve Friedman, the guy who turned the* Today *show around, to produce* USA Today *on TV. Could you refuse a show like that?"*

"Can *USA Today* Be Saved?" by Joe Morgenstern,
The New York Times Magazine, January 1, 1989

The Gannett news conglomerate, which owned *USA Today,* had built a state-of-the-art studio in one of the twin towers of its headquarters in Rosslyn, Virginia, across the Potomac from Washington.

USA Today: The Television Show was to be the electronic arm of "the nation's newspaper." It was the most eagerly awaited show in memory. With such an illustrious band of creators how could it go wrong?

One of the gilt-edge résumés belonged to the show's producer, Steve Friedman. "The reason they hired me," he recalled, "is that I did the *Today* show. And they had modeled the *USA Today* newspaper after the *Today* show. Not only that, the way they *presented* the paper was like a TV screen." Good circular logic—the TV show was based on a newspaper that was based on a TV show, right down to its vending machines.

What *USA Today: The Television Show* presented was called "infotainment." The problem was that the show didn't manage to either inform or entertain.

USA Today: The Television Show (the name later was changed to *USA Today on TV*) was one of a series of attempts to marry television and print. And it never seems to work very well. Lots of people have tried it—*People* magazine, the *Reader's Digest,* Time Inc., and *USA Today.*

"You can't really marry the two," insists Steve Friedman, who brought me aboard to replace himself. "There's a reason you can't do it. The two mediums are incompatible. A lot of money has been flushed down the tube in trying to do it. When you talk to print people, they think good TV is putting them on television."

I must have seemed a sensible choice when the show stumbled at the gate. *USA Today on TV* was trying to blend the cultures of print and TV. I understood the print culture better than anyone from the print side who was on the show. And I had been a capable show fixer at *Entertainment Tonight.*

When *USA Today on TV* first appeared, *E.T.* was in its heyday and it was the show that most insiders figured *USA* was going to knock off. So much for the art of prediction. Remembering the show's promise, Steve Friedman says today: "Yeah, the show had a great pedigree. . . . But most new TV shows don't work."

Friedman asked me to visit the show and help reshape it. Soon after, I quit my job at Prodigy for the position of managing editor at *USA Today on TV.*

■ Disaster Relief Sought for <u>USA Today</u> TV

Arlington, Va.—*Can a still-born television series be resurrected?* USA Today: The Television Show *will attempt to answer that highly expensive question Monday. . . . Monday is the date set for "a major relaunch" of its struggling series. . . . It's designed to persuade people who tuned out on the show to tune in again . . .*

One of the best show doctors in television, Jim Bellows, is now in charge at the series' headquarters here, just across the Potomac from Washington.

To fully understand the task facing Bellows, it's necessary to look back at what has happened so far on USA Today: The Television Show. *If you're the kind of person who likes train wrecks, you'll enjoy the trip.*

Lee Winfrey, Knight-Ridder, January 4, 1989 ■

Recently Steve reflected on the favorite moments that he shared with me: "It was when Jim looked at the rundown for a show and said: 'Does that fill a half hour? Is that enough to fill a half hour?' He was in doubt because he didn't see any real substance there. He saw nothing but smoke and mirrors. And Jim is a substantial guy. And he always wondered how you could actually go out there with what we had some nights."

Shortly after I came aboard, Steve left for Gannett's offices in New York and started working on plans for a 24-hour comedy station.

I installed myself at the River Inn in a tiny apartment, and shuttled back to my wife and daughter in New York on weekends.

As it turned out, I was being assigned to mission impossible. Of course, I had undertaken more hopeless missions, in at least three technologies. The joy is the journey, not the goal. So, to work.

It seemed to me that the show was too much like the *Today* show. I set out to rev it up—create more human conflict stories, more drama, more action pictures, more immediacy and urgency. I tried to make it more focused, more substantial. I tried to create an exciting, helpful news show about what unusual things were happening in the U.S.A. today.

I knew we had to give a special dimension to the news. This was not *Entertainment Tonight* and it was not Rather-Brokaw-Jennings. We had to have an *edge* to our news stories, something that compelled people, night after night, to want to see us.

When I was editing the *Washington Star,* the *Washington Post* was my nemesis. Now the *Post* was the local paper covering my return to the capital. Carla Hall, a *Post* reporter, paid me a visit. We had lunch at Windows, a restaurant in a Rosslyn high-rise. I ordered a Stoli on the rocks and an overcooked grilled tuna plate, gazed out over the cliffs above the George Washington Memorial Parkway, and reflected on the TV medium.

"There seems to be a feeling in television that you should be screaming and there should be a frenetic pace," I told her. "I think I go pretty fast, but not like these twenty-five-year-olds."

Bellows Can Fix It

Jim Bellows, who was once brought in to revive Entertainment Tonight *when critics were complaining that it was all form and no content, said Wednesday that his focus will be much the same with his new patient . . .*

When it premiered, USA Today: The Television Show *was calling itself TV of the future: Awash with graphics, quick stories, quicker polls and factoids, it was the ultimate in high-tech TV for the young, video-fluent generation. It did not work . . .*

Bellows is 65. He is not video-fluent. He spent most of his career in newspapers. . . . "I've certainly always felt that it's a lot easier to fix something than to start something up," Bellows said. "I think I can help this work."

Jay Sharbutt, *Los Angeles Times,* October 14, 1988

Wrote Carla: "Tall and lanky, his suit coat doffed for a beige sweater in the newsroom, he has a physical image that conjures up a Jimmy Stewart of about the same age. [I would have preferred Henry Fonda, but I'll take it.] Bellows' talent appears to be a clear and sharp vision of how to make stories interesting and focused. And he is dedicated to shaking things up to the point of recklessness."

Carla Hall asked me about the muckraking days of journalism when her *Washington Post* was breathing down my neck. "I think the newspaper's job is to print the news and raise hell," I said. "How many newspapers are raising hell?"

I told her that I wanted to have fun. And I feel you can't have much anymore in newspapers. More and more today, they are edited for the bottom line.

Perhaps that's why television intrigued me. Its power and reach were amazing. I have always tried to bring passion to my newsrooms—and that's what drew me to television. That and the fact that I was running out of competitive newspapers in large cities. The driving force of many of TV's hottest new shows was a sense of *outrage* and *passion,* while newspapers had grown much too dispassionate.

So what of my new rescue mission to *USA Today on TV*? Wrote Carla: "Bellows loves helping the underdog, and certainly this show was an underdog, if not an outright cur . . ."

At the beginning, the show's young staff, most of them in their twenties, loved the experience. It was like they were mounting a gangplank onto an ocean liner before a glorious voyage. "People had the feeling of being reborn, of being touched by a wand," one staffer told Joe Morganstern for his cover story in *The New York Times Magazine*. The staff was jubilant at the daily production meetings. Then the ratings dived and the critics attacked.

When I arrived on October 13, 1988, I discovered that for a show named after a newspaper, it was a little short of newsmen. According to the *Times Magazine* story, there was only one "seasoned journalist" on the staff. That was Joe Urschel, who came from *USA Today*. Urschel recalled that he was "probably the only seasoned *print* journalist. A lot of the staff were *TV* journalists. They had worked at CNN, the *Today*

TV Guide Gives Us a Second Look

The first few shows were pretty much a mess . . . leaving viewers wondering what on earth was going on. The premise seemed to be that after a couple of generations of watching TV, the American viewer has the attention span of a flea and the intellectual level of a sea slug. . . . Recently Jim Bellows was hired. . . . But the show's predilection for reporting the results of its namesake newspaper's reader polls ("Parenting is: Easier than expected—7%; Harder—53%; As expected—7%) still tend to highlight its triviality and fitful pace.

More recently, USA Today, with more solid mini-exposés and off-beat interviews, seems to be striving to be a news-oriented, half-hour version of 60 Minutes, and that's not at all bad. . . . We suggest that viewers who have seen the show in its early stages and found it wanting, or just plain confusing, try it again.

Merrill Pannitt, November 19, 1988

show, and other shows. I never thought the staff lacked for talent, it lacked for direction."

The show had a whole medley of problems. One was its audience. As Urschel expressed it, "The show was based on a newspaper that was popular with male baby boomers, and it was going into a time slot that was dominated by older women and down-scale adults."

Another problem was competition. Tabloid TV was in full flower, from Geraldo Rivera to Maury Povich's *A Current Affair*, with *Inside Edition* about to premiere. So *USA Today on TV* had some heavyweight rivals.

On Monday morning I held my first meeting with the staff. They were no longer feeling reborn and touched by a wand. In fact, they were depressed and bewildered. They had loved Steve Friedman and I felt like Gregory Peck replacing the popular commander in *Twelve O'Clock High*.

"I need all the help I can get," I told them quietly. "I promise you that the show is going to improve."

In contrast to the flashy Friedman, I am your standard oracle. I gesticulate, I express ideas with my palms, I grimace and mumble and laugh. Joe Urschel remembers that meeting: "Everybody was trying to figure out what Jim meant when he said, 'Put a nice ribbon around it' or 'Wrap it up this way' or 'It's missing, it's missing, it's missing. . . .' And he said, 'It doesn't have any . . . you know, it doesn't have any . . .' He never actually got to the word you're waiting for him to say. But somehow you knew what he was talking about. He had an amazing way to communicate through apparent confusion."

I realized that *USA Today on TV* was going to have to be more of a tabloid presentation of the news—but tabloid in the very best sense. The new shows that were coming on, like *Hard Copy*, were a sleazy kind of tabloid. But I thought *USA Today on TV* could succeed by being a tabloid that was combative, sophisticated, edgy, smart. Not sensational or groveling.

Though I appear not to be able to articulate what I want to say, people usually know what it is that I want, even though I sometimes can't verbalize it—or choose not to.

And irrespective of my powers of articulation, I know how to motivate good writing. And I relish the role of the combative underdog. God knows I have played it often enough.

So I wandered the newsroom and talked to the youngsters who seldom ever looked at a newspaper. They got their news from TV. So with my mumbles and gestures, my assorted scowls and grins, I acquainted them with some basic laws of journalism.

"Bring out the conflict in this story," I would say. "Be curious. Try to find stories that are fresh and unusual. And get the detail."

I kept reaching for drama in the news. And the critics and the station owners seemed to feel that we were getting better. The show was becoming a mix of timely news, human interest stories, useful facts, and a touch of glitz. My biggest job was to give the show an identity in the crowd, give it a distinctive point of view. But time was running out . . .

The people at Gannett were very comfortable with me at the beginning. I was one of them. A journalist and editor with ink in his veins. But it was tough to do a hard-driving show and call it *USA Today on TV* because the newspaper *USA Today* wasn't very hard-driving. But I wanted to get viewers. Steve Friedman recalled, "Remember, that was the heyday of Geraldo, and I think to compete, Jim tried to do a hard-ass show and call it *USA Today.*"

Steve is right to an extent. The show probably did not reflect *USA Today*. It wasn't an apparent copy of the newspaper—though it had a lot of the paper's qualities: It was quick, it was easily digestible, it got around the country, it didn't spend a lot of time on policy issues, it was a show about real stories with some inherent conflict, stories that people were interested in. It was *unusual* content.

We improved the show markedly in the ratings. But in the process, the Gannett people got worried that we had become too much of a tabloid show. A real schism developed between me and the Gannett folks. When the *New York Times* ran a page one story about two lesbians in Ohio who were in a custody battle about the child they were raising, I ordered up a piece for the show and ran it. Al Neuharth, the head of Gannett, fulminated. He was quoted as saying that such stories, running on *USA Today on TV,* were ruining the image of the newspaper.

The First Daily Newsmagazine of the Air

Jim wanted to create the first daily, legitimate newsmagazine show on the air, and he figured he had found his vehicle; it just needed some work under the hood. He reduced the number of anchors [from four] to two. He changed the lineup of the show to have fewer small items and focus on a few main stories each day. He changed story selection to more visceral topics.

The mood in the newsroom improved. The advertising was better because the show was better. The numbers improved. But most of all, it was great fun. . . . And then one day, Jim was gone. I was never quite sure what happened. There was never really any formal explanation. Without fanfare, Jim slipped out at the end of one day and went up to New York to ride out his contract at GTG's office in Manhattan. People literally cried as he left.

Tom Jones

■ Tom Jones developed a series of print and
   radio ads for the show's launch week.

Neuharth exploded in a letter, saying that under my control, the show was drifting away from the basic concept—it must return to reflecting the newspaper.

Gannett had made it clear at the outset, he said, that they would only underwrite a show with content that reflected the image of the newspaper. "It would be far better to fail with a show we can be proud of," he concluded, "than to win the ratings game with a show we're ashamed of!"

Without any discussion, I was removed from the helm and moved to their New York offices as a "consultant" in March 1989.

In his recent memoir, *Tinker in Television,* Grant Tinker presented his view: "We had hired Jim for his editorial skills, which were considerable, but we forced him into the de facto role of executive producer. The show's ratings were at their peak on his watch, but there were two problems, only one of which we knew about at the time. The program was wildly over budget. . . . The problem we didn't know about until later was that the editorial changes Bellows had made ran counter to what Gannett wanted."

When I was removed, I wrote a letter to Al Neuharth that I never sent. It read in part: "My feeling is one of great sadness. We were just beginning to hit our stride with the ratings up and the show poised for a second year . . .

"When I was suddenly given word of my replacement, it was quite a stunning disappointment. And I still have not been given a sound reason or cause for my replacement. A sad, surprise ending."

I recall my farewell party when the black hand had fallen on my shoulder. Joe Urschel remembers it, too:

> Jim left at a point that the morale of the show was on an uptick, people were optimistic. There was a sense of turnabout, the ratings were up. People had a lot of respect for him, and when we found out he was leaving, we put together a quick going-away party—we bought some champagne and some food, and we were going to have a little reception and give him a sendoff. I remember he came out of his office and he mumbled something about he really didn't want to do this, and he really had to be going. He just sort of arrived into the room in the way he always did. And he was tearing up, and the entire staff was. And then he just left. So we were left there with all the champagne and food and we were just totally morose.

In April Gannett brought in as executive producer a man named Tom Kirby from their Oklahoma City TV station. He would be replaced in July by still another Gannetteer, Jack Hurley, as the revolving door continued to spin.

When I was transferred to Gannett's Manhattan office, and then fired, it was without severance pay and without a contract payout that would have involved several hundred thousands of dollars. So I hired a lawyer and threatened suit for $1.8 million dollars. A short time later, I traveled with Keven to Vermont for a party that Gary David Goldberg was throwing. Gary was the father of such delightful TV fare as *Family Ties* and *Brooklyn Bridge*. At the party I bumped into Grant Tinker on the veranda. We said hello and a little later he took me aside and asked if I'd be satisfied if they paid out the contract terms. I said sure, and the matter was settled; a big check arrived a few days later. Thank you, Grant, thank you, Gary.

In January 1990 the show died and the title *USA Today on TV* was erased from *TV Guide's* schedule. Since its highly promoted premiere, the show had spent $50 million and become the biggest broadcasting debacle in recent history.

Recalling the failure, Steve Friedman recently said, "The show didn't work, in my opinion, because we were never able to get the editorial muscle that we needed to do stories. The idea was—the paper was going to do the journalism, and we were going to put it on TV. But we were never able to figure out how the paper did the journalism. Whether we should have believed they didn't do any—sort of like the *Reader's Digest*, where they read everything and put it in a condensed form. Or maybe we weren't smart enough to figure out how to do it."

USA Today on TV was distinguished in another way besides the extent of its losses. It was the first great experiment in trying to accomplish what they now call "convergence." Convergence is a very hip

---

◼ My Lunch Dates Impress the Staff

Jim was a very connected guy in Washington from those days at the Star. *And we had at the TV show a very young staff, certainly not a sophisticated Washington policy wonky staff. We weren't getting kids of the* Washington Post. *They were young and fresh. Jim had probably the greatest list of lunch dates every week that you could possibly amass. He would go home on weekends, but he lived here in town during the week. So his secretary would come in and say something like: "There's a Mr. Greenspan on the phone. He's wondering if you still want to have lunch with him today—is that something you want to do?"*

Joe Urschel, supervising producer of *USA Today on TV* ◼

business term in large media companies these days. That's where you have a newspaper, you set up a Web site, you try to do some TV news feeds, you feed news about your newspaper stories to your local TV station. In the utopian view, everybody is working together and it's all the same news product.

It's interesting that what we did on *USA Today on TV*—what we got killed for by critics and the public—everybody has since adopted. The banners on the stories, the people walking on newspaper headlines, the monitor walls, the quick stories, the rapid pace. It's funny, what they all said was terrible, now they are all doing.

Steve Friedman finds one other bit of wisdom in the failed enterprise we shared. With some bemusement, Steve recently recalled:

"I was at one of those big dinners in Washington that the president was at—the Radio & Television Correspondents Dinner. And I'm standing there, and who comes up to me but a Gannett executive who was against the deal with the Grant Tinker Company, a guy who was against putting *USA Today* on television, a guy who couldn't wait to sell the studio . . . and he grabbed me and hugged me. So, America is the greatest place in the world. You can lose $50 million of their money and they actually don't hate you!"

It was just a matter of time before the editor who had labored for various eminent publishers—Jock Whitney, Otis Chandler, William Randolph Hearst—would work his way around to the publishing tycoon who owns the *Times* of London, the *New York Post,* and HarperCollins books, not to mention Twentieth Century–Fox film studios, the Fox Television network, and Fox Cable News.

Not content with all that, Rupert Murdoch had bought *TV Guide* in 1992, hired a British editor, Anthea Disney, and together they had saved *TV Guide* from hitting the iceberg. Anthea really cleaned house. One of her most imaginative changes was to make a certain 70-year-old editor the head of their Los Angeles bureau.

Murdoch wanted *TV Guide* to be the powerful force that it had once been. The magazine had been going downhill and had undergone a descent into trivia. Anthea Disney wanted a Los Angeles bureau that would have the respect of the TV industry, and a bureau chief people knew. I guess she felt that if the bureau was headed by a traditional journalist, the magazine might take on some needed gravity.

When I arrived early in 1992, I brought in a staff of establishment reporters—people who actually wanted to come into the *TV Guide* office. Before my arrival, that had not always been the case. There was one writer who came in every three or four months if the weather was good. Veteran journalists on the staff were edging toward the door. The L.A. bureau was not an office that was run *in* the office. Writers would do walk-ons. I changed that a bit. I was used to running a newspaper, so I knew how to run a magazine with newspaper deadlines. The screensaver on my office computer bore one of my favorite mottoes: "Begin at once, and do the best you can."

I tried for more interesting stories, free of puffery, as I had done a decade earlier at *Entertainment Tonight*. Articles such as "The Stars' Ten

A Stormy Relationship

When I first worked with Jim at the Los Angeles Times, *he was more like a father figure. I was 23 years old. We had a very troubled relationship. I was wild and he would call me in and say, "Shape up or ship out." We did not have a great relationship. Because he expected a lot more than I was able to give at that point.*

Then we had this second chance when we worked together at TV Guide. *And we collaborated. You could bounce ideas off Jim, and you know immediately whether it was a good idea or not.*

He was a fountain. He was in before everybody, clipping all the newspapers and magazines, and reading everything. And by the time you came in, he had 25 story ideas. "What about this? . . . Look at this Wall Street Journal *. . . What about this in the* New York Times? *What about this?"*

But if you didn't perform for him, if you didn't meet your deadlines, if you did less than your best, he was not someone you wanted to work for. Because he is unforgiving if you are not doing your best.

Mary Murphy

Tips for Summer Vacations" were less welcome. I preferred articles like the one our ace writer, Mary Murphy, wrote: "Roseanne—The Lucy of the Nineties." It was about comedy, but it contained a lot of hard research about the troubled world of TV's most prominent comedienne.

In 1994, *TV Guide* decided that they wanted something other than what I could give them—they were entering a more computerized era of editing. They wanted a younger man who was more at home with computers, which was their constitutional right. I wasn't all that adept at the technology.

I tried to clear the path for my successor, Vince Cosgrove. I brought him into the picture so that no one felt alienated. I told the bureau staff that Vince was going to be great for the magazine, that he was going to be a wonderful editor, that he was just what they needed. And he has certainly worked out well.

CHAPTER 19

◆

The Geezer and the Kids

The phone rang. It was Will Hearst, grandson of William Randolph Hearst.

"I want you to meet someone," he said. "It's a guy named Joe Kraus. He and his young pals have invented a search engine to find things on the Internet. It's a new start-up company and it would be competing with Yahoo!, the leader in the search field now."

Underdogs are my life, I thought.

"What would I do for them?" I asked.

"They think that people will want to understand what's out there on all those Web sites. It's an editorial job, and they don't know anything about editorial content. They're technical people."

"Sure, have them call me," I said. "What the hell."

A few years before I had built a bridge for Will Hearst that brought him back into the family business. I hired him for the *Los Angeles Herald-Examiner* and put him in charge of graphics. So he was returning the favor.

When I'd created editorial content for Prodigy six years earlier, the Internet was mainly an electronic bulletin board where academics posted their research so that colleagues anywhere in the world could share it instantly. By 1993, though, businesses had discovered the Internet, and the then-nascent World Wide Web, and were trying to define their commercial potential.

But what was this search engine thing? Well, Joe Kraus and five class-mates fresh out of Stanford, with a sack of rice for nutrition and an electric dryer to ward off the chill, had invented it in a San Jose garage. "It" was search engine technology that was supposed to be better and faster than whatever Yahoo! used to enable subscribers to locate their quarry in the trackless jungle of the Web.

So at the beginning of 1994 the 72-year-old editor met with the 24-year-old techie. Joe Kraus studied my résumé and asked me some questions about my work experience, although it was clear that he wasn't a big newspaper reader.

Then he asked, "What do you do to relax?"

"I play a little golf."

"Where?"

"At the Bel-Air," I said.

"My grandfather plays there."

"Oh, what's his name?"

"Archie Haljun," he replied.

"The dentist," I said. "I've played with him."

And that's what I remember most about our first meeting: "The grandfather thing," which is also the title of my friend Saul Turteltaub's recent book.

And now here's what Joe remembers about our meeting:

"When I met Jim, I'm thinking—how do I convince this guy that what we're doing is worthwhile? I hope I don't look like an idiot. Jim seemed like a guy who could make it happen for us—give us instant credibility. I mean, we were a bunch of 24-year-olds running around, trying to hire people who knew ten times more than we did about editorial. What we *did* know was that our technology was great."

Joe Kraus and his friends sensed there was real money to be made if they could tell people where things were on the Web. Their search engine was able to direct people to maybe a third of the millions of Web sites that were out there, and according to Joe and his partners, it could do it faster and better than Yahoo! But Joe realized that he would need some good reason for people to come back to his group's engine—beyond Yahoo!, there were rivals like Lycos and Infoseek. Joe had been looking for a way to make their engine more than a mere navigation device. (They called their software "Architext"—they would later change its name to "Excite.")

Thus the techies turned to the ancient mariner. I would be the point man in their effort to make their software distinctive. Joe Kraus wondered: What if we could bring to the Internet some of the color and snap this guy brought to old-fashioned print journalism?

I called Digby Diehl. I had worked with Digby at the *Los Angeles Times,* the *Los Angeles Herald-Examiner,* and Prodigy. He knew his way around a computer—certainly more than I did. I brought Digby along to my second meeting with Joe.

It was the first trip for both of us from L.A. to Silicon Valley—Mountain View, to be specific. I was candid with Digby: "Sometimes they can be overwhelming with their tech-talk. I certainly need another pair of eyes and ears to evaluate what they're talking about."

The young partners had their offices in a big industrial park, a stark white structure with tinted windows—it gave no clue about its tenants. Joe and his pals were working in four rooms in a small part of an upstairs floor. It was their first set of offices, and the place was spartan,

---

The Millionaires Next Door

What do you get when you combine raw brainpower, 80-hour workweeks and 50-pound sacks of rice and beans?

Just four years out of Stanford, the founders of Excite still marvel at the wild rocket ride that blasted them from the Stanford dorms to millionaire status at the tender age of 25. But in a world of unbridled hype about the high-tech revolution, these guys are authentic. . . . Now a sobering reality stares the young entrepreneurs in the face. Excite made it big because the founders devised a powerful way to help a new world of Internet users find what they wanted among millions of websites. But in the race to cater to the digital hordes, the company is up against life-threatening competition.

Stanford *magazine, May–June 1997*

even by old-fashioned newspaper standards. They were still installing the phones. Digby and I wore sport jackets but were tieless, as a concession to our youthful hosts. They wore T-shirts and jeans.

We sat down with the half-dozen guys who had started this whole thing. The purpose of the meeting was to bring me up to speed on what they hoped to accomplish, so I could provide them with the *content*.

Joe wasn't too sure exactly what we were looking for, and he spewed tech-talk and drew diagrams on an erasable white board with various colored markers. I guess I understood perhaps half of what he said.

At one point Graham Spencer, who was *the* technical genius of the group, took over and explained the process. He communicated perfectly, provided you were well versed in computer technology and the intricacies of Web sites.

I looked at it like a journalist.

"It seems to me," I said, "that what you need to do is make this exciting for readers and users."

But more than the jargon puzzled me. I didn't quite understand how they were going to make any money, if anyone could use their technology without paying for it, and all they would be doing for income was selling advertising space to other Web sites—none of which were too prosperous. How would this make money? I was to learn.

I had been thinking about the search-engine process, as much as I understood it. Someone who went to the Architext Web site and used their technology to locate, say, manufacturers of rustic pine furniture, or information about a pop star, would quickly be provided with a list of Web sites, each of which had a link that would let the user click once and be transported to the site.

But that list culled its description of the site from the words *on* the site, so it really didn't tell a user much at all. It struck me that if each Web site was, in effect, an entertainment or educational "program," then what users needed was a sort of *TV Guide* of the Internet—listings that would give a concise summary of each site.

The Architext guys agreed with my notion. Okay, they said, give us about 100,000 Web site reviews, and how fast can you do it? How about yesterday?

I knew the reviews had to be young and hip, bright and sometimes irreverent, because if I had come away from my meeting with one impression, it was that this was a young person's game.

I told the Architext kids that I could put together a network of journalists to provide these site reviews. Sometimes my means of expression is elliptical. I can be as incomprehensible as any techie. So I'm not sure that they were entirely getting what I was saying. It was not the most communicative exchange.

I was certainly in a different world from these youngsters. They were incredibly technically oriented. At that time, the entire Internet was technically oriented. This was before the mass of people began using the Web. These 24-year-olds were not *verbal* people. I've had a lot of 24-year-olds in my newsrooms, because at the *Star* and the *Her-Ex* they were just about the only people I could afford to hire.

In the newsroom we had a sense of community. We shared a language of excitement and commitment to telling great news stories. The news business runs on that kind of energy, the kind that comes from kids with dreams and drive. These computer kids were smart, but they weren't verbal in the way I was used to.

Driving back to the San Jose airport, I confessed that I had understood maybe half of what they had said. Digby confessed that he was equally at sea.

When I got home I went to my Rolodex. It seemed to be a great opportunity for some journalists. My Rolodex is a who's who of journalists young and old, each with his or her own voice, some still in journalism, some writing books, some practicing publicity, some working as consultants, free-lancing in the corporate world . . . a range of activities. We were setting up a far-flung network across the country with about six staffers planned back East and another 14 on the West Coast to get things started. It was an easy sell.

I started making calls and signing people up night and day. For that matter, I started getting calls from the Architext crew at all hours. They were incredibly driven, incredibly enthusiastic, and extremely focused. They never seemed to sleep. They had cots in their offices, and very little sense of time. They thought nothing of calling at three in the morning.

> ■ Grace Lichtenstein Recalls How Legends Met
>
> *There was a story in the* New York Times *business news section in 1994. In it Joe Kraus talked about building a great editorial staff. I wrote him an e-mail note saying that I had pretty good credentials and would like to be a part of such a group. You called. You introduced yourself on the phone, and I blurted out: "You mean the legendary Jim Bellows?" And you said, "Are you the legendary Grace Lichtenstein?"*
>
> *I was terribly pleased you recognized my name and thought to myself, "Jeez, maybe there is a place in that brave new World Wide Web for us wily veterans."*
>
> *Despite the fact that Excite canned its great editorial staff in one fell swoop, I never forgot the fun we all had making good money and being clever, most of the time without getting more formally dressed than a bathrobe and without leaving our living rooms.* ■

Joe Kraus was a little surprised by the extent of my network: "It was amazing. He hired all these editors and he did it *overnight*. He just picked up the phone and *BLAM,* we had twenty editors writing reviews."

I told everyone I called about the brave new world that beckoned, how we were needed to bring some sense into the technical world of the Internet. The old media were going to meet the new media. Journalists would teach techies the magic of words, and they in turn would teach us the magic of the Internet—while paying us to learn.

I worked with Digby in assembling a stylebook for our writers. I was using *TV Guide* as a model of the effective use of brevity. You had to pack a lot of impact into a few words. I had learned at Prodigy that computer users weren't going to read very much.

So I set a 40-word maximum for our summaries. If you wrote less than that, fine. But 40 was the limit. Writing short is a skill all its own and, interestingly, it was the younger writers I brought aboard who found it easiest. Maybe they had been trained by the rat-tat-tat of quick TV news items; maybe shorthand comes naturally to the young.

Here's part of what our stylebook said:

"Be descriptive, convey personality, be concise, show some style, display some attitude. . . . Keep it crisp, a little irreverent, write with flavor." (That's 21 words.)

We set up a national network of editors and writers linked by computer modems. I sought journalists experienced in specific areas— sports, food, politics, business, science, health, and entertainment. There were ten major categories, and dozens of subcategories. I hired thirty writers, and later made ten of them managers.

As they churned out reviews, we were operating under the goofy code name "Bnoopy"—a name that even a dedicated Web surfer wouldn't stumble on. These former newsmen and women called themselves "Bnoopsters," and for them, it was a pretty good deal: They were paid on a piecework basis for part-time work they could do in their bathrobes at home. The paychecks for staffers usually ran between $400 and $700 a week, depending on how many hours they were willing to work.

At the beginning, however, the company was being financed by just a few venture capitalists in Silicon Valley, and the contributors' paychecks were sometimes delayed for weeks as the company waited on infusions of capital. Another hurdle was technical: Contributors had computers of varying ages, and connections with the Web at their homes that ranged from very slow to moderately fast.

All the reviews that were produced went into "the bank" in the Bnoopy system, and I could view them on my computer at my home in Los Angeles or at the cubicle they set up for me in Mountain View. At any time day or night I could correct the reviews or send them back to the writer for rewriting. It was a marvelous technical development for editorial management because the writers were all over the country, and—again—the "community" of the computer world was successful.

But management long distance sometimes has its drawbacks, as Joe Kraus overheard once when he passed by my cubicle:

"I'm walking by and Jim is on the phone with somebody, and I listened. Apparently the guy had made a spelling mistake, and this was the third time Jim had to tell him about it. Jim is at the end of his patience, and I'm 24 and thinking, 'The guy made a *spelling* mistake.

Come on, it's no big deal. It's the *Web.'* The guy on the other end didn't just let go of it. He started to fight Jim. And I could hear the guy's voice saying something like 'You know, I really think you're being—' And Jim growled, 'You're done! You're done!' and hangs up the phone. And I'm like, 'Wow, is that how it works in the newspaper business?'"

As Architext cruised toward the date when its whole operation would go up on the Web—which was the point at which they changed their name to Excite—funding became more regular, so much so that the company gave each contributor a $1,500 hardware allowance to defray the cost of a new computer (more expensive then than now), as well as a special ISDN modem that would allow our editors to download at up to ten times the speed they were accustomed to.

About six months after we started, it was time to go beyond the virtual office. I thought we needed to have our editorial team meet one another—most of them knew one another only from e-mails and phone calls—and meet Joe.

We gathered at my house. I've hosted a lot of editorial meetings, but this one was different from the rest. One of our editorial managers, Larry Dietz, described it as "one of the most delightful business gatherings I've ever attended—a true representation of the word 'collegial.' I'd worked for Jim on *Entertainment Tonight,* the first time that Jim had reinvented himself in an area where he hired people who were unfamiliar with the technology at hand. And there were some killer egos in the room. But the Excite crew seemed genuinely cooperative, without competitiveness, perhaps because we were all writing anonymously, so there weren't any stars. And that feeling continued."

We met every month or two. Mary Pitzer found that "those gatherings were the most fun and educational part of the job. Even though we worked alone at our homes, we were a team. And those meetings were a big reason why."

They had the chance to meet the parade of founders and executives, most notably Joe Kraus. They would go home energized by the vision of the future—but one thing troubled Mary: "The focus was always on technology. Content was always secondary." Her fears turned out to be prophetic.

One of our other managers, Alex Auerbach, who had been a financial reporter at the *Los Angeles Times,* asked Kraus the multimillion-dollar question: Where was the cash flow to come from? Kraus's answer was significant. The Excite Web site would attract a lot of eyeballs, which would make it a great spot for advertising. Moreover, if a visitor asked for automobile-related sites, the technology could automatically place a car ad on that page of listings. And couldn't a premium be charged for referring such a motivated visitor? Moreover, deals were going to be struck so that a Web site receiving an order from someone taken to the site by Excite would pay a few pennies for the referral. Those few pennies per transaction would add up.

Some of the journalists who were between 40 and 45, along with their 72-year-old honcho, found it a little strange to have a 24-year-old boss. But Joe handled himself as well as any 40-year-old. When, at the end of the meeting, Joe asked around for a lift to his parents' house in Encino, he was suddenly transformed into a college student bumming a ride.

The meetings crackled with fun, but they had a serious side. These people were all distinct personalities, articulate and sometimes opinionated. We got into some heated discussions about where we were

---

Ex-citations: Excite's Editorial Style Guide

Be descriptive. *You are a writer in cyberspace. For most of your readers this is alien territory. Give them some familiar guideposts . . .*

Convey personality. *This is not the Yellow Pages. Show some style in your language. Give me some attitude. Write like yourself. Not cute. Not flip. Be knowledgeable, intelligent, honest, amusing . . .*

Emphasize freshness. *Is there something new or special about the site? Help your reader see how this fits into his or her life today.*

Be concise. *Is every word necessary? Is each word the most accurate and energetic word you could use?*

going with our reviews, and especially, as the start date grew imminent, how they should be organized.

We needed to organize the Web site summaries in ways that would
make them easily accessible to people who were using this kind of
directory to find what they wanted on the Internet. Looming over us
was the specter of the search engine Yahoo!, which was open for business, attracting a lot of visitors, and which had a highly developed
hierarchy of Web site categories. We didn't want to mimic Yahoo!, so
our discussions went on late into the night. It was almost librarian
talk—we were creating our own Dewey decimal system.

Finally we were in a crunch, so three managers—Tim Robinson, Ben
Cosgrove, and Larry Dietz—met at Excite headquarters for a two-day
blitz to create a hierarchy of the reviews. Dietz remembers that day:

> When Tim and I got to the offices we practically tripped
> over a couch that was jammed into the entranceway. It
> was obvious from the crumpled blanket that it was used
> as a bed. Ben had gotten there before us, and had started
> to create a structure. While the work was almost nonstop,
> we benefited from Ben's sense of humor. He wrote one of
> the best reviews we ever had. One of his areas was human
> relations, which meant he was in charge of reviewing what
> were then only a few sex sites on the Web. The search spi-
> der that grabbed sites for all of us to review had come up
> with a chat group on bestiality, something like alt.sex/
> animals. Ben's review was: "Lassie! Go home! Quick!"

About a week before the launch, it suddenly occurred to the lawyers
that no one had bothered to lock up all rights to these reviews in perpe-
tuity. What if the site was a great success and the managers demanded
a piece of the action? So a deal was struck: Our free-lancers would become permanent, part-time employees. Their weekly pay was increased
to $1,000. They would be given stock options. All twenty signed up.
(My own special incentive options would become fully vested when
we finished 100,000 reviews, or in four years.)

Now, writing snappy Web reviews may seem humble duty for the guy who edited the *Trib* and the *Star,* but for me the challenge was to bring quality and integrity to it, no matter what the length. Besides, I felt that site reviews were just the beginning for our team.

We were going to broaden what we did. I added features from daily polls and discussion groups to historical quotes and interactive cartoons. And though Excite had no interest in creating a Web news service, we planned to supply site reviews to newspapers so they could create regional site listings of their own. Excite signed content agreements with the *Los Angeles Times,* Reuters, and the Tribune Company. Two of our managers, Tim Robinson and Larry Dietz, recorded one-minute news features about the Web that Tribune Company newspapers added to their group of phone-information recordings that were made available to readers.

It was too good to last.

The Excite kids came to the conclusion that nobody really wanted to read descriptions of the sites. People wanted to *go* to the site and make their own determination about its value. No matter how witty or trenchant the description of the place, they didn't care. And where a newspaper can continue to run a feature that isn't as well read as others but is considered to be prestigious, or well written, at Excite, the numbers were all that counted.

Counting on one hand, not enough visitors to the Excite site were clicking on the reviews. Counting on the other, those reviews were costing a million bucks a year.

The kids were concentrating on making their search engine as fast as possible. Sparkling prose wasn't going to bring more "eyeballs" to their site. They buried the reviews, making a visitor have to click through a page or two to get to them. Overall visitor numbers went up. Review visitor numbers didn't.

So they pulled the plug.

Joe Kraus called a meeting in January 1998 at a motel near LAX. Everyone assumed it was to announce a new direction for Excite. A new CEO, George Bell, who'd come from consumer magazines, was on

---

New-Media Nightmare

Reporters, writers and editors headed West to teach the techies a thing or two about content. So why all the hangdog looks now?

Sighs Michael Kinsley, former editor of The New Republic *and now editor of Microsoft's on-line magazine,* Slate: *"Content is not going to be the killer app on the Internet, at least not in the near future." . . . Silicon Valley isn't scrambling to hire old-media hounds anymore. . . . Don't look for want ads in* Editor & Publisher *or* Columbia Journalism Review *. . .*

Old-media types may yet play a role on the Net but it's likely to be a bit part . . ."

Fortune, June 22, 1998

---

board. But the packets stacked in front of Joe weren't good news. The assembled editors were given a choice—be laid off and accept the vesting of 3,000 of their options, or move to the Bay Area and go to work for Excite full-time at the same $1,000 a week. Not surprisingly, all but two—Tim Robinson and Marnie Davis—elected to take their walking papers.

Digby Diehl recalled that day: "I was stunned. We thought we were an integral part of their plan. They had led us to believe that we were playing an important role in the direction of the company. Yeah, we probably needed some fine tuning, but we thought we were doing something *important.*"

It was a surreal scene. There was a luncheon buffet in the meeting room. Mary Pitzer said, "I remember thinking I ought to eat something, because the gravy train was ending."

Joe Kraus and his partners had come to believe that there is what they called "a utility-oriented approach to the Internet for most people. . . . You didn't need to take a whole lot of *joy* on your journey to the destination you wanted. Your attitude was, Get me there and get me there quickly. For services like Excite, it wasn't about great writing."

The stock, meanwhile, had fallen, then risen again. Some of our people who had not cashed in their first options had a nice bonus from their part-time work. Most sold their shares at once; but the company kept growing, and the stock price rocketed. Those who left early missed the big payday when Excite was bought by @Home and the stock split and split again.

Taking the longer view, however, after the Internet boom peaked in January 2000, those shares kept tumbling and by September 2001 they were worth less than a dollar a share. On September 29, 2001, the *New York Times* ran the story of At Home filing for bankruptcy: "The At Home Corporation, a once-mighty Internet portal turned high-speed access provider, filed for bankruptcy protection today, a victim of shrinking on-line advertising revenue and the collapse of the dot-com bubble."

Excite was a company that sprouted in two years from an idea dreamed up in a dorm at Stanford to an enterprise valued in the marketplace at $750 million. For a time it was the second most popular site on the Web, attracting more than 20 million visitors a day. The other part of the young men's vision—the important part, having to do with cash revenues—didn't work out as well. There were ads, but nowhere near the projected numbers, and little referral income materialized. Excite entered into a lot of alliances, but by then my contract had expired, and I, too, was gone, although I had to wave a lawyer at George Bell to receive all my contracted-for options, most of which I'm happy to say I sold before the stock bottomed out in the fall of 2001.

However, it was a phenomenal period in the history of journalism and communications. A battalion of mostly white, mostly young, mostly male techies made a fortune, although it's not clear how many of them managed to cash out before their particular stock collapsed. It was one of the most dramatic eras of technical innovation in the century. It forced traditional newspapers to again think about their mission—they were already grappling with the fact that evening news on TV gave most people a quick overview of the big stories the night before morning newspapers were delivered. Now the Internet gave Web surfers the chance to call up headline news in real time from their workplace computers.

Of course, some newspapermen are asking about the Internet's ability to distort the news. They point out with dismay how quickly print

Tim Robinson Tells of Exciting Ride with His Excite Stock

The April day in 1996 when Excite went public was, well, exciting. Another reviewer, Margaret Leslie (Marney) Davis, and I went to Yamashiro, a Japanese restaurant overlooking Hollywood and drank champagne—but most of all, we fantasized about the potential value of the 6,000 stock options we had been granted at 3½ cents a share and which would be vesting over the next four years. What if it went all the way to $20 by the end of that period? That would be $120,000. And, as more champagne took effect, what if it hit $50? That would be $300,000.

The stock, priced on IPO day at $17, promptly dropped to $6 and stayed in that range for quite a while. Then, in January 1997, Joe Kraus—the 24-year-old nonengineer on the founding team, with whom we had most closely worked—summoned us all to a motel near Los Angeles Airport. The packets stacked in front of him weren't good news. The editors Jim had assembled were given a choice: be laid off and accept full vesting for 3,000 of their stock options, or move to the Bay Area at the same rate of $1,000 a week. All but Marnie and I did the former, and became ex-Exciters.

The stock, meanwhile, was back in the $17 range—some cashed in then at that rate, which, at $51,000, was a nice bonus for what amounted to an 18-month free-lance job.

However, the company kept growing—and the stock kept rising. Excite was bought by @Home. The stock split twice. Those same 3,000 shares would have become 12,000 shares. If sold at the highest price of $60 a share after those splits, they would have been worth $720,000 instead of $51,000.

And, for me, who stayed at Excite for the full vesting period, my original 6,000 shares would have become 24,000 shares. If I had held them all, and sold them at the post-split high of $60, my "what's a URL" phone call from Jim would have turned into $1,440,000.

But, alas, I didn't—and it didn't.

In fact, the company declared bankruptcy five and a half years later with the stock at 14 cents.

Robinson and Davis were two of
our writer-editor-managers.

reporters jumped on the Clinton scandal and ratcheted it up to nuclear-explosion size overnight. Reporters driven by the speed of the Internet to get a story into circulation rapidly trumpeted the sexual allegations and trampled rules of ethics in chasing the story. But as Jack Shafer said in *The New York Times Magazine*, "When the deadline whistle blows, things get messy. . . . Technology is neutral. . . . The Internet is a tool with the same good and bad aspects as any other."

Today there isn't a lot of sparkling prose on the Internet.

I guess it was no surprise that it would be the techies who would decide the relative importance of prose versus technology. And it was the techies who had the clout, while itinerant editors and writers were the underdogs.

Underdog—there's that word again.

■ Excite Has a Midlife Crisis

Internet pioneers Joe Kraus and Graham Spencer are wondering what to do next. Both are 29 years old. The startup they founded in 1993 along with four Stanford dorm-mates has grown into Internet media success story ExciteAtHome, they're multimillionaires and they've ridden out the delirious '90s boom to a soft landing . . .

"It was time to try something new," says Spencer, a tech wizard whose innovative search engine technology helped make the Internet accessible to the masses . . .

For Kraus and Spencer, the bust is a personal story. They've watched as the decline in Internet stock valuations took shares of Excite, which traded at a 52-week high of $50, down to a humbling $4.77. They've seen their colleagues and rivals, once lauded as heroes of the New Economy, become the butt of Jay Leno jokes . . .

Kraus and Spencer both realize their next venture won't match the thrill of starting a company with four friends and growing it into a 3,000-strong corporation. . . . Kraus wants to fulfill his fantasy of just being a kid for a while.

"Most of my friends went backpacking in Europe in their 20s. I missed that," he says. He's heading to the Himalayas.

SiliconValley.com, March 2001 ■

But, despite the fact that our role at Excite was short-lived, I was delighted to have been invited to the party—especially at an age well past retirement for most people.

And—at last I had a nest egg. Better late than never! I tried to express my gratitude to Will Hearst a few years later about providing me with the means to financial security. In his characteristically graceful way he said, "Well, Jim, what goes around comes around."

CHAPTER 20

◆

Last Word, and the Towers

I wrote the first draft of this last chapter before September 11, 2001. My opening sentence was "I would call my attitude about the future of journalism 'guarded optimism.'" Today, a few weeks after that tragically defining moment in our history, I am removing "guarded" in this final draft. Not that there are no reasons for concern when we look at the future—and I intend to touch on those—but my optimism has been totally vindicated by the way the media have responded to September 11.

Last summer I was talking about the future of journalism with the Pulitzer Prize winner David Halberstam, Bill Kovach of the Committee of Concerned Journalists, and my longtime friend Dick Wald, with whom I have worked for years in newspapers and television. Dick said that the current state of what we report reflects "the absence of any national crisis. The cult of celebrity has taken center stage from the reporting of serious significant events that directly affect all Americans."

He predicted that such an "event" was inevitable in the next decade. In fact, it came to pass within weeks. Being as objective as I possibly can in the initial aftermath of the terrorist attacks on New York and Washington, I have to say that I am very proud of my profession.

■ Mitch Albom on the Media After 9/11/2001

How newspapers, TV, and the Internet will be changed for years to come by the Twin Tower tragedy. *See page 317.*

Overall, the newspapers and broadcast media have done an excellent job of reporting in the midst of monumental confusion, mass shock, and overwhelming sorrow. The coverage has been restrained and respectful, informative and involved, comprehensive and compassionate, as the story continues to unfold.

Newspapers have exemplified what the print media do best—thorough and accurate reporting on all aspects of a huge story from the geopolitical to the personal. The news divisions of all the networks have been responsible and responsive, resisting the sensational and the purely voyeuristic.

But let's look ahead. Why am I optimistic about the future of journalism? First, because I'm optimistic by nature. I believe that the importance of a free press as a public service will always be valued and protected. Second, I'm optimistic because the quality of writing and reporting has improved a lot over the last 50 years. And third, the proliferation of sources of news is a good development—it gives more control to the people and less to the historic gatekeepers.

As a lifelong maverick, that appeals to me.

The role of a free press in maintaining a free society is self-evident. The first responsibility of newspapers, in particular, is to be the eyes and ears of the public—an early-warning system. This requires more emphasis than I see right now on crusading journalism—spotlighting societal problems and public and private corruption, and giving a platform to the folks who have solutions to offer. Americans count on their newspapers to bring important issues to their attention. And throughout the history of journalism in this country, I think we've done a pretty fair job. But I do worry that the focus on this sacred trust is blurring.

I see better writing and reporting in the top newspapers today. Good reporting means paying attention to details, exploring conflict, revealing the human dimensions that make a story accessible. It's best if the reporter leaves the judgment of those facts to the reader or viewer.

Above all, stories should be *interesting*. And newspaper stories will be interesting if the reporter is *curious*. If there's one single quality that a reporter needs it's curiosity. A flood of questions should arise about any story the reporter is assigned to cover:

How did this happen? Why?

Who could shed light on it?

How does it relate to my audience?

How can I best communicate that?

Is this just an isolated event or is there more to the story?

Do I have all the details?

I think the high-speed access to information via our computer screens will mean that most of us will get the "news" we care about by pushing a button. We won't have to pore over pages of newsprint to get the facts we want: the weather in town and in the city we're traveling to; the stock price of what we own and what we're watching; the ball scores of our favorite teams. And the day's headlines will be customized for us while we sleep, all in living, colorful, moving words and pictures via fiber-optic cable.

Of course, the problem with the Internet as a source of news and information is that the writers, reporters, and content providers who decide what material travels through cyberspace don't necessarily follow the traditional rules of journalism. As Halberstam says, "Is there as much energy in the editing and verification process, or is it more a bunch of people scrambling for attention?"

Mitch Albom weighs in brilliantly on the "morphing" of newspapers and computers elsewhere in this chapter. I think David's concerns about editing and accuracy are valid, especially in view of recent reports that hackers have successfully altered the content of Yahoo! News Service stories.

But if electronic news and information is the preferred delivery system of the future, our government had better make damn sure that every household has the basic equipment, rather than worrying about another pipsqueak tax cut!

So, where does that leave the daily newspaper? I think it will become a source more of commentary than of news. As the world shrinks and becomes more complex, we're going to need more in-depth analyses and a spectrum of commentary from experts. We're going to need a broader horizon to scan for events that impact us, in addition to personal screens that are servants of our self-interest.

That "broader horizon" is what concerns David Halberstam. He said in the discussion referred to earlier,

> I grew up in an age of pluralism in newspapers and magazines. One of the things that has happened in our society in the last 30 years is the decline of the general-circulation magazine that took you outside of your own narrow interests. But, those publications that provided opportunities to be informed about things you didn't even know you care about, have been replaced by niche magazines addressed to doctors who can fly and fishermen who can fly-fish in salt water, among other tiny affluent special interests.
>
> These ever-smaller communities of common interests cause more separation between people. The result is that people become more conspiratorial in their view of their society, their neighbors, and their government. Narrow magazines perpetuate isolated communities.
>
> I like general circulation. I like the newspaper as a reflection of the larger community, local, national or international.

Now to the *guarded* part of my optimism.

I have a lot of concern about several media trends. One of them is the pursuit of wealth and the glorification of money. Another is the confusion about traditional standards of fairness and accuracy. And I'm positively alarmed about the concentration of ownership across all types of media—from newspapers, magazines, and books to TV, radio, and the Internet.

Let's talk about money first (everybody else does). Money is the culprit in all three of these trends. Magazines, TV, and radio have long been fixated on wealth and celebrity in their reporting. The amount of money that people make is a bigger story than the jobs they do. There is an avalanche of stories about money—how to make it, how to keep it, how to make a fortune.

Naturally this obsession with money influences reporters and editors.

Twenty-five years ago a young columnist I hired at the *Washington Star* got a big laugh when he said that he had gone into journalism "for the money." That's not a punchline today, when the desire for wealth compromises journalists who cover the financial markets and other journalists become stories themselves by virtue of their incomes.

The most pernicious effect of money madness in newspapers, though, is the crumbling of The Wall between editorial and advertising. For generations, editors and publishers alike have honored the importance of denying advertisers the ability to influence editorial content. This is changing, and I put the blame squarely on the shoulders of the editors and reporters.

It's in the genes of publishers to push against The Wall. They expect resistance. Good publishers welcome it. But too many editors today don't push back hard enough. And it shows in the product, as well as in the growing disrespect of the public for the media.

What's also disturbing to me is the recent development of editors becoming publishers. Whoever thought that was a great idea? In the best of all possible worlds, editors aren't even remotely qualified to be publishers, and vice versa. Nowadays many journalists brag as much about the stock price of their megamedia parent company as they do about their Pulitzers!

The almighty buck also plays a big role in weakening journalistic standards of fairness and accuracy in reporting, and editorial judgment about what to cover.

The downside of a profusion of media outlets is that everybody doesn't play by the same rules. This never used to bother newspapers—the newspaper world managed to adjust to the trauma of TV stealing their jump on the news without losing its soul. It led to the death of lots of afternoon papers—I attended a couple of the funerals—but most of the remaining papers retained their identity and their integrity.

I'm afraid that newspapers have a perilous grasp on their souls today. They are competing in the lowest-common-denominator race with tabloids, trash TV, shock-jock radio, and the rumor-plagued Internet. They are fighting for eyeballs, advertising dollars, and a thumbs-up from Wall Street for maximizing profits (not serving the public) as their primary goal.

Don't get me wrong. I don't think newspapers should shy away from tough stories, exposés, or gossip. My newspapers didn't! Reporting on things that people may consider unsavory, impolite, or invasive is a right we have—one that goes along with our duty to judge the data, fact-check the story, and balance the reporting. Of course, we make mistakes, we don't always get it right, but I have the uneasy feeling that we tried harder in the past.

The worst thing about media concentration is the silencing of diverse points of view—all those lovely shades of gray. It's true that if people don't like their newspaper, they can watch TV, turn on the radio, or read a magazine or a book. But when the same company owns all those outlets, there is a real danger that all those media will be singing the same song.

A possible antidote to this conformity, however, is the Center for Public Integrity in Washington, founded by Charles Lewis, a former CBS *60 Minutes* producer, to pursue important stories that the networks view as "too expensive" to uncover and report.

In the ten years since its founding with funding by philanthropic organizations, the center has broken major stories by using the resources of the World Wide Web and the talents of like-minded investigative reporters.

Remember—lots of my optimism stems from my confidence that there will always be mavericks like Charlie Lewis among men and women who see themselves as guardians of the free press and see their profession as a calling, not just a job.

There is another threat to free speech and the free flow of information in the way our government lately has been letting big business concentrate ownership, take control of our communications outlets, and destroy competition.

This reconfiguration of the media has also led to the diminishment of the news product within the clashing cultures and values within these new megacompany partnerships. The people in charge do not cherish the First Amendment and a free press. Their focus is on managerial concerns, not editorial integrity. Because entertainment attracts a mass audience, too often news takes a backseat when investment funds and available resources are allocated. As well, TV news producers are pressured to add more "entertainment value" to their news.

Bill Kovach told us that a 2000 study by the Project for Excellence in Journalism found that since 1977 straight news as a percentage of stories in newspapers had declined from 61.1 percent to 30.7 percent and on network television from 51.4 percent to 34.3 percent.

There are several hundred fewer newspapers today than there were 20 years ago, and 2,500 fewer newsroom employees than in 1989. Many existing papers are owned by chains that the government is inviting to own more TV stations in the same markets.

This country has grown and prospered because of competition in the press. The public deserves a variety of views on important issues in the world, the nation, and the city. As the voices diminish in number, our lives are diminished, too.

But we're a feisty people. The British called us troublemakers during our revolution. Americans treasure their values and their hard-won freedoms. That's why the optimist in me wins out when I look ahead. Young men and women—mavericks like me—will see to it that their own and other voices are heard in the years to come. But it's important that they also understand the ethics of a free press. It's up to those of us who have benefited from the traditions we were handed to pass them on.

That's one of the reasons I wrote this book.

But here we are, deep into my "last word," and I haven't scratched the surface on my gratitude for my life in journalism. I encourage those of you burning with idealism to climb aboard. A career in news will let you change your world, and if you do it with passion and zeal, make it better. And you'll have more fun that you ever dreamed work could provide.

Passion, dedication, fun, the sense that you are making a difference—those are goals worth chasing, in life and in work.

Matter of fact, the concept of "zest, excitement, and pizzazz" as essential ingredients of one's work life seems to have disappeared. From everything I read about work today, it appears the fun has gone out of it for most people—except, perhaps, for those very brief moments before young entrepreneurs with great ideas get bought out by lumbering corporations or are demolished by the market.

Woven into the bunch of stale old newsmen's stories in this book, I have tried to put a subliminal message to young people on just how much joy I had at work, despite all the stresses and disappointments. I have tried to show how to love what you do—not just the money you make—and how to use work to create a rich and rewarding life, instead of being used by work and risk having no life at all.

So maybe you should think of this as a "how to" book on having fun and finding meaning and success in your work life, as seen through the eyes and jobs of a guy who has had it all.

Well, you'll have to excuse me now. I've got to be going. I've devoted two years to this backward book, and looking behind me is not my style. As I enter my 80th year, I'm looking ahead to new challenges. Got anything that needs starting or fixing?

Mitch Albom's View of the Future of Media After September 11, 2001

When terrorists hit the World Trade Center on September 11, 2001, they rocked the world of the everyday American.

Inadvertently, they rocked the newspaper world as well.

The first attacks, in New York City, came at 8:45 A.M. Many morning newspapers, at that point, were still yet to be read. On the West Coast, many were yet to be delivered. But with the first plane's fiery impact, all those newspapers were rendered obsolete. Who cared about anything else at that point?

Some papers rushed out "special" afternoon editions, bold headlines shouting "ATTACKED!" These were well intentioned, but hopelessly outdated even by the time they were printed. For most newspapers, a full-scale effort didn't reach America's front lawns until 20-plus hours after the tragedy.

And by that point, the event had become what all news events are destined to become if newspapers don't adjust—a TV story.

Print is second class.

This leads to a very important question for those of us who love our inky business: How do we keep up? In a CNN world, where pictures of war come almost instantly, how does a product that requires writing, layout, pagination, printing, shipping, driving, and porch-tossing even hope to remain vital?

Here's one newsman's suggestion: by morphing.

By changing form. By breaking traditionally held concepts.

And by playing to our strengths.

Which are? you ask. People. Personnel. Skills. The average newspaper reporting staff dwarfs even that of CNN, let alone local TV news. And the writing and reporting skills of print versus TV—not to mention the sources— are solidly in favor of print.

Our weaknesses?

The medium and the timetable.

How to fix that?

Change the medium and the timetable.

Medium first. Let's be honest. Newspapers' best hope is not on paper, it's in the air. Cyberspace. The Internet. I have heard the hosannas tossed to the lovely feel of the printed page, the rustle of papers as you flip them on the subway. Yes, yes, yes. And you know who usually tosses those hosannas? People who grew up reading newspapers. Not kids. Not teens. Not young professionals who have been clicking longer than they've been page-turning.

Newspapers need to realize that paper is slow, printing is slow, delivery is slow, and slow is death. I envision a newspaper of the future that not only runs on-line, but runs around the clock.

Which means we lose another long-cherished tradition: the deadline.

No more "Get it in by 11 P.M. so we can reach the outer suburbs by sunrise."

Uh-uh. Now it's get it in by 3:47, so we can have it up on the "refreshed 4 P.M. page."

I am serious. I see newspapers updated hourly. Full updates, not just a new opening sentence on a news story. You don't expect to get the same show on CNN at 4 P.M. as you do at 7 P.M., do you? Why expect that with newspapers?

Better to let a reader subscribe to a "new" newspaper every hour. Reporters could work in shifts, instead of everybody being on during the day and sleeping at night. News happens around the world at night. Why not have an 8 A.M.–4 P.M. shift, then a 4 P.M.–midnight shift, then a midnight–8 A.M. shift?

This would enable newspapers to do what they really need to do, update everything. Don't roll round the same tired column that no longer makes sense given the events of the day. Have a fresh new column up there.

Don't carry on the same old feature, when something has already changed with the profile subject. Run a new, updated feature. Same goes for op-ed pieces. Obituaries. Even TV listings in the case of "special" programming.

Mostly, we need to break the pattern of people reading the newspaper once in the morning and forgetting about it—or pretty soon, all we'll have left is the forgetting-about-it part. Remember, our advantage is resources. We should use them around the clock. Make readers believe they are getting something they can't get anywhere else—not even on the websites of

CNN or MSNBC, which tend to use newspaper reporting as their backbone anyhow.

This raises another important advantage for print: opinion. TV news has reporters. TV news has graphics. But, despite the proliferation of "analysts," there is very little thoughtful and succinct commentary on TV. Maybe because everyone is so busy firing questions.

This gives print an advantage. Readers get addicted to their columnists; they need to see what they are going to say. Newspapers should jump on that relationship. Which means the columnists and the opinion writers will need to be even more plentiful and more prominent in the newspapers of the future.

Imagine if, at 6 P.M., after your favorite baseball player was traded, you could read your favorite columnist's take on it, instead of waiting until the next morning.

Imagine if, following a terrible day on Wall Street, you could read a thorough economic analysis at night, before the markets reopened.

Imagine, if Madonna begins her new tour in L.A., reading a review just an hour after the show was over—with photos and perhaps a sound clip?

If you can't imagine this, then, sad to say, you are part of the problem, not the solution. Because all this is, in some way or another, already being done on the Internet. Only it's not being done by newspapers. It's being done by entrepreneurial Web-meisters who do not feel duty-bound to old-fashioned ideas of what newspapers must be.

And these Web-heads are soaking up audience every day.

Now, don't panic. I love the finger-staining ink pages, too. And there is no reason, in the foreseeable future, to do away with a morning print edition of the paper. From comics to coupons to box scores, there is a true and real value to it.

But think of that morning paper on September 11th which contained news that, before 8:45 A.M., may have seemed important.

One minute later, it couldn't have been more trivial.

Newspapers can be a lot of things, but they can never be trivial. Not if we want to see the one thing that keeps us all going: tomorrow.

■ Mitch Albom is the longtime sports columnist of the
Detroit Free Press and author of *Tuesdays with Morrie*.

ACKNOWLEDGMENTS

◆

The title of this book is *The Last Editor,* not *The Last Writer.* Hence, I owe a special debt to the many fine writers who have helped me write it. One of the greatest gifts of my life has been to work with so many wonderful writers. They have made me look good throughout my career and they are still doing it!

First among the writers who lent a hand with this book is Gerald Gardner. So much success depends on timing, and it was my good fortune that Gerry had the time free to translate my mumblings, my files, and the memories of my friends into a coherent story, full of conflict and irreverence.

This book also owes a lot to the cooperation and prose of the people I have worked with through the years, who have made my peripatetic career a joyful adventure. Their names march proudly across the end sheets of this book, in alphabetical array. From Mitch Albom to Tom Wolfe, they constitute a who's who of literary and media America. They have turned my memoir into an oral history of the golden age of journalism and made of my autobiography a sparkling anthology.

Keven Bellows, my wonderful wife of 30 years, knows me better than I know myself. That is normally a disquieting situation, but in a book of this kind, such knowledge is precious. Her keen insights coupled with her gift for language have enriched this book immeasurably, and her devotion and encouragement have been invaluable.

Then there is Dick Wald, my good right hand at the *Trib,* my colleague at ABC News, and now a professor at the Columbia School of

Journalism. His recollections, especially of the meeting with Bill Paley, and of other auspicious occasions added flavor to my story. Mary Anne Dolan, whom Keven refers to as my office "wife," has been a big help, too, especially in evoking our days at the *Washington Star* and inside the Hearst empire. And Jim Fain, the first of my press mentors, helped me by recalling my cub reporter days in Columbus, Georgia, and the elephant wars in Atlanta.

Then there are Digby Diehl, Ron La Brecque, and Steve Zousmer, each of whom lent a hand in the circuitous evolution of the book, in the early days before I found my way into Gerry's hands and the home of John McMeel at Andrews McMeel Universal.

Sterling Lord is my old and dear friend and literary agent, who first gave me hope by saying, "Thank you for sending me this marvelous proposal" and molded the early chapters so wisely.

I also want to thank filmmaker Steve Latham, who produced the fine PBS version of *The Last Editor.*

My debts, as usual, are beyond my ability to acknowledge them.

So I must thank you all in the same way I have always instructed you, with a shrug and a gesture and a laugh.

INDEX

◆

An "n" following a page number refers to a footnote. Page numbers in *italics* refer to sidebars.

Mitch Albom • Joe Allbritton • Martha Angle • Agnes Ash • Bill Baggs • Ted Beitchman • Keven Bellows • Mark Benerofe • Martin Bernheimer • Ray Bradbury • Ben Bradlee • Omar Bradley • Jimmy Breslin • Bubbles • Art Buchwald • Peter Bunzel • David Burgin • Richard Burton • Mary Langer Butler • Rubin Carson • Charles Champlin • Dorothy Buffum Chandler • Otis Chandler • Bill Chanin • Marian Christy • Tom Clark • Clark Clifford • Paul Conrad • Norman Corwin • Judith Crist • Loyal Davis • John Denson • James Dickenson • Digby Diehl • Larry Dietz • Barry Diller • Mary Anne Dolan • Maureen Dowd • Rick Du Brow • Mel Durslag • Rowland Evans • Jim Fain • Clay Felker • Mitchell Fink • Jim Flanigan • Bob Flick • Jane Fonda • Mary Lou Forbes • Don Forst • Steve Friedman • Lindsay Gardner • Daryl Gates • Robert Gehorsham • Jack Germond • John Goldhammer • John Goldsmith • Barry Goldwater • Richard Goodwin • Barry Gottehrer • Caroline Graham • Katharine Graham • Samuel Green • Ed Guthman • David Halberstam • Jim Head • Will Hearst III • Henry Heilbrunn • Heloise • Ernie Hitz • Woody Hochswender • J. Edgar Hoover • Barbara Howar • David Israel • Tom Jones • Marty Kaiser • Walter Kerr • Howard Kleinberg • Dick Kluger • Joe Kraus • Ron LaBrecque • Louise